OUR KNIVES
WILL SAVE US

OUR KNIVES WILL SAVE US

Dispatches from a White Mountain Apache Chef

+ + + +

NEPHI CRAIG

PENGUIN PRESS NEW YORK 2026

PENGUIN PRESS
An imprint of Penguin Random House LLC
1745 Broadway, New York, NY 10019
penguinrandomhouse.com

Designed by Christina Nguyen

LIBRARY OF CONGRESS CONTROL NUMBER: 2025050761
ISBN 9780593831908 (hardcover)
ISBN 9780593831915 (ebook)

Printed in the United States of America
1st Printing

The authorized representative in the EU for product safety and compliance
is Penguin Random House Ireland, Morrison Chambers, 32 Nassau Street,
Dublin D02 YH68, Ireland, https://eu-contact.penguin.ie.

For the Master Teachers in my life: my children.
May you find evolving strength, determination, and
vitality in understanding your dad. . . . I love you.

For my mother, Mariddie; my father, Vincent;
my brothers Dustinn and Shiloh.

Dó religion a'ted'da—*it's our way of life.*

CONTENTS

INTRODUCTION

THE CULINARY ART OF SELF-DETERMINATION

The sun hung low in the sky as I turned on to the path leading from Whiskey Flats to the neighborhood we'd always called Nobody's Home. It was barely eight o'clock, a frigid morning in February, and the air smelled of juniper smoke from people's cooking fires. I pulled my beanie down over my ears and hurried across four lanes of highway.

I was looking for the tall guy who had told me he would buy one of my high-end chef's knives. I'd met him the night before, completely faded. I didn't remember his name, but I could picture his face. He had been wearing a black T-shirt of some death metal band I'd never heard of, sneering while I told stories about cooking a Native food dinner in Osaka, Japan, like he was sure he'd caught me in a lie.

I pushed away the familiar sting of shame. Once again, I had managed to completely fuck up my life. I had no job, no apartment, no money—I was a grown man living in his mother's house. No one in my life, not even my seven-year-old son, could rely on me.

I turned up the dirt driveway that led to the compact white-brick house where we'd partied the night before. My head was pounding. The yard looked much less inviting in the daylight, its patchy grass littered with crumpled cans and empty Natural Ice boxes. As soon as they saw me, a couple of sleepy, skinny Rez dogs stood up and barked, baring their teeth. I reached for my pocketknife, but just then a small Apache grandma rounded the side of the house. She was wearing a maroon camp dress and little black penny loafers, her gray hair tied back and pinned up.

"Aaaah-HEY!" she yelled.

Instantly, the vicious dogs turned into mild puppies, wagging their tails as Grandma scolded them in Apache.

"Weh'Zhanh," she said, and they scampered away.

I folded up my knife, stuffing it back into my front pocket. The old woman started peppering me with questions.

"Uhhhhhh, I can't really speak Apache," I stammered, a refrain I had repeated many times over the course of my life. One more thing to feel ashamed about.

The woman fixed me with her glare, an expression every Apache kid knows. It meant, *You should know better. Who are your parents?*

"Kay-yeah," she said, reluctantly switching to English. "Nobody's here!"

She started walking back toward the side screen door.

"Wait!" I took a few steps toward her. "Do you like to cook?"

She turned around, confused. It was such a random question coming from an Apache dressed all in black, from my sneakers to my Wu-Tang hoodie.

"I'm friends with your grandsons. I was here last night, and they said they wanted to buy my knives," I rushed on.

She kept her piercing eyes on me.

"Or that you might want to buy one, 'cuz you cook chaaaaamp," I lied.

The old woman's face softened. I detected a grin. I figured I would bat away the last of her suspicions by telling her who my people were.

"Whiskey Flats, yu," I fumbled. "Mariddie bi'zhaazhé. Nephi Craig, o'zeh. I'm selling my knives."

Before I could say another word, she turned away and walked inside the house.

I stepped up onto the concrete stoop, steadying myself with a deep breath. I was getting sicker by the minute, jittery, and it was going to get worse if I didn't get another drink soon. I needed cash to stay fucked up—I couldn't give up so easily. When I knocked, the clattering sounds inside stopped. I pulled myself up straight as the door creaked open.

"They're not here, I told you." Grandma's tone was sharp.

"That's okay," I replied, giving her my friendliest smile. "I want to sell you a chef's knife. Let me show you. They're really good quality."

She considered for a moment, huffed, and waved me in.

The house smelled like fried potatoes and coffee. It was a comforting smell, but I was too hung over. It turned my stomach.

"You guys were too loud last night," she scolded, leading me to her kitchen. The layout and décor were similar to my parents' house—small, clean, and cozy.

"Where'd my sons go?"

I tried to respond in Apache. "Doo hwaa bígósį da." *I don't know.*

The old woman sat down at her oval table, wrapping her hands around a yellow mug. Like every Apache elder I knew, she had serious crow's-feet.

"Let me see the knives then."

I placed my backpack on the chipped Formica and pulled out two black leather cases, each holding a ten-inch Yanagiba slicer, along with a rectangular wooden box containing a fluted eight-inch Japanese chef's knife. I opened each holder, revealing red velvet lining and three gleaming blades.

Grandma's eyes opened wide. "Shhaaaang, they're so pretty!"

I lifted one of the slicers out of its case and presented her with the handle.

She turned the knife, looking down the bevel to check its straightness. "Where'd you get these?"

"I bought them a few years ago," I told her. "They were handmade by this old Japanese man whose ancestors made samurai swords."

Her eyes widened. "You were in Japan?"

"Yeah, I'm a chef." I could hear the pride in my voice. "I've cooked all over the world—London, Germany, Brazil. I was in Japan a couple years ago."

My mind drifted to the old knife-maker's tiny shop, with its smell of incense and steel. I'd spent that afternoon skateboarding around Osaka before heading back to the Imperial Hotel, where, a few days later, I had cooked a banquet showcasing Native foods. I loved everything about the city—the late-night eats, the towering temples, the chefs who worked alongside me with quiet reverence and respect.

"Kay-yeah, what are you doing out here drinking and partying too much?" The old woman's stern voice pulled me back to the present moment. "Why are you selling these? They're special."

Before I could answer her, she got up and tugged open a drawer.

"Look at my knives." She held up a couple of worn Old Hickory knives that looked like they were a few decades old.

"This one's my favorite," she said, pulling out an eight-inch Chicago Cutlery fillet knife. "It cuts potatoes and meat gooood!"

I checked it out, running my thumb along the side.

She grinned again. "See. I keep it sharp."

Part of me wanted to sit with Grandma all morning, bonding over our shared appreciation for a well-honed blade. I'd tell her about learning to cook with my White Mountain Apache mother and my Navajo grandma, and about my experiences working in high-end kitchens and meeting other Indigenous chefs like me in Seattle and São Paulo. I was certain she would understand when I told her how, ever since my father had died the previous spring, my knives just didn't seem that important anymore. I had relapsed, losing my first executive chef job. I'd been bumming around the Rez for months. Nowadays, I'd explain, fine dining was the last thing on my mind; I was lucky if I could scrape together a dollar or two to buy a bag of chips or a greasy burger.

Instead of saying any of this, I took a sip of the coffee she had poured me. I needed to get high again.

"I'm selling these long slicers for eighty dollars and this chef's knife for sixty dollars," I said. Each of them had cost me a few hundred.

Grandma gasped. "Kay-yeah, I don't have that much money!"

She carefully lifted the chef's knife up from its box. "I like this one 'cuz it's pretty and you said potatoes won't stick to it." She took a deep breath and looked me dead in the eyes. "Hol' on. Wait here."

I stood still, trying to stop my hands from shaking. A rack of freshly washed breakfast dishes sat next to the scrubbed-down sink, and a row of Apache dolls lined the windowsill.

Grandma returned clutching a small beaded purse. "All I have is forty-five dollars," she said, plucking out a few folded bills.

My heart sank, but I needed the money. I consoled myself that, judging by how she treated her favorite fillet knife, my fluted Japanese blade would be going to a good home.

"All right, go for it then," I said, putting the knife back in the box and grabbing the cash. I jumped up to leave, almost forgetting my backpack. The woman handed it to me and accompanied me to the door.

"Don't open any El Pato cans with that knife," I joked over my shoulder.

Grandma was still watching me when I turned back on to the road to make the short trek over to the bootlegger's house, where I knew I could buy a twelve-pack of beer and a liter of Barton vodka, AKA rot gut, for cheap. After that, I'd stop by my dealer's place and talk him into taking both of my Yanagiba slicers in exchange for an ounce of weed and an eight-ball of coke.

By ten a.m. that morning, I was down to my last knife: the gorgeous, mahogany-handled santoku with the words APACHE CHEF carved into the blade. No matter how bad things got, it was the one thing in my life I wasn't willing to sell.

\+ + + +

When I found myself walking the familiar streets of Whiteriver, Arizona, in the winter of 2011, looking to pawn off my knife collection to anyone who could pay me in cash, I was not in a healthy state of mind. Deep in my addiction, I was confused, angry, heartbroken, and disillusioned. I had forgotten what had carried me through other difficult moments in my life—my passion for cooking and, more specifically, the strength I derived from learning about foods that were indigenous to the Americas.

In the years leading up to that bleak morning, I had done everything that a young, ambitious cook should do, working in high-end restaurants down in Phoenix, traveling across the country and around the world doing cooking demos and tasting dinners, making industry connections.

In the span of a year, all that had fallen apart. Since the previous summer, I'd been teetering on the edge, drunk and high most of the time. I was lost.

Back then, I couldn't have known how my training as a chef would ultimately save my life, giving me the tools to stabilize, dream big, and live in sobriety for fifteen years and counting. I was incapable of imagining that one day I'd be back in my hometown—not just alive but thriving—running a beautiful café specializing in Native food. There's no way I would have believed that I'd be working as an addiction recovery specialist in my community.

All I knew was that, even at my lowest, I was desperate to hold onto my most prized chef's knife. It was the one thing that kept me tethered to reality.

Even as my life and my recovery took many wild swerves, transporting me from the Rez to one of the fanciest restaurants in the country, all around the globe and back again, cooking was a constant. But it was cooking with *Native foods* that truly showed me a new way to live. Working with the Indigenous cultivars that have long nourished our people—seasoning with acorns, popping amaranth, or brewing wild tea—ultimately helped me find my way back from the brink.

I didn't learn any of this in culinary school. During my formal education as a chef, the subject of Native foods never came up. The message I received from teachers and mentors, again and again, was loud and clear: When it came to cooking, all things French reigned supreme.

Instinctively, I knew there was more to the story. When I was growing up, my parents instilled in me a profound love for family, home, and culture. I knew that when it came to Native communities and ceremony, food was a very big deal. It was at the center of many of my most vivid memories—and of every gathering, joyous and sad.

Once I started working in the professional food world, when I was just eighteen years old, I decided to educate myself as much as possible about Native food traditions, making a name for myself with this specialized knowledge. But I had no idea how far this journey would take me—or all the ways it would alter the trajectory of my life.

+ + + +

There is nothing simple about the story of Indigenous food in the Americas, which is both violent and terrible but also ordinary, beautiful, and poetic.

From the moment they first made landfall, European colonizers used food as a weapon of mass destruction, burning fields of quinoa and forcing Indigenous farmers to slave on cocoa plantations. In an effort to starve the Native Americans of the Great Plains, white settlers massacred many millions of North American buffalo between 1870 and 1890, piling the animals' skulls into monstrous mounds reaching up to the sky. All across the United States, federal soldiers rounded up our Native American ancestors like cattle, pushing them into prison camps, many of which later became reservations.

Fenced in and barred from foraging, fishing, hunting, and farming, Indigenous peoples were intentionally cut off from the calorie-rich landscapes that had fed them for millennia. Native communities—who had been eating fresh, seasonal foods long before farmers' markets were a thing—were now forced to stand in line for military rations, subsisting on commodity foods like white flour, sugar, and blocks of orange cheese.

The aftershocks of all this colonial violence continue to reverberate. Poor nutrition and poverty have resulted in shockingly high rates of diabetes, heart disease, and other illnesses among Native Americans. Ongoing injustice rears its ugly head everywhere: poor mental health, suicide, and addiction.

Still, our food traditions endure. Growing up, I participated in Apache ceremonies where we feasted on traditional dishes like Dįjįįzhi, Acorn Stew, and racket bread cooked on juniper and oak coals. I was also taught that many of the things we ate regularly at home, like corn, squash, and beans, were "Native foods," but I was too busy being a rowdy kid to give it much thought.

I wasn't alone. The fact that most non-Natives, and many Natives as well, would be hard-pressed to put together a list of Native American foods—that's colonization in action. It wasn't until I was in my twenties, deep into my self-directed learning, that I began to grasp the profound connections between Indigenous foodways and our way of making sense of the world.

It was only when I started cooking in high-end restaurants, back in 1998, that I realized how many of the foods we routinely consume—often with little thought to where they came from or what memories they carry—are Indigenous cultivars, crops that were planted and used as food and medicine by Indigenous peoples as far back as 8000 BC. The erasure of our ancestors' contribution to food history doesn't change the fact that Indigenous cultivars have shaped the world in significant, lasting ways.

The Native foods have changed me, too.

When I first became a line cook, I worshiped at the altar of fine dining, aspiring to work my way up the ladder and create dishes that were technical and intricate. But taking a deep dive into the stories of tomatoes and chocolate and corn shifted my focus to the human aspects of cooking. These foods laid the foundation for my recovery, teaching me about the tangible, tactile ways that cooking can be a way to participate in healing and revitalization.

For me, success no longer looks like working at a Michelin-starred restaurant. It looks like Café Gozhóó, the small restaurant I run on the White Mountain Apache Rez. It looks like the clean, open kitchen I designed to facilitate collaboration and communication between my all-Native staff. Success is a giant Apache squash grown by Apache farmers at Ndée Bikíyaa, the People's Farm, a beautiful operation down the road in Whiteriver. It's lining our shelves with jars of different dried beans and chilies, and hanging corn and wild tea from the ceiling to dry.

All of us, Native or not, are in recovery from the disease of colonialism, a system built on a set of beliefs that erode our humanity and harm the earth. Our intimate relationship with the foods we eat has been lost, but we can start to heal by reclaiming it.

Getting curious about ingredients we use every day provides a sort of spiritual nutrition, offering a tangible vision of a more gentle, more vibrant future. Food has the ability to connect us to each other. It can point us back home.

We can all learn from the cultivars that have been part of this landscape for centuries. We have so much to gain from listening to their stories—and from telling our own.

ONE

SUMAC BERRIES, ACORN STEW, AND THE FORCE

I was born in the northeastern part of Arizona, the ancestral homeland of the White Mountain Apache people. Nestled along the foothills of our sacred mountains, my hometown of Whiteriver is the largest community on the Fort Apache Indian Reservation, with several thousand residents spread out across dozens of small housing tracts.

Like every other Indigenous community in the United States, Whiteriver is a place steeped in tragedy, violence, and hardship. It's situated just down the road from the remnants of the fort where the U.S. military launched its campaign to stamp out the Native American renegades of the so-called Apache Wars. At the same time, Whiteriver is also a beautiful and magical place, encompassing the wettest watershed in Arizona, where blue spruce, pine, cedar, and oak color our world, giving us all four seasons.

To a kid, it was paradise.

Our family of five—Mom, Dad, my older brother Dustinn, baby brother Shiloh, and I—lived in a neighborhood called Whiskey

Flats, which got its name from Old Man Whiskey, who had once owned the surrounding land and now lived alone next door. I didn't know much about him, apart from the fact that he kept his house lit with an old kerosene lantern and only spoke Apache. My parents both grew up speaking their Native tongues—Apache and Navajo—but they never formally taught us their language. As teenagers, both of my parents had been sent away from the Rez to Utah as part of the Mormon placement program, finishing high school in predominantly white schools. I know they watched their own parents struggle to learn English and communicate with white people, and they wanted to equip their sons to succeed in a changing world.

The brick houses on our street were all built in the 1970s, so when I was born, in February of 1980, they were still pretty new, with tidy yards, recently planted trees, and perfectly smooth sidewalks. From the outside, our house, where my mom still lives, looked just like all the others on the street, but inside it was different. My dad built a beautiful glass-front cabinet in our dining nook and replaced the linoleum flooring in the living room with soft, forest green carpet. Our house was cozy and welcoming, a gathering place for birthday celebrations, graduation parties, and holidays.

During the eighties, the neighborhood was bursting with little Apache kids, and we all traveled as a pack. Floyd and Lloyd, the twin brothers who lived directly across the street, became my best friends, and this tall, smiley kid named Delmore, who was two years older than me, became like an older brother once Dustinn got too cool for us.

Delmore's mom worked at Whiteriver's only movie theater, and she'd sneak us in and hook us up with free popcorn. The movies we watched in that little theater—everything from *Gremlins* to *The*

Breakfast Club—offered a window into the American world, teaching us that the nuclear family was the most important social unit and exposing us to suburban neighborhoods with big, fancy houses and shiny, new cars. We were ingesting the fantasy of the American dream long before we understood that that dream wasn't meant for us, that it had been built on our people's destruction.

I remember watching *Red Dawn*—about a group of teenagers who fight to defend their town from a Russian invasion—and then pretending the same thing was going to happen to us, training in the woods with my buddies. Of course, none of us were old enough to pick up on the irony of the film's tagline—"No foreign army has ever occupied American soil . . . until now."

Most days after school, my friends and I would run around in the hills behind our houses, but in summertime, our favorite activity was sneaking down to the river where our people had camped for centuries. We called it Down Below, pronounced as one word—*Downbelow*.

Everyone would tell their parents they were going to someone else's house to hang out, and, when my mom wasn't looking, I'd stuff my backpack with a towel, a military-issue canteen, and a can of Beanee Weenees or sardines. I always carried my pocketknife and a lighter with me just in case, like my father had taught me.

We'd run down to the cattle guard next to the two-lane county road that cut through the reservation, and, when the coast was clear, we'd duck into the bushes and clamber through the drainage ditch to the other side. After maneuvering through clumps of jumping cactuses and cholla, yucca, juniper, and oak, we'd scoot down these huge lava rocks on our butts before turning around and climbing down backward, feeling into the foot holes. Once we were all down, we'd stash our bags under a bush and make our way barefoot across slippery basalt. We spent hours Downbelow splashing around in the cold water, the orange sun pouring through the towering ponderosas.

The river taught us how to be White Mountain Apache: strong and self-sufficient. Once we were done swimming, we dried off and collected kindling, making a fire so we could warm up the tinned rations we'd packed. On the way back home, we'd look for a stand of skunkbush to pluck tsínk'ózhé. The sour pop of the native red sumac berries made our lips pucker just like they probably did to our ancestors when they went foraging. My mom loved tsínk'ózhé, so I always made sure to carry an empty Ziploc in my pack so I could bring some home. The fruit reminded her of her childhood, she'd told me once, when she and her sister used to collect berries, which the "older ladies" would use to make refreshing Apache Kool-Aid.

+ + + +

My mother, Mariddie Johnson Craig, was my first cooking instructor and so much more. From a young age, I saw the impact she had on other people in our community and how much they respected her. She treated our neighbors and the people in our community with love, generosity, and kindness, delivering food to Old Man Whiskey—who was crazy about her pineapple upside-down cake—and organizing a caroling group during Christmas, where she'd hand out small paper sacks containing fruit, hard candy, and hazelnuts and almonds still in their shells.

My mother is someone who chooses her words carefully; people have always leaned in to hear what she had to say. She bought me my first journal, encouraging me to record events and feelings and emphasizing that memories and thoughts were very important. I'd see her at the kitchen table, filling her own journal with her beautiful handwriting. She had volumes and volumes of stories from her life written down.

A nurturing presence to everyone around her, my mother was the oldest of five children. She grew up in a home impacted by crushing poverty and hardship; even before her parents died from complications related to alcoholism when she was in her early twenties, she held the family together, acting as the matriarch and helping raise her two younger siblings who had fetal alcohol syndrome. She taught herself to cook, and by the time she became a mother herself, she knew how to make a delicious meal—even when there was very little in our fridge or pantry.

Some of my happiest early memories involve baking with my mom, leafing through her copy of *The Good Housekeeping Illustrated Cookbook*, with its glossy, golden-brown soufflé on the cover, looking for a recipe to make with whatever we had on hand. During one of these kitchen sessions, she told me how she'd discovered her love of baking when she lived with her foster family in Utah. Some of the recipes we prepared, like my favorite chocolate chip cookies, actually came from her foster mother, a friendly, soft-spoken white woman with crinkled eyes whom we kids called Grandma Bush. I imagine that, for my mother, who grew up in a chaotic environment, Grandma Bush's home would have seemed especially calm and orderly. I can see now that, by inviting me to cook with her, my mother was sharing an important discovery—that the kitchen could be a warm, safe place, a little slice of heaven.

My parents actually met in Hawaii, where my mom was a student at Brigham Young University and my dad was stationed with the Marine Corps. The story goes that when my father first proposed to my mother, she said no.

"You have no direction in life," he recalled her telling him.

My dad, Vincent Craig—a well-known singer-songwriter who performed across Indian Country—regularly recounted this story during his shows. He'd tell the audience that, after this rejection, he had returned home, to Crownpoint, New Mexico, where he climbed the nine-story water tower, intending to end his life. Instead, he watched the sun rise over the Navajo Nation, realizing that he wanted to live and be a positive influence on the people around him. He climbed down, went back to his mom's house, shaved his beard, and cut off his long black hair, marching into the Navajo Police Department and telling them he wanted to help pursue justice in his community.

By the time I started elementary school, my father, a lifelong learner, had decided to enroll at the University of New Mexico and deepen his knowledge of Indian law and legal issues on and off the reservation. Once he started taking those college classes, it was just us three boys and my mom during the week. Our family budget, which had always been tight, got even tighter, so my mom and I started selling our baked goods to neighbors for extra money. We'd make triple batches of chocolate chip cookies and brownies, portioning them in little plastic baggies, and I'd pull our red Flyer wagon from house to house, a mobile bakery.

A former Marine Corps sharpshooter and sergeant who could build or fix anything, my dad was impressive in many ways, but he wasn't much of a cook. He was ingenious and creative, though. I recall how he once stuck a few cans of Beanee Weenees in the engine of our truck when we went on a camping trip. At the end of a long drive, we arrived at our campsite, where he proudly presented a hot meal, serving us the mini hot dogs and baked beans with a box of crackers.

Once or twice a year, when my mother packed up her paisley bag and left for a few days to visit some relative or attend a conference on behalf of the tribe, she left my father in charge. I really loved those boys' weekends, not least because we got to eat my father's signature dish, a mix of over-browned, crunchy ground beef and a can of Campbell's mushroom soup served over sticky green spinach noodles—the ultimate comfort food.

"All right, boys, Camouflage Goulash is ready," my father would yell. "Come and get it!"

My brothers and I would drop everything and run to the kitchen; the first one there could snag the most generous portion.

"Boys, this is made by a real United States Marine," Dad would say, ladling his trademark concoction into our bowls. He'd smile, then shout, "Oorah!"

My dad's mother, Grandma Nancy, was the best cook I knew. I always loved driving up to visit her in Crownpoint. She was a typical Navajo grandma, small and loving, always happy to see us. She showered us with kind words and hugs, and her house was always bathed in amazing aromas from the bread baking in the big adobe oven in her backyard and whatever was bubbling on the stove.

One day, my brothers, cousins, and I were kicking up dust in her yard when Grandma marched out with a couple of my aunties, holding bowls and towels. I watched her walk up the driveway to a skinny sheep that was tied up to a stake. She looked down at the animal, mumbling a prayer under her breath, then pulling a giant knife out of her apron pocket.

My eyes got real big. "Whoa, Grandma's a ninja," I yelled, trying to get my playmates' attention.

She looked over at me, putting a finger to her lips, then turned back and, in one quick motion, swiped the blade across the sheep's throat, snapping its head back and taking a bowl from one of my aunts to catch the blood.

The other boys went back to running around, but I stood there staring at my grandma's red-stained hands, watching her spend the next half hour or so taking the animal apart methodically. She was the first person I'd ever seen butcher an animal, and from her precise, confident motions it was obvious she'd done it many times before.

I'd only ever seen Grandma Nancy as this sweet, loving person, and then, suddenly, she took a life to feed us, committing this violent, bloody act with serious reverence. By that afternoon, she had mutton cooking on the grill, and the skin of the dead animal was hung and stretched out to dry on her clothesline. Everyone was chatting as my grandma giggled and baked more bread. It blew my mind that this was the same person.

I also learned a lot from my mother's grandpa, Joseph Carley Ivins, my great-grandfather. Grandpa Ivins was born on the White Mountain Apache Reservation in 1899, eight years after its establishment by the U.S. government, and when he was eight, he was put on a train and sent to Pennsylvania, where he attended the infamous Carlisle Indian Industrial School, whose founder coined the phrase "Kill the Indian, save the man." My dad—who recorded an album called *Boarding School Fish Stories* when I was eight—made a point of telling us how Joseph and his friends always held on to their languages, as well as their values and beliefs. As a teenager, my great-grandfather managed to leave Carlisle and stay with friends down in Anadarko, Oklahoma, where he learned traditional Native farming techniques. Eventually, in his early thirties, Joseph finally made his way home, where he planted a lush garden down by the river.

I spent hours in that garden with my great-grandfather and my mother's brother, Uncle Duwayne, digging for snails and learning how to weed, fix the irrigation lines, and sing to the plants. Joseph's garden was about the size of a swimming pool, but it seemed enormous to a little kid like me. Surrounded by dense, wild vegetation, it opened up into neat rows of corn, beans, tomatoes, and squash—four foundational Indigenous cultivars that changed the way the world ate forever, even if I didn't know that at the time.

There was a line of rose bushes with giant, fragrant flowers and a pear tree I loved to climb. Near the garden was an old ceremonial site where, every summer, a Sunrise Dance was held to celebrate a girl who was coming of age. I'd sit up in the tree listening to people drumming and singing, enjoying the aroma of roasting corn and eating a perfectly ripe, sweet, soft pear. I remember feeling so happy and safe.

We gathered in Grandpa's garden for family campouts, birthdays, holiday gatherings, and, always, for harvest time. It was a place of abundance. In Indigenous communities like ours, poverty and scarcity have always fostered resourcefulness and creativity, and for Grandpa Ivins, planting a vegetable garden was a tangible way to care for the people around him and shield them from hunger. Years later, when I attended culinary school at age eighteen, I was taught that food separated people—by nationality and class, by gourmand discernment—but growing up, I saw how it drew people together. Even when it was hard to come by, food was something that was meant to be shared.

+ + + +

As a kid, I couldn't fully grasp that my mom and dad were pillars of the community. They were just my parents. But years later—when my mother campaigned for, and won, a seat on the White Mountain Apache tribal council in 1998, with my father by her side—I understood that they were a power couple, two people whom others looked up to for guidance and wisdom.

By the time I came around, my Navajo father had earned the respect of the Whiteriver community as a principled and caring police officer. As the founder of the White Mountain Apache Police's Mountain Rescue unit, he channeled his military experience into training a team to extricate people stranded on huge cliffs and at the bottoms of deep canyons. Four years before I was born, in 1976, my then twenty-six-year-old father risked his life to save the passengers in a truck that had been washed away during a historic flood. He climbed a giant cottonwood tree, running a line from its trunk to the bridge where the vehicle was lodged in the raging water.

Around the time I went into elementary school, my dad started recording music and touring Navajo Land. I often accompanied him, sitting among a rapt, all-ages audience as he sang songs and told charming, rambling anecdotes that dealt with life on the Rez and our peoples' history. My experiences at those shows confirmed what I had always known: My father was the best storyteller in the world.

He first talked to me about the Apache scouts when I was five years old. Our school was putting on a play for the community and we kindergarteners were tasked with performing the Apache War Dance. I was so excited that my classmates and I would get to wear the type of regalia I'd seen the ceremony dancers wear and I was thrilled to hold a bow and spear and have my face covered with war paint. There was just one problem, though—all the other Apache kids had leather moccasins, but I did not.

Luckily, my dad was unfazed. The night before the performance, he told me to put on my sneakers and come into the living room. He knelt in front of me, wrapping snug strips of tan canvas around my shins and over my shoes and sewing them up with thin rope he carried in from his backyard shed.

When he was done, my dad stood to stretch his back, admiring his handiwork. I must have looked dubious, because I remember my dad placing his hands on my shoulders and looking me square in the eyes.

"Those other moccasins are good," he told me, "but this—this is how a lot of Apache scouts would have done it."

I shifted my weight from side to side, stamping my feet just like our teacher had taught us. I wanted to make sure my running shoes would stay covered.

"Do you think they went to the store to buy them?" My dad chuckled, a familiar sound I loved so much. "Real scouts made their own moccasins, taking a long piece of buckskin and sewing it to a rawhide base, then lacing them up tight to protect their legs from scrapes and cuts and prickers. Boys and men were required to learn how.

"An Apache scout ran for hundreds of miles," my father continued. "If one of their moccasins ripped, they knew how to quickly wrap and fasten it with whatever they could find, maybe a tough piece of wild grass. Then they'd grab a piece of jerky from their pouch and just keep running."

He paused for dramatic effect, leaning in close and dropping his voice.

"Apache scouts could glide through the forest without making a sound. They could sneak up on anyone and they wouldn't know what hit 'em. No way you could do that with some store-bought moccasins." He slapped his hands on his dark cowboy jeans.

I smiled, marching in place without making a sound. "What did scouts do?"

My dad's lips tightened underneath his bushy mustache.

"They helped the U.S. Army track down their enemies. The white soldiers wouldn't have lasted a day up in these mountains. If it wasn't for them scouts, your ancestors would have probably been marched off their land with all the other tribes around here. Who knows if they would ever have been allowed to return . . ."

He shook his head, looking a little sad.

A lot of what I learned about the history of Indigenous peoples in America I learned from my dad's songs, and also from his comic strip, *Muttonman*, which ran in numerous publications like *The Apache Scout* and the *Navajo Times* and was popular enough to be featured in a special exhibition at the Smithsonian. The day that he fashioned my makeshift moccasins, my father introduced me to the trauma that hovered over our community. I remember envisioning lean, intense-looking young men like the teenagers I saw hanging out in front of the local high school gliding silently through dense forest. I imagined how their hearts pounded as they tried to outrun unseen dangers and make their way back home.

+ + + +

Depending on who's recounting the history, the Apache scouts might be cast as traitors, or they might be portrayed as heroes. The truth, of course, is messier, infinitely more human, and gut-wrenching.

In my dad's telling, it began with the British, who arrived and tore through the tribes on the East Coast in America, leaving millions of people dead. Closer to home, on the West Coast, it was the Spanish conquistadors who wreaked havoc, arriving, lost, in 1492 and pushing their empire all the way up through Mexico and then moving even farther north, establishing the territory of New Mexico in 1598.

"You see, son, by the eighteen hundreds, our people in the Southwest, in Dinétah and Pueblo Land, had already been in contact with Spaniards for about twenty years," he told me. "But up in their remote home, the White Mountain Apaches were protected."

That started to change around 1848, at the end of the so-called Mexican-American War, when the United States took over territories that included parts of Apache Land.

"Nobody asked us if they could take the land," he continued, "and things got even worse when they discovered gold out this way."

By 1860, the U.S. government was circling closer and closer to our White Mountains.

"Can you imagine what it was like to be alive back then?" my father would ask, a question he repeated often, teaching us that history was personal. "Your ancestors would have been always moving, always hiding, watching the world all around them changing."

My father's people, the Diné, were forcibly removed from their ancestral homelands in 1864 and marched at gunpoint to Bosque Redondo. That event, which came to be known as the Long Walk, resulted in the mass deportation of ten thousand Navajos, more than a third of whom died of exhaustion or starvation, or were shot at close range when they were unable to keep up. The U.S. Army committed similar atrocities with the Yavapai and Tonto, two neighboring Western Apache tribes, who were rounded up in a concentration camp down in San Carlos, Arizona.

I remember listening to the lyrics of my dad's song "Someone Drew a Line" for the first time, and thinking about how so many of the Indigenous peoples in our region had been targeted and uprooted. The song opens with the mournful sound of my father's harmonica, and then he sings about how his grandfather used to take him up into the mountains in his youth and tell him the legends of long ago.

"Between the four sacred mountains, we lived in harmony, and now you tell us that we have to go," it continues. "Because someone drew a line."

This threat of displacement, my father explained to me, was the thing that would have struck the greatest terror in my ancestors' hearts. Nourished by a vast landscape that stretched from the desert canyons around Cibecue, with their cactuses, manzanita bushes, piñon trees, lizards, and roadrunners, all the way up to the peak of Mt. Baldy, our people based their entire culture around belonging to the White Mountains. Throughout our childhood, my brothers and I were taught that we derived our strength from this sacred place and that we should be proud of who we were and where we lived.

"When people ask you, you tell them that you're a White Mountain Apache," my mother always told us.

Having married into a matrilineal society, my father—a proud Navajo—spoke about Apache culture with serious admiration. He was the one who opened my eyes to the Apache scouts' heartbreaking compromise. Following in the footsteps of other Indigenous communities from Alaska to Florida who had collaborated with the colonizers in the hopes of being spared the worst of their brutality, some young White Mountain Apache men opted to enlist with the U.S. military and help track down Indigenous resistance fighters like Geronimo, Naiche, and Nana, who were striking back against white settlers across Arizona and New Mexico.

As an angry teenager, all I could see was how humiliating it must have been to put on a military uniform and fight alongside white soldiers, knowing that you might be ordered to kill other Apaches and that you would comply because your people's future depended on it. It was only once I became a parent myself that I was able to see the Apache scouts' sacrifice for what it truly was—the ultimate act of love. If it weren't for the scouts, I wouldn't have gotten to spend long summer days down by the same river they bathed in or savor the flavor of corn cooked deep in our soil. I wouldn't be raising my own children in the same landscape that shaped me.

In 1891, in return for the White Mountain Apaches' service, the U.S. government established the Fort Apache Indian Reservation—which was later renamed the White Mountain Apache Tribe Reservation—on 1.6 million acres of our ancestral territory.

This is where our people live to this day.

+ + + +

Throughout Apache Land, autumn means acorns. Families gather in truckloads and drive in caravans to their favorite spots along the Mogollon Rim, a two-hundred-mile-long rock shelf that is home to many groves of Emory oak, bushy trees that are unique to our part of the world.

When I was young, I looked forward to the joyful racket of my aunties and grandmas gathered around our dinner table, cracking acorns and howling with laughter. Just like generations of White Mountain Apache women before them, my mom and her relatives would venture out on a crisp morning and return hours later to sort through their haul.

The fruits of the Emory oak—Apache acorns, to us—are unusual in that they can be eaten straight out of the shell, like sunflower seeds. While most acorns are high in tannins and must be leached before they're eaten because they're unpleasantly acidic, Apache acorns are a little bitter with a sweet afternote. I like to think it's the same with Apache people: We can be fierce and intimidating, but once you get to know us, we're friendly. Our flavor is complex.

The relationship between acorns and Apaches runs deep, featuring in our people's creation story, which I learned as a young boy. In the time before we were Apaches as we know ourselves today, there was a huge flood, and Changing Woman—our original matriarch, whose Apache name is Saan bigesha—survived by floating in an abalone shell and eating the seeds of corn and sunflower and grass and acorn. This is why Acorn Stew is the ultimate Apache food, something that's served at every community gathering and ceremony.

It's a simple dish: bone broth, meat, acorns, and, often, pieces of squash. As is the case with Indigenous cuisine across the board, there's little to no documentation of what our White Mountain Apache ancestors actually ate, so it's hard to say whether Acorn Stew was part of their repertoire. The Acorn Stew I grew up with was usually prepared with beef, which would only have been possible starting in the 1800s, after white settlers introduced cattle to our region; our ancestors might have used elk or deer meat. What makes this stew unique is the taste of the Apache acorns, which season the broth as it's cooking. The soup is then finished with generous spoonfuls of acorn flour—a yellow powder that we use to season everything we eat, our version of sea salt.

Back when I was young, I didn't care for the funky taste. (My buddies and I used to joke that Acorn Stew was the dish that Yoda served to Luke Skywalker in *The Empire Strikes Back*, when he takes him to his hut on the dreary planet of Dagobah, intent on serving him "good food" rather than the dried rations he carries in his pack. "How you get so big eating food of this kind?" Yoda asks, after taking a little bite and spitting it out.)

As an adult, I was finally able to fully appreciate the force of this traditional dish—the best way I can describe the flavor is how roast beef and horseradish work together, fatty richness accompanied with a sharp bite. Once I began traveling abroad as a professional chef, I often incorporated Acorn Stew into my tasting menus, carrying shrink-wrapped packages of Apache acorns foraged close to home in my luggage.

We share a geography, us Western Apache tribes and the Emory oak; it's called Western Apacheria, a vast expanse that stretches from what we now call Arizona over to Texas, and from Colorado all the way down into Mexico.

But after our traditional homelands were stolen and divided, my ancestors lost the ability to roam freely. As wild, abundant spaces were replaced with white towns, rich subdivisions, golf courses, and strip malls, the places where our people once foraged became so-called private land, and, today, many of the traditional spots for gathering Native ingredients fall beyond the boundaries of our reservation. The largest stands of Emory oak trees, for example, sit within the Tonto National Forest and near the town of Payson, whose population is about 97 percent non-Native. Officially, my relatives and neighbors could get in big trouble for gathering Apache acorns, although that doesn't stop us. We continue to harvest acorns responsibly, getting them at the right time and only taking as many as we will use.

An oak tree must reach its twentieth birthday before it can produce acorns, and some don't fruit until they're fifty. Like us, Apache acorns need strong roots to thrive. Acorn trees yield fruit only during a very limited span of time, so you need to monitor the weather and trees carefully if you hope to gather them. As a chef, I view our acorn gatherers as the Apache version of the celebrated white-truffle hunters of Alba or the divers who extract sturgeon roe for caviar. These people are collecting a precious food, one that we consider both a staple and a luxury, a gift from the land.

Just as the White Mountain Apache people have stayed put, surviving colonization, so has the acorn. Our fates remain intertwined.

+ + + +

In the second grade, I got my first skateboard, ordered from the back of one of Dustinn's skate magazines from a company called

California Cheap Skates. I had ticked off the box for the metallic Tony Hawk model, which, when it arrived, turned out to be hot pink, but I didn't care. That board symbolized freedom, expanding my world far beyond Whiskey Flats and reinforcing the Apache values of toughness and resourcefulness.

I started riding with a crew of young cats that had a reputation as being "doo da'dits'a da" guys, an Apache word that translates to something like rowdy.

We spent our afternoons crisscrossing Whiteriver, and I loved learning the names of all the different neighborhoods, which, when I think about them now, are a brilliant representation of Apache humor. Jurassic Park was situated in a thick stand of ponderosa pines and mixed conifers, and Ben Gay was where a lot of old people used to live. Lifesavers got its name because the houses were all different colors, and Beverly Hills, a cluster of newer, relatively big houses with great views of the mountains, was home to our beloved tribal chairman, Ronnie Lupe. There were neighborhoods called Dark Shadows, Nobody's Home, Knots Landing, and Smurf Village. I really liked the name Eightball, which I didn't know at the time was a reference to where you could score drugs.

Skateboarding helped me see our Rez with fresh eyes. It was unlike any of the places I'd seen in the movies, both wilder and more gritty. It was unique, just for us.

Often, while we were skating around, we'd hear a *whirr* and stop in our tracks to watch a helicopter or an airplane take off from our local airport. "Wonder who's sick now?" one of my buddies would ask.

All of us had heard the stories.

"So-and-so got hurt in a car accident."

"So-and-so got beat up real bad and they're getting flown out."

"So-and-so is very sick and they're flying him down to the hospital in Phoenix."

I can't remember a time in my life when we weren't going to a funeral or wake almost every week. We lost people in our close circles to murder, suicide, car wrecks, addiction, and illness, often at shockingly young ages. It was terrible—and completely normal. Like all Indigenous people, we existed in a state of perpetual grief. I have so many memories of attending Apache wakes, multiple-day events that take place outside in a camp erected for the occasion where, alongside the wailing and laughter, there was always food being prepared over roaring open fires to feed the hundreds of people who showed up.

Later, in my twenties, once I started listening to the lyrics of an Indigenous hip-hop group called Antithesis, I realized that we Rez kids had grown up in a sort of prison or war zone. We were locked in an ongoing battle with the monster of colonialism, a powerful shapeshifter. Colonialism was woven into almost every aspect of our contemporary Indigenous lives, starting with the fact that we lived on federal trust lands, where we had to get permission for everything from building houses to farming. Our families could never truly own their homes, never build equity. Driving through Whiteriver and the neighboring reservation towns, you saw very few small businesses—securing a bank loan on the Rez is virtually impossible—but you passed plenty of churches.

There was a direct correlation between land theft, the loss of food sovereignty, the crushing poverty that ensued, and the extremely high rates of preventable disease, mental health issues, and substance abuse that plagued our community. There was a direct correlation between organized religion and the loss of our language and culture.

You could draw a straight line connecting our people's history to the air transports and funerals that disturbed children's play.

✢ ✢ ✢ ✢

I got my first taste of alcohol the summer after I turned eight. My friends and I were hanging out down by the cattle guard when a pickup truck rolled by with a crew of shirtless Apache guys sitting with towels draped around their necks, like they were on their way back from the river or a hard day's work in the sun. One of them opened a big orange cooler and, next thing we knew, a can of Budweiser fell out of the truck, hitting the ground in front of us and hissing and spraying.

We ran into the middle of the road and I picked up the dented, spraying can. I remember sticking out my tongue to catch the spray and grimacing. It tasted disgusting, like rotten apple juice.

I didn't know then that alcohol was a problem at home. I saw people in the community drinking all the time, at friends' and relatives' places and out on the streets when I skateboarded around the different neighborhoods, but never in our house. In addition to instilling in us a deep pride in our Indigenous heritage, our parents raised us Mormon, rounding us up to go to church every week. (I was the only one to get a Mormon name—Nephi is an important character in the Book of Mormon.) Mom and Dad had started going to church when they were children, before they were sent away on the Indian Placement Program, which had its peak in the sixties and seventies. Alcohol was forbidden in my parents' adopted religion. Every Sunday, we sat through sermons about purity, righteousness, and perfection. I wrestled with doubts from a young age, but my parents' firm belief in the Church definitely instilled fear in me. I worried that I would end up separated from them for all eternity, banished to hell while they hung out in the Celestial Kingdom.

My mother's hatred of alcohol ran deep. She'd never even taken a sip of it, she told us. Growing up, I overheard her talking about how her parents bootlegged Home Brew, a concoction of fermented ground corn, yeast, sugar, and water that could be extremely potent. She and her sister Charlotte, my aunt, sometimes talked about the scary people who came by to drink at the house, about the threat of violence. I knew it made my mom sad that her brother Duwayne and her sister Berlinda had been born with fetal alcohol syndrome and struggled to live full, independent lives.

"Drinking took away my childhood and destroyed my family," she once told me. "I'm not going to let that happen to you."

One day, not long after I'd spat out my first taste of beer, I was digging in our pantry for snacks when I found a six-pack of Coors cans shoved behind some unopened boxes of oatmeal.

"Dustinn!" My older brother was sitting at the dining room table, sketching medieval battle scenes in his notebook. "Check out what I found."

Dustinn walked over, and instead of being pleased that I'd found this cool contraband, his face turned red with rage.

"Damn it," he said, snatching the beer from me. I was stunned, trailing behind him as he walked out the door to our backyard.

Dustinn pulled the cans from the plastic rings, throwing them one by one onto my dad's meticulously organized woodpile, where they exploded dramatically.

"You better not tell Mom!" he yelled at me. Tears streamed down his face, which made me cry as well.

That was the first time I became aware that my dad was a closet drinker and that this was probably the reason for my parents' nighttime arguments, which had increased steadily as I moved through elementary school. Learning that my dad had a problem with alcohol made me sad. I thought we were different, that drinking was something that tore other families apart.

+ + + +

A classic middle child, I was wedged between my intelligent older brother and sweet baby Shiloh, our family's cute mascot. Sometimes, I felt like my parents overlooked me, especially once I got a little older. Back then, it seemed like the only time I had their undivided attention was when I got in trouble and they would sit me down for a serious conversation.

The truth is I liked being known as "the tough one." Even though I was shorter than most of my friends, I was faster and stronger. By fourth grade, I had already been beaten up in a couple fistfights, but not before landing a few punches of my own.

As a kid, I listened closely when my dad and his brother Harrison sat with their father, Bob Etcitty Craig, and discussed their time in the service. Dad and Uncle Harrison were both marines and my grandpa was one of the Navajo Code Talkers, the small, secret band of marines who created a complex code based on the Navajo language, helping the Allies transmit secret messages and win World War II. I particularly loved my father's story about stepping off the bus at the Marine Corps recruit depot in Camp Pendleton and being greeted by screaming drill instructors. He'd imitate them perfectly, describing how all the young men around him looked terrified as they lined up to get their heads shaved.

"I stayed calm," he said, repeating this story at his shows. "It was just like boarding school, and those drill sergeants were just like the Dorm Mothers who issued uniforms and shaved the little Navajo boys' heads."

The comparison would make the audience roar with laughter, a humorous way of addressing a serious topic.

When I grew up, I told myself, I'd become an elite soldier, too, stoic and brave. I loved all things military. I played toy soldiers for hours with my cousins, turned every stick into a weapon, and wore camo clothes almost every day. I remember listening to the Nas lyric "Aimin' guns in all my baby pictures," and thinking, *Yeah, that's like me.* I think I always saw myself as a bit of a rebel.

My parents were so respected in the community, accomplished and articulate. Expectations that I would be a good boy were high, but, especially at church, it felt like I was going through the motions. Left to my own devices, I was drawn to things that, at the time, were considered edgy and fringe, things my parents didn't understand—skating, tagging, punk music, and rap.

It didn't help that people often commented, "You come from a nice home and family," which was usually followed by the question: "Why are you like this?"

I felt like a caged animal, desperate to run wild.

+ + + +

Right around the time I finished the fourth grade, our tribal leadership changed over and my dad lost his job in Whiteriver. Thanks to his great reputation and legal training, he quickly found a new position as a chief juvenile probation officer with the Navajo Nation's judicial branch. In the summer of 1990, my family packed up our home and moved up to Window Rock, Arizona, one hundred and eighty miles to the northeast.

I did not welcome the move, and, at school, I quickly developed a reputation as a troublemaker, falling in with a rough crowd, including some junior high kids. A few weeks in, I brought some bottle rockets to school, setting them off behind our classrooms at lunchtime to impress my new friends. The principal called in the Navajo Nation Police, who handcuffed a fifth grader. My parents grounded me for two weeks—no skateboarding, no friends, no TV. They also gave me the silent treatment, which made me feel scared, lonely, and unloved.

I resented being ripped away from my friends in Whiteriver. I was still getting to know our neighbors and the kids in my school, and I spent a lot of time alone, walking to school each morning with my beloved Rez dogs Frybread and Beans, who had made the move with us, nipping at my heels.

A few months after the fireworks incident, I was hurrying home to make myself some instant ramen after school. Our new house was twenty minutes from the elementary school, and, once I got close, I'd whistle for my dogs and they'd come running, excited to accompany me for the last stretch. That day, I noticed a stranger sitting up ahead by the side of the road. As I passed by him, he jumped up and grabbed me by the arm, putting his other hand on the scruff of my neck and pushing me toward a thicket of gnarled juniper trees.

The man, who looked to me like he was in his twenties, not young but not old, pulled out a knife and pointed it at me. He spoke calmly and slowly, telling me everything was going to be okay and that he wanted to be nice to me.

Acting out of sheer panic, I lunged to get the knife, thinking I didn't care if I cut my hands. The stranger dodged and squeezed his clammy hand around my neck.

"Want me to cut out your fucking eyeball?" His voice had deepened to a scary baritone.

I remember looking up the hill, willing someone to come walking along the trail or spot us from the four-lane highway that was less than a hundred and fifty yards away. I looked up at the overhead power line that I could see from my bedroom window. I was so close to home and safety, but in great danger. I went limp with fear.

The next few minutes passed in a slow-motion blur. The man asked me to give him a hug, drawing the word *please* out in a way that made my stomach turn. I reluctantly did what I was told, feeling my eyes stinging.

"Sit down next to me," he said, still pointing the knife at my face and patting the big white rock behind him with the other hand.

"Kiss my neck . . . Kiss my lips."

I winced, pulling away. "Don't." My voice trembled.

"Just touch me here," he said, moving my hand onto his thigh.

The second I heard the sound of his zipper coming down, something in me snapped.

I swung my fist, punching him in the throat.

I remember the sound of the knife pinging as it fell out of his hand and hit the rock before thudding to the ground.

I started running—downhill. Among my friends and family, I was known for my ability to go full speed down steep terrain, weaving in and out of trees, never falling or getting hurt. Now, I darted out of the thicket, springing over large rocks and ducking under low-hanging trees. I whistled, loud, for Frybread and Beans.

I could hear the guy running behind me, yelling at me to wait, that he was kidding, that he would give me money.

Finally, when it was clear he couldn't keep up with me, he cried out, "Don't tell anyone, you little shit!"

I never looked back as I ran up the slope toward my house. When I couldn't hear his footfalls anymore, I yelled, "Fuck you," my voice surprisingly loud.

I stopped at the top of the hill, bending over and placing my shaking hands on my knees. I was in shock. The first thought that sprang into my head was *I'm in big trouble*, and then the shame fell over me like a disgusting, snot-colored blob.

Frybread and Beans came running over, wagging their tails and jumping up to greet me.

"I was calling you, fuckers!" My tears welled up as I kicked the dirt.

I unlocked the door and went straight into the kitchen, staring at the clock on the microwave. I didn't want ramen anymore. I felt like I might throw up.

It was two forty-five. Dustinn was still in school, and it would be a couple of hours still before my parents got off work and picked Shiloh up from day care.

I remember running back to my bedroom to grab my pocketknife and the T-ball bat I kept in my closet. I sat outside the house under the basketball hoop in our driveway, feeling scared, angry, powerless, and, above all else, deeply ashamed.

My mind raced, trying to decide who I could enlist to come find this guy with me and beat him down. My older brother wasn't a fighter, my little brother was too small, and I couldn't tell any of my new skate-rat friends. I could hear them laughing in my head, telling me I wasn't strong enough, I was a pussy, I probably liked it, I probably wanted it, I probably let it happen.

The thought of telling my parents was the most terrifying. I was convinced they would tell me that what had happened to me was all my fault.

"That's why you don't wander around like that." In my mind, my mom's tone was sharp and angry. "You know better."

If I'd had my doubts before, I now knew for a fact that—if the three levels of Mormon afterlife were real—I was definitely not going anywhere nice.

As the minutes creeped by, I remember getting more and more angry. *Nobody is going to help me*, I told myself. *Nobody is going to believe me.* Even with all the funerals I'd attended and my growing awareness of the apocalypse my people had experienced, I had still believed that, at its core, the world was a good place. But something broke inside me that afternoon.

+ + + +

I did my best to continue living my life like a ten-year-old, but I was no longer the same Nephi. I did everything I could to forget about the ugly secret festering inside me. By the end of fifth grade, I had discovered inhalants, and by sixth grade, I was regularly smoking weed. Once I started at Tsehootsooi Middle School in Fort Defiance, I spent less time at home, staying out for hours skateboarding around Window Rock and getting high in the drainage ditches with my friends. My grades plummeted.

I knew my parents worried about me, and it made me sad, but then I remembered how they would never understand, and I'd feel angry and resentful again, especially toward my dad who—when I needed him most—couldn't do a thing to protect me. Whenever I got into trouble for cutting school or fighting, he sat me down and asked me what was wrong, and I'd just sit there, silent and seething. Even when the conversation was loving and he begged me to open up, I refused to say much. I was terrified of the feelings that might pour out if I opened my mouth. If nobody knew the shameful truth, my young brain reasoned, nobody could hurt me with it.

During my freshman year at Window Rock High, I was invited to my first house party, in St. Michaels, the large housing tract across the highway from our neighborhood. I remember walking into a smoky living room of wall-to-wall teenagers and immediately spotting this girl I knew from school, the cutest Navajo girl I'd ever seen. One of my friends had told me she liked me, but I was too intimidated to go and talk to her. Instead, my friends and I stood in the corner, sparked up a joint, and started talking shit. At some point, I looked over to see my crush sitting on the couch with her friends and staring at me. She was holding a large can with a gold-and-red label, and, with her other hand, she gestured for me to come over.

Ever since I'd discovered my dad's hidden six-pack, I had told myself I was never going to be a drinker. I was on my own shit, bumping Cypress Hill, a *real* smoker like B-Real and the crew. But when I sat down next to my crush and her friends offered me an "OE," I grabbed the bottle of malt liquor like it was Mountain Dew.

"I always drink forties on the weekend and shit," I bluffed, cracking the tab and taking a big swig.

It tasted awful—sweet, thick, and fizzy—but, after a few more sips, I felt warm all over, like I was sitting by a campfire. A few Olde Englishes in, all my anxiety melted away. That had never happened with weed. I felt happier than I had in years, speaking easily to the prettiest girl in the room, making her giggle. Next thing I knew, we were both standing outside and I watched as the moon suddenly swerved.

I hit the ground, opening my eyes to see her squatting above me, asking if I was okay.

I raised a hand to my head, pulling it back to see that it was covered in blood that looked black in the moonlight.

I woke up the next morning in the backyard of the party house, covered in my own vomit. Somehow, the pretty girl was still there, worried about me.

I sat up, a little embarrassed, but I quickly pulled myself together.

"I'ma mob out now," I told her, and made my way back home.

I was a fourteen-year-old blackout drunk, but I had finally found something that wiped out my painful emotions.

+ + + +

I wasn't a total fuckup.

I continued going to church with my parents where I participated in a youth group. One time, around Valentine's Day of my junior year, we played a game where you trap an orange under your chin and try passing it to the person next to you without using your hands or dropping it. When our leaders instructed us to arrange ourselves in a circle, a girl I recognized from school quickly slipped in next to me. I had noticed her and her friends hanging out in the courtyard during lunch, watching my friends and me skate, but we'd never really talked. She seemed like a good girl who probably shouldn't be hanging out with someone like me, but that day I observed her looking at her friend across the circle with a tight-lipped, nervous expression that implied she might be interested.

Her name was Kim and she was two years younger than me, a slim, pretty Navajo girl with a huge smile who played on our school's softball team. We started dating toward the end of that school year, and, although I remained as wild as ever, I liked hanging out with her, getting to know each other and listening to music. I introduced Kim to Wu-Tang Clan and all of my favorite hip-hop groups, and she played me the mellower stuff she liked, mostly Lauryn Hill and Erykah Badu. One of her favorite songs, Eric Clapton's "Wonderful Tonight," became "our" song, and I remember that once, when we were hanging out on the hood of her dad's car looking up at the night sky, it came on the radio. I flashed her a big grin and howled at the moon, letting the sound bounce off the huge sandstone cliffs around us. For the first time ever, I thought I might be in love.

There were other things that I cared about, even if I was busy playing it cool. There was a "No Skateboarding" rule at Window Rock High School, which I thought was ridiculous, so I decided to start a petition. After my friends and I gathered hundreds of signatures, we got the rule overturned. A couple years later, on one of our trips back to Whiteriver, Dustinn and I raised enough money to build a skate park in town, which also felt like a major accomplishment.

Another passion of mine was *Great Chefs of the World*, the TV show I discovered in eighth grade while flipping through the channels one day. There on the Discovery Channel, I saw this burly guy with a big, bushy mustache wearing a crisp white coat with shiny buttons running down both sides of his chest. He was wearing a tall white hat that looked like a cigarette filter.

I dropped the remote on the cushion beside me. The man was standing behind a stainless steel table with about a dozen small white bowls full of colorful ingredients arranged neatly around him. What caught my attention was that he was holding a big knife, like the one that Michael Myers has in the *Halloween* movies.

Even though the man was speaking English, an American narrator would provide a voiceover every few sentences. As a Rez kid, I found this amusing. I was proficient in interpreting thick Apache and Navajo accents—I didn't need help understanding French mustache man.

"Dis chef knife is not being suitable for somefing like fluting mussrooms," he said. I'd later learn he was referring to a classic technique for marking the top of a mushroom with a grooved spiral pattern.

After the entrée segment, another chef—who the narrator said was from Switzerland—came on to make a dessert. The chyron underneath him read *Pastry Chef.*

"Whooaa . . . there's different kinds of chefs?" I spoke to the television. "That's rad."

Up until I started watching *Great Chefs*, I assumed cooking was mostly a girls' thing because that's how it was in my life. But most of the professional chefs on television were men. I remember wondering if they, too, had learned to cook from their mothers.

From then on, I was hooked, watching the show regularly all the way through high school and teaching myself to do things like julienne potatoes into thin matchsticks.

Before this, my obsession had been skateboarding videos. It was amazing to see skaters doing tricks in all these different cities, and I liked that, no matter if they were in Tokyo or Paris, they all dressed in similar clothing: baggy jeans, oversize T-shirts, and sneakers. There weren't many things like that, where it didn't matter who you were or where you came from, whether you were rich or poor, Black, white, or brown. In the skating world, if you were good, you could go around the world thrashing.

It seemed to me that the same thing was true of trained cooks. No matter where they were from, they almost all wore the same uniform—white coat, white hat—and they all used the same cool-sounding lingo, words like *julienne* and *demi-glace*. I liked to make my parents laugh by clowning around in the kitchen, pretending to be a Rezed-out chef with a thick Navajo accent.

"An den you take da budder and put it in a reeeelly hot fryin' skill-let." I'd purse my lips, pointing them at the frying pan in my hands. "You godda fry da meet reeeaaaallly goot until its golen brown!"

It wasn't like I had any dreams of being a chef after high school, though. By my senior year, it wasn't clear if I'd be graduating at all. My grades were awful and I was three credits short. I remember my guidance counselor, Mr. Arviso, a goofy Navajo with chunky, square bifocals, telling me that I wasn't "university material" and that I should be looking at trade schools or the military.

"You don't want to end up in prison, do you?" he said.

"Hell, no." I looked over at the wall where he kept handouts and brochures in wire files.

"What's this?" I reached over, fishing out a pamphlet for Kendall College. What had caught my eye was an action shot of a young person in a tall white paper hat holding a pan over an orange-blue flame. She had an intense, concentrated look on her face.

"You . . . like cooking?" Mr. Arviso sounded shocked, like I'd asked if I could date his daughter or something.

I had to admit, the idea of learning how to be like the pros on *Great Chefs* was intriguing, but I was done with school. I tucked the pamphlet back in its place and agreed to attend weekend classes so I could graduate on time. I wanted to head down to Phoenix and make just enough money to hang out, drink forty-ouncers, score weed, and skate. I couldn't wait to move out and live on my own. Once I turned eighteen, my parents wouldn't be able to stop me.

From February of that year, 1998, I hunkered down, determined to stay out of trouble and just finish school.

Thankfully, my cousin-brother Lyle came through for me. He had graduated a year earlier and moved to the city, and when we talked that spring, he invited me to come live with him. The construction company he worked for was hiring and he said he'd put in a good word.

By May, my bedroom walls were almost bare—I'd taken down all my Wu-Tang Clan, Gang Starr, Tribe Called Quest, and *Trans-World SKATEboarding* posters and rolled them up in a cardboard tube. Pretty much everything else I owned was already crammed into three duffel bags.

My mom and auntie Charlotte had agreed to drive me the four-and-a-half hours down to Phoenix right after school ended. The night before we were set to leave, I found an empty Etnies shoebox under my bed and filled it with photos and special objects, including an eagle feather and a small glass jar of yellow pollen gifted to me by an Apache medicine man. I also packed a handful of the acorns my mom and aunties had collected during our trip up to Whiteriver that previous fall.

Most people in America didn't even know you could eat acorns, which told me that we Apaches were distinctive and *badass*.

Acorns would remind me of home.

TWO

DUMBASS IN A NECKERCHIEF

The aroma of browned meat and caramelized onions mingled with the weed smoke wafting in from the living room, where my Navajo cousins were sitting around talking shit. I cranked the can opener, pulled the lid off the tomato sauce, and dumped it into the pan.

"Hey, someone pass me the spliff," I called out, rummaging around in the cabinet where we kept a few spices and a stash of ramen packets.

My cousin Lyle popped his head into the tiny kitchen, which fit only one person comfortably. I'd been living in the apartment for a few weeks, long enough to know that Lyle and I were the only two who ever cooked. Whenever the other guys would tease us about it, we'd shut them up with an insult.

"That's why I have a girlfriend and you don't," I told my cousin-brother Rufus when he razzed me.

"Yeah, it's not just 'cuz you're a punk-ass beeyatch." Lyle backed me up, his voice playful. "Girls get hot when they hear a guy can cook."

I took a couple of tokes, stirring the meat sauce with my other hand while Lyle lingered in the doorway.

"Whatcha got there, Nephi?" he asked, craning his neck to check out the jars of garlic powder and oregano I'd pulled out. "You sprinkling weed in the sauce? Is that your secret ingredient?"

"Tcha-right! I don't need to get no one high to get them hooked. My sauce is just better than yours."

It was an ongoing riff between us—who made better pasta. Lyle used diced green peppers and premade marinara sauce. *No contest there.*

My mom taught me her simple but delicious recipe before I got to the third grade and, by now, I knew it by heart: slice an onion into rounds before crosscutting it into small squares, then fry it up with a small block of ground beef. Mom used a can each of tomato sauce and tomato paste, along with garlic powder and dried oregano. The finishing touch was a couple of drops from my dad's bottle of Tabasco.

Lyle's gift, which I was big enough to admit, was being able to bake from scratch while blazed. We'd all be wiped out from smoking a couple of joints and he'd say, "Fuck it, I'm gonna bake a cake," and disappear into the kitchen for an hour. Slouched on the sofa, we'd hear him opening cupboards and mixing ingredients; the smell of batter would give us the serious munchies. We'd devour Lyle's creations straight from the pan.

When it came to spaghetti sauce, though, I was the champ.

I was definitely high now, floating and dreamy. I picked up the aluminum can of tomatoes I'd just emptied into the pan, staring at the label and chuckling. With its vineyards, villas, and pointy cypress trees, the illustrated countryside looked nothing like Whiteriver or

Window Rock, but just like some of the Italian chefs I'd seen interviewed on *Great Chefs*, I, too, had learned how to make a mean pasta from my *mamma*.

+ + + +

The one-bedroom apartment I shared with Lyle, Rufus, and whoever else needed a place to crash during the summer of 1998 was on the second floor of a gated apartment complex in east Phoenix, around Thirty-second and McDowell. There were two mattresses on the floor of the bedroom and a pullout couch in the living room. We rotated sleeping arrangements—we'd grown up together, so it was no big deal.

Our apartment was a typical bachelor pad. We tacked up pictures from different skate and hip-hop magazines; one of our older cousins, Aaron, hung a Shania Twain poster because his girlfriend at the time wouldn't let him put it up in his own apartment. The whole place was sparsely furnished. We ate at a small round table pushed against the glass sliding door that led to our narrow balcony or—if there were more than three of us, which there usually were—we'd sit around the low, secondhand coffee table.

During the workweek, my cousins and I woke up at the crack of dawn, piling into Lyle's brand-new dark blue Dodge Dakota, his pride and joy, and driving to that day's worksite. Since I was new and one of the shortest guys on the crew, my job was installing air-conditioning units, climbing into the rafters to run the wires and cables in the 120-degree heat. We kept it pretty chill during the week, but every weekend we'd have people over and stay up all night partying.

Like every other skate rat I knew, my main ambition was going pro or getting sponsored so I could score free gear. A bunch of my skater friends from Window Rock had also made the move to Phoenix, and we'd go out and skate together as much as possible, exploring different spots like the parking garage at Scottsdale Fashion Square and the massive drainage ditches in North Phoenix. We loved heading out at three or four in the morning, the best time to avoid cops and security guards, searching the cityscape for architecture that we could skate and destroy.

On paydays, my cousins and I sometimes splurged on dinner at one of the Mexican food trucks we drove by on our way home—back then, before food trucks were cool, people called them roach coaches—but most evenings, Lyle and I took turns cooking, feeding a rotating cast of friends, girlfriends, and anyone else who happened to be around. We baked chicken, fried eggs, sautéed vegetables, and made a lot of instant ramen, experimenting with different toppings like carrots, green onions, fresh and pickled chilies, or leftover meats, basically whatever was in the fridge.

I loved feeling confident in the kitchen, and it was a satisfying feeling, feeding people I cared for. I was in my element, living out of my duffel bags and partying all the time.

+ + + +

That first summer in Phoenix slipped by in a haze of alcohol and smoke. One Sunday night in the middle of August, me and a bunch of my cousin-brothers were hanging out on our narrow balcony around midnight, chugging Olde English, and we ran out of cigarettes. We were all totally wasted by then, but decided it would be all right to drive to the Circle K less than a block away. Back then, we drank and drove so much that we rarely gave it a second thought.

In high school, I was known as the guy who could drive everybody home no matter how drunk I was. I'd figured out that—if I was seeing double—I could cover one eye and make myself see one line on the road. Now, I walked into the living room where Lyle was stretched out on the couch, trying to sleep, and placed a hand on his shoulder.

"Yo, Lyle, give me your keys."

At first, he mumbled to leave him alone, but I kept pestering him, knowing that he loved that truck and was happy for any excuse to ride in it. Eventually, he sat up, rubbed his eyes, and mumbled that he'd come with me.

When we got to the store, I ran in; by the time I got back, Lyle was passed out cold.

I turned the key and pressed play on "The Death of John Smith," one of my favorite NOFX tracks, blasting the volume.

"Wake up, fool!" I looked over at my cousin, then pulled out of the parking lot, making a fast left-hand turn.

The collision was fast and violent. I hadn't even seen the sporty Mazda approaching the intersection. The little blue car bounced off the hood of our truck, spinning across the six-lane road.

I cut the wheel hard to the right, smashing into the curb. Lyle came to, pale and panicked. I was happy to see he wasn't hurt, but I could tell his truck was wrecked. The gears were making this horrible grinding sound, and as we hit the curb and came to a stop, I saw that the entire front was crumpled.

Before I could cut the engine, this big white guy swung open the driver's-side door and pulled me out of the truck, pinning me down on the ground and putting his knee on my back.

"You're not going to get away, you piece of shit! Don't fucking move or I'll smash your fucking teeth into the pavement," he yelled at me as I kept calling out to make sure Lyle was okay.

Eventually, the mobile DUI unit showed up and the cops took down statements from various witnesses and called an ambulance for the Mazda passenger, who was badly injured. They booked me on the spot and the Department of Public Safety officer on the scene offered to drive Lyle and me home.

I was still in handcuffs when he walked us up to the door. Rufus and Aaron were awake and they looked scared when we walked in, pulling themselves up straight. The apartment was a mess, with empty forty-bottles on every surface, but luckily there was no visible evidence of drug use.

After opening our fridge and doing a quick sweep of the place, the officer uncuffed me and handed me a printout of my arrest sheet and a slip of paper with the details of my arraignment, which was ten days away.

"You're in some serious shit." The room was silent. I felt my cousins' eyes on me.

"I hope you take this as a hard lesson—get your life in order and don't miss your court date."

"Yes, sir," I mumbled. I knew that when it came to law enforcement, the less I said, the better.

As soon as the officer left and we heard him thumping down the stairs, Aaron spoke up. "Tha fuck happened? Are you guys all right?"

Lyle shook his head. "We got in an accident. The truck's still at the scene—it's totaled." He started pacing around the room. "FUCK, I should have drove! How are we going to get to work?"

I felt like a worthless piece of shit, saying, "I'm sorry, bro," over and over.

"You're lucky you weren't hauled off to jail," said Aaron, who was older and knew that DUI and drug charges usually got you thrown behind bars. He looked at the cheap clock hanging on the living room wall. "Shit, we gotta get up for work in two hours," he said, patting me on the back.

It was my night to sleep on the floor, but I was jacked up on adrenaline. I lay on that thin mattress, feeling sick to my stomach, trying to calm my whirling mind.

Will my cousins lose their jobs now that our ride is gone?

How can I make this up to Lyle?

What is going to happen to me?

What will I tell my parents?

+ + + +

Right around my thirteenth birthday, after I was caught getting high with my friends and the school informed my parents about multiple unexcused absences, Mom and Dad made me come back to Apache Land with them, to visit my auntie Charlotte. The drive was mostly silent, and when we got to East Fork, my dad turned off the main road, driving up a steep hill to an unfamiliar yellow house.

"Where are we?" I asked, looking around the dusty yard with its yucca plants and jumping cactuses.

"Come, son," was all my father said.

An old man I vaguely recognized from the Sunrise Dance ceremonies I'd attended answered the door, ushering us into his living room. He was a medicine man, someone people came to for help. That day he was wearing large tinted eyeglasses and a plaid shirt tucked into his Wranglers. He gestured toward the scratchy couch, where I sat down between my two parents, and eased himself into a large leather armchair.

My mom spoke Apache in urgent, serious tones while my dad nodded in agreement and made the occasional comment, also in Apache. I couldn't understand most of what they were saying, but I knew for sure they were talking about me since their conversation was peppered with English words like *suspension*, *Window Rock*, and *skateboard*.

I'm in serious shit this time, I thought to myself, *because now I'm in trouble the Apache Way!*

The medicine man listened intently to my mom while I sat slouched and stone-faced, my black beanie pulled low. I wanted everyone to see how pissed off I was to be sitting there instead of hanging out with my friends.

All of a sudden, the old man sprang up from his chair and disappeared down the hall. He returned a few minutes later carrying a scuffed, olive-green tackle box, which he set on the low redwood table in front of us. I watched as the old man sifted through compartments of colored stones, razor blades, mirror shards, string, markers, and jars of colorful beads, staring at his gnarled brown hands with their giant knuckles.

Finally, he pulled a bundle wrapped in buckskin from the bottom compartment and placed it between us, carefully unfolding the fabric to reveal a handful of beautiful eagle plumes.

"Take one, shichoo," he said, using the Apache word for grandson. His kind tone took me by surprise.

I considered the different feathers in front of me, but the choice was obvious. I picked up the speckled caramel-brown one that faded into white. It was fluffy at the base of the stem, the most elegant thing I had ever seen.

"Heey-yeeeeaaaahhh!" The medicine man sounded pleased.

My mother, father, and I all leaned forward as he took a golden strip of deer sinew and wrapped it around the feather, then plucked an oval piece of turquoise out of a matchbox and tied it to the shaft with a tight, graceful knot.

The medicine man looked up from his work, sticking me with his bright, coffee-colored eyes and switching to melodic English.

"We are Apaches," he told me in a raspy voice. "You are White Mountain Apache even though your dad's a crazy Navajo."

The two men laughed, like old friends. I couldn't help but grin.

"You and the eagle feather, you chose each other. And I chose this big turquoise bead because I can see you need big protection.

"Us Apaches are prayerful people. We do everything in prayer, and it doesn't matter what language you pray in and it doesn't matter what church you go to," he continued.

I looked back up at him. I appreciated the concept that it wasn't necessary to attend church in order to pray. I've carried the medicine man's next words with me ever since that day:

"The mountains are our church, the land is our church, the stars are our church," he told me.

"What matters is that you pray to Bik'ehgo'ihi'dán," he said, using the Apache word for God.

He pulled out a small bottle of yellow pollen.

"When you pray, use this and the eagle feather. Together with the deerskin and the turquoise, they will protect you."

He handed me the jar.

"Heey-yeeeeaaaahhh," he whooped. "This is Apache power!"

The medicine man gestured for us to stand. He put his hands on my shoulders and turned me to face east, saying a prayer in our Apache language while holding my newly tied plume.

I closed my eyes. I could hear both of my parents gently weeping and sniffling. I didn't feel like I was in trouble anymore. I felt deeply cared for, being blessed for the journey to come.

The medicine man finished his prayer and handed me my feather. When we got to the front door, he reached out to shake my hand. His grip was incredibly strong, his skin dry and rough.

"Keep it close," he said, nodding to the feather in my other hand. "It'll even protect you when you're on that skateboard."

The night of the accident, the memory of that day came back to me with startling clarity. I got up and tiptoed over to the narrow shelving unit we'd found next to the dumpster, picking up my Etnies box and taking it out with me to the balcony. I lit a cigarette and thought about opening the lid to take out my precious eagle feather, picturing how I would twirl it around in my fingers and pray for protection. But that felt like a bad use of Apache power, so I just finished smoking, staring at the box gloomily.

\+ + + +

I lasted only another day or two more at the construction job. I felt too ashamed to spend that much time around my cousins. I tried to stay out of the apartment as much as possible, getting faded with my skate crew at their houses every night, and sometimes even during the day.

A few days before I was scheduled to appear in court, Dustinn—who was married with his third kid on the way and living about twenty minutes away in Scottsdale—came by the apartment after everyone else had left for work.

I hadn't told anyone in my immediate family about the accident, but one of our older cousins had called my older brother to tell him I'd gotten into some trouble. I answered the door, rubbing my crusty eyes. The place was a mess—crushed beer cans and overflowing ashtrays everywhere, half-eaten cartons of ramen and some greasy pizza boxes littered every surface. I didn't want a lecture, so I made up an excuse about a friend sleeping over.

"I'll put on some shoes and come out to you," I said, my voice low and scratchy.

We walked silently through the hallway and down the stairs, opening the front gate. The temperature was already in the high 90s and I felt sick, so I suggested we sit down on the curb and talk.

Dustinn got straight to the point. He'd always been the solid, responsible one out of our pack of brother-cousins.

"What the fuck, Nephi? Are you okay?"

"Yeah, man, I'm all right." I lit a cigarette and took a long drag. I pulled a mini of Jack Daniel's out of my cargo shorts pocket, lifting it up like I was making a toast. Dustinn grimaced.

I grinned, trying to defuse the tension. "I'm going in front of the judge in a few days and I'm gonna be fucked. I'm just trying to get a head start."

Dustinn didn't laugh, but he didn't tell me off, either. Instead, his voice got real soft. "Why don't you just come live with us, bro? You just graduated and you're already fucking up your life. We love our brothers and shit, but fuck, dude . . ."

I took another drag, staring across the street at the cars in the parking lot. It was impossible for me to look at him. "For real?"

Dustinn put a hand on my shoulder. "Of course. You're my little brother."

I thought of all the people I knew who were locked up, the classmates who had already died. For the first time since the accident, I let myself cry. I didn't want my life to be over.

Dustinn said I could move in as soon as I wanted, and I thanked him. I told him I'd check in with him as soon as my arraignment was over.

+ + + +

I reported to Maricopa County Superior Court on a hazy Wednesday morning, riding the city bus alone because I thought there was a good chance they might take me into custody and I didn't want anyone to see that. I'd stashed the medicine man's plume in the front pocket of my backpack.

Sitting in the air-conditioned courtroom, my face was burning hot. By this point, everyone in my family knew that I drank and smoked and used drugs. My parents had been trying to talk with me about my self-destructive patterns for years, but I had no interest in having those conversations. When I finally called my dad to tell him about the accident, he was excited to hear from me, immediately cracking some joke, but as soon as I delivered my news, he got quiet. I sensed the unbridgeable distance between us. When he asked whether I was facing jail time, I could hear the worry in his voice. I felt like a real loser.

The judge called my name, snapping me back to attention. He read out the charges against me: "Drinking as a minor. Possession of marijuana. Aggravated DUI."

I swallowed.

"Two counts of aggravated assault with a deadly weapon."

What the hell? I thought, my panic growing. The public defender assigned to me leaned over, explaining that, according to the law, a vehicle is considered a weapon when driven by a drunk eighteen-year-old.

We left the hearing and went down the hallway to a small meeting room, where my lawyer suggested we try to plead down to a high misdemeanor.

"If the charges stick, you could get three to five years in prison," he explained. "But you're young and you don't have a criminal record. There's a chance the judge will cut you some slack."

It turned out to be good advice. We struck a plea bargain with the prosecutor in the pretrial meeting and reported back to the courthouse for sentencing.

The presiding judge riffled through the papers in front of him before clearing his throat.

"There's a whole life ahead of you, young man. Perhaps you can construct something out of the wreckage and make something great of yourself, just like your namesake." *A Mormon judge.* The feather was protecting me, after all.

I looked down at my shoes and mumbled, "Yes, sir."

He sentenced me to three years of probation on the condition that I remain drug- and alcohol-free and become a full-time student or employee.

I suspected *skateboarder* wasn't a job that would fly with the judge, but I thought back to the brochure I'd seen in Mr. Arviso's office. Maybe cooking would be a good profession for me?

I liked how the chefs on TV artistically carved vegetables into unique shapes and made chocolate sculptures and apple swans. I thought it would be a great experience working in an immaculate, steel kitchen, wielding my sharp knives. Plus, I wanted to travel. Thinking of all the idyllic locations I'd seen on *Great Chefs of the World*, I imagined culinary training might, at the very least, get me to Italy or France.

I looked into my options and found out that Scottsdale Community College had a culinary arts program. The school was about three miles away from my brother's house, close enough that I could get there on my skateboard. I was nervous filling out the application, especially when it came to the section about relevant work experience. I hoped that honesty would work in my favor—I wrote that I'd been cooking pretty much since I was able to reach the counter.

Miraculously enough, I got in.

Since I'd already missed the fall deadline for tribal scholarships, I had to borrow money from my brother and my parents to scrape together the first tuition payment. They were excited to see me focused on a goal, and happy to help.

Once I was officially registered, the school sent me a list of equipment I needed to purchase before the first day of classes. I took the bus to a uniform store on the west side of Phoenix, in the hood.

The shop wasn't very big, but there were racks and racks of nursing scrubs, rent-a-cop uniforms, and military fatigues. I found a small selection of chef's uniforms all the way in the back, and picked out the cheapest items I could find: a simple white chef's coat with plastic buttons; a pair of standard, checkered pants; a pair of black slip-resistant shoes; and a neckerchief.

I went into the dressing room and put everything on, following the instruction sheet that explained how to roll and tie the neckerchief around my neck. I came out and stood in front of the mirror, choking back a laugh.

What a fucking dweeb. I looked like the kind of kid I would have given mad shit to.

I caught my eyes in the reflection. *It's either this shit or fucking prison*, I told myself firmly. I'd take my chances looking like a dumbass.

+ + + +

The first week of culinary school, it became clear to me that I was totally out of place—and not just because I was the only student on felony probation.

Pretty much all of my classmates were white, and before class, they'd talk among themselves about their "vision" for their future and what type of "operation" they planned to run someday. A few of them drove nice cars and complained about the lack of student parking, or bragged how their parents were going to help them open a restaurant after they graduated, though most of us seemed to be from working-class families.

Every other student seemed to know the vocabulary our teachers threw around, words like *risotto*, *ganache*, *cassoulet*, and *turbot*. I caught a couple of them smirking when I raised my hand and asked what a *bistro* was. When our teacher talked about *vichyssoise*, the strangest word I had ever heard in my life, I didn't dare ask about it. After class, I headed over to the library, where I looked it up in the dictionary.

What a crazy-ass word for potato-leek soup, I thought.

I had never heard of most of the dishes our instructors rattled on about, let alone tasted them. Many days I asked myself what I was doing there. Although we were in the heyday of quote-unquote Southwestern cuisine, the stars in the space were white dudes like Rick Bayless and Bobby Flay—in all of the reading we did at school, I never encountered a single mention of an Indigenous chef. I didn't find any in the magazines I devoured on my own time—*Gourmet*, *Bon Appétit*, and *Food & Wine*—either. I felt like an outsider, an imposter. What did people like me have to do with great food?

Despite all those hours of watching *Great Chefs of the World*, I had no real concept of the restaurant world. On the rare occasions my family went out to eat, we usually ended up at a Chinese buffet recommended by a local in whatever town we were visiting. Back when I was in elementary school, my dad took me and my buddy Delmore on a road trip to Phoenix, where I ordered stir-fried octopus off the menu at the restaurant we ate at. Neither Dad nor Delmore would even try a bite, which, I remember, made me feel very brave. Another time, I convinced my mom to take me to a sushi restaurant. I knew about the Japanese staple from *The Breakfast Club*, where the rich, snobby girl, played by Molly Ringwald, is teased by her classmates for bringing sushi for lunch. I found the notion of eating raw fish interesting, but in reality I thought it was gross. I forced one roll down and couldn't eat anymore. The rice vinegar, the wasabi, the slightly mushy rice—I've since grown to love sushi, but back then it just seemed cold, strange, and complicated. It wasn't for me.

Sitting in the classroom, I felt that way again. As I jotted down the ingredients for a classic béchamel or Mornay sauce, I thought about how, for many Native people, the main reference point for cheese was the big orange block of government cheese that came in a brown box and looked like something out of an army surplus store. That cheese was a staple of my youth, along with the Commodity Beef Stew, which came in a silver can with black labels indicating which "food groups" were represented—icons of an apple, a carrot, a slice of bread, and a piece of meat with a bone sticking out. The cans of Meatball Stew were my favorite. They came in a thick, delicious brown gravy, and the meatballs looked like the ones Freddy Krueger put on his pizza that had the little screaming faces of his victims on them: *Noooooooo, don't eat meeeeeee!* I would pretend I was Freddy and devour the tasty mystery meat.

When our instructors showed us how to make a perfect omelet, I thought about how my mom made her own delicious version by dissolving powdered milk in water and then mixing that with the powdered eggs that came in white and silver paper bags, printed with an image of a hen and a few eggs. I especially loved when she fried up a can of salty canned pork and folded it into the eggs.

The only time I felt in my element during those early days of cooking school was in our Knife Skills class. Knives were a constant in my life—I was the proud owner of dozens of different Swiss Army knives and buck knives, and I had multiple versions of the so-called Rambo knives from the eighties that came with a "survival kit": matches, fishing line, a plastic rain poncho, and, inexplicably, chewing gum. A few times, I had "borrowed" my dad's KA-BAR, a relic from his days as a marine, using it to sharpen sticks into spears and arrows. My dad believed every boy needed a knife, and he taught us to be careful and respect them.

It was second nature, taking good care of the Wüsthof chef's knives I'd purchased before school began. I kept them extremely sharp, always putting them in their blade protectors and keeping the whole set neatly rolled up in my black knife roll.

I also took to heart the classic kitchen motto *Shut up and cook.* Whenever one of our instructors snapped at us to respond only with a "Yes, Chef" or a "No, Chef," I instantly thought of one of my favorite movies, *Full Metal Jacket*, and the scene where Gunnery Sergeant Hartman says, "The first and last words out of your filthy sewers will be 'sir.'" Then the recruits respond with "Sir, yes, Sir!" My classmates seemed offended or annoyed, but I—the son of a United States Marine who had gone through the Devil Pups program at Camp Pendleton—found it amusing, even comforting. My classmates had no idea how much easier this was than doing drills in the sun.

I could be as quiet as I wanted in our Knife Skills class, letting my work speak for itself. *Julienne*, *bâtonnet*, *brunoise*, *rondelle*, *chiffonade*. I mastered the different cuts much more quickly than any of my classmates, and I liked learning about the different types of kitchen knives and their uses, memorizing the various elements of a knife: the spine, the pommel, the rivets, the tang. All of these terms became an exciting new language that I picked up easily.

Around the same time, I learned that *cuisine*, a word I'd never really understood, means *the food that represents a people.* Our teachers used the word often, primarily to lecture us about the "Great Cuisines of the World," which—surprise!—all happened to be European, part of the "Old World," an ignorant colonialist label that would have definitely made my Apache ancestors chuckle.

The culinary program at Scottsdale Community College was established by Chef Dominic, a real old-school guy who was our head instructor. Chef Dominic was tall, six feet two, closer to seven feet with his chef's toque on. Before he started teaching, Chef Dominic had worked in the business his entire life, and he created exquisite classic French dishes, taking special pride in his stocks and sauces. After a lifetime in the kitchen bent over plates and work counters, he had a hunch in his back, and he loved to cuss and flash you his yellow smoker's grin. To him, I could tell, we were all a bunch of stupid rookies. I never knew if Chef Dominic liked or disliked me—or if he saw me as just another useless turd.

One day, early in the school year, I asked Chef Dominic the question that had been bubbling in my brain for weeks.

"Hey, Chef, is there such a thing as Native American cuisine?"

He laughed in my face.

"I know you make fry breads and boil stews," he said in his fancy accent that I could never place. "That's about it."

His condescension really pissed me off. Based on what I knew from growing up in Apache Land and the Navajo Nation, I was positive there was a lot to learn about Native American food traditions. I expected more from a culinary school teacher, especially one working in a region with a rich Indigenous history. In that moment, I decided to seek out this knowledge myself. The skateboarding, graffiti-writing, Wu-Tang Clan–loving, Navajo/Apache punk in me was excited to go on an underground journey to answer all kinds of questions: What were Native people eating before they came into contact with white Europeans? Where and how did they get their food? How did they grow and trade it? Each time I encountered a new ingredient during class, the first question that popped into my mind was: Is it Native to the Americas or not?

I spent every free moment that fall trying to educate myself about my culinary roots, consulting librarians at community colleges and public libraries around Scottsdale and Phoenix and scouring the book sections in the thrift stores where I shopped for clothes and CDs. I read encyclopedias, gardening guides, and sociology texts, chasing down mentions in footnotes. I checked different magazines, journals, and newspapers, seeking out interviews with Indigenous experts and food practitioners. Once it became clear to me that much of our food history had been forgotten or erased, I committed myself to piecing it back together as best as I could. I was determined to bring the truth back to the table.

+ + + +

The entire time I attended classes at Scottsdale Community College, from August 1998 to May 1999, hardly anyone acknowledged the fact that we were sitting within the confines of a Native American reservation, the Salt River Pima-Maricopa Indian Community. There was no mention of Native American people at all. We'd been wiped off the map.

The same, it turns out, can be said about the seminal foods native to the Americas. Hardly anyone knows the truth about them.

Take the tomato. I learned, at eighteen, that it actually originated as a wild plant in the mountainous regions of Mesoamerica, within the present-day territories of Ecuador, Peru, Bolivia, and Chile.

I was shocked to find out that the poster child of Italian cuisine was indigenous to the Americas—a Native like me! What else, I wondered, had been kept from us? I scoured every book of food history and cultural anthropology I could get my hands on to learn the story of this ingredient that loomed so large in our classical training.

All the varieties of tomato that we know today evolved from a species called *Solanum lycopersicum* that dates back around eighty thousand years. These plants produced tiny, inedible fruits that were small, somewhere between a tack and a cherry. Eventually, some seven thousand years ago, these wild tomato plants were domesticated, and by the time the Aztec Empire was founded in the fifteenth century, tomatoes were an important ingredient in the cuisine of the Indigenous peoples of the region. Its Nahuatl name was tomatl, and it was the base for many sauces, soups, and stews.

Historians often frame the story of a tomato as a big mystery, speculating whether the tomato plant ended up in modern-day Mexico by chance—thanks to migrating birds, for example—or more intentionally, through human migration or trade. Remembering how my great-grandfather Joseph Carley Ivins religiously saved and exchanged seeds, it seemed clear to me that tomatoes did not arrive in Central America by accident. Reaching for explanations like bird shit seemed . . . like a heap of bullshit.

European colonizers would have first encountered the tomato sometime around 1519, when they infiltrated Aztec territory. As the Spaniards were laying waste to the Americas, razing the land and killing its people, they were also extracting Indigenous cultivars and sending them back to their homeland, thousands of miles away. Over the next one hundred years, the tomato plant would travel from Spain to Italy and beyond, eventually making its way to Asia, most likely via the Spanish colony in the Philippines.

In Europe, the tomato was initially treated as an exotic oddity; many people worried it was poisonous, and used it primarily as an ornamental plant. Botanical writings from the time completely omitted the fact that the tomato came from the Americas. Take for example Italian botanist and physician Pietro Andrea Mattioli's 1544 leaflet, where he described a novel type of eggplant that had arrived in Italy, which was bloodred or golden colored when mature and could be divided into segments and cooked in oil, seasoned with salt and black pepper. A decade later, Mattioli coined a new name for this "eggplant" of mysterious provenance: pomi d'oro, which translates to *golden apple*.

Works of art and cookbooks from the seventeenth century show how, despite initial hesitation, the tomato was eventually adopted as a kitchen staple in both Spain and Italy. Tomato sauce first appeared in a cookbook released in Napoli around 1692, but by 1891, when Pellegrino Artusi published his famous overview of recipes from every Italian region, *La scienza in cucina e l'arte di mangiar bene*, tomatoes were featured throughout its pages.

By the time I enrolled in culinary school, in the late 1990s, there was no question about the tomato's status as a cornerstone of Italian cuisine, but not a single person I talked to, including the chefs hired to educate us about the fundamentals of cooking, seemed to realize or care that before the brutal colonization of the Americas, Pasta Pomodoro and Bolognese simply didn't exist. The plant's Indigenous origins had been carefully erased, as had the deliberate pattern of European powers appropriating Native foods—and reaping their gastronomical rewards through violence and theft.

+ + + +

Without tomatoes, there would be no ratatouille, a French peasant food turned bistro classic, which I learned how to make at my first restaurant job.

Almost as soon as I started culinary school, I realized that I needed to make some money. From the beginning, probation was difficult for me, and I failed one of my early drug tests, which meant that I was now subjected to random testing. I tried to stop smoking weed, but I was constantly pushing my luck, going out at night drinking. My brother had two little boys and a newborn daughter; he didn't drink or allow it in his home. I knew he hated it when I rolled in drunk. I was desperate to move out on my own, and I also needed to start chipping away at all the fines and court and probation fees. I owed several thousand dollars.

In October, I attended a hospitality job fair hosted at the community college. I walked around all the booths set up in and around the cafeteria, carrying a bulky backpack stuffed with my kitchen uniform, knife roll, and skateboard.

I filled out applications for hotels like the Princess, the Boulders, and the Hyatt Regency Downtown, but the only person I chatted with that day was this tall white dude wearing a white chef's coat embroidered with two maroon horseshoes turned back-to-back. The logo looked like the one for DC Shoes, the skate brand.

"Cool chef coat." I pointed.

"Thanks," he said in a hardcore Midwestern accent, his thin lips turning up at the corners. "You looking for a job?"

I nodded. "I applied to a bunch of places."

He handed me an application. "Are you in school here?"

"Yeah," I answered, and then trying to sound professional, I added, "So, like, uh, what kind of food do you do?"

"Mediterranean-style cuisine inspired by local southwestern ingredients, with a lot of French influences," he said, sounding like a robot—nasally and serious and uptight.

"We're a new property up in North Scottsdale, about a year old. We do breakfast, lunch, and dinner. We're looking for people to fill out our team."

As it turned out, the robot's name was Chris Olson, the executive chef at the Country Club at DC Ranch, and he was the only person who called me back.

Two weeks after the fair, I went in for an interview, and, two days later, he offered me a job as an entry-level cook making nine dollars an hour. I was thrilled.

After that, my days were fuller than ever. Every morning, I was at school, filling my head with fundamentals and theory. At one o'clock, I'd haul ass to my job, where I'd hold down a station all night.

+ + + +

The Country Club at DC Ranch provided me with a crash course in the realities of restaurant kitchens. It was busy, noisy, and hot. I was getting my ass kicked by the mise en place—there was so much to prepare before we opened for dinner at five. Like most newbies, I was put on the garde manger station to start, preparing salads and apps, but I quickly got moved to the expo station out in the dining room—where I wore a goofy-ass puffy gray chef's hat and was in charge of firing pizzas and specials in a wood-burning oven—and then on to the grill station. I made it my goal to work my way up to the sauté station.

No one had to tell me that the sauté station required more skill than the others. Each night, I'd stare in wonder at the dishes they put out: perfectly cooked halibut, salmon, striped bass, and red snapper; glistening plates of bay and diver scallops; delicate risottos, handmade pasta specials, and mouthwatering cioppino, a tomato-based seafood stew. That station was in charge of sauces and broths as well: rich mushroom broths, fish fumets, truffle butter, and shrimp stock. The first time I tasted a beurre blanc with Meyer lemon, I felt like I was tasting a cloud on a sunny day: creamy and fluffy with a refreshing tang. The entire dinner service appeared to revolve around the sauté station, where both the executive chef and the sous chef focused their attention. It was the only place in that kitchen where a line cook could tell the chefs what to do.

The grill station was also its own universe. Our executive chef Chris Olson held daily service meetings where he'd hand out printouts describing the daily specials for each station. Most weeks, he'd get whole sections of cow and cut them himself on a meat band saw at a butcher shop across the street. On any given night, I'd be putting out amazing dry-aged porterhouse, Kansas City, New York, or T-bone steaks, along with tenderloins and chops. I learned how to prepare great gratins, mashers, and risottos, and discovered the magical world of mycology, learning how to pan-roast chanterelles, morels, wood ears, black trumpets, maitakes, and porcinis, drawing out the umami flavors of all the different mushrooms.

At DC Ranch, I cooked vegetables I'd never heard of growing up on the Rez: Broccolini and broccoli rabe; cipollini and Vidalia onions; turnips, rutabagas, sunchokes, and celery root; arugula, Swiss chard, endive, and mizuna. White asparagus was a miracle.

One night, an unfamiliar word appeared on my specials sheet: *ratatouille*.

"Tha fuck is that?" I mumbled, trying to sound it out: "Rat-at-oily?"

The sous chef snickered, but thankfully Chef Chris didn't hear me. He turned to me and I clicked my pen, ready to take notes.

"We're gonna do a rustic ratatouille for the dry age. Large-dice some zucchini, yellow squash, and see if there's any baby eggplant left on Deidre's station." As usual, Chef Chris was all business. "Take twenty Roma tomatoes, split them and char them on the grill. Small-dice a yellow onion, sweat it in a pot with raw chopped garlic until fragrant, hit it with a spoonful of tomato paste, and cook it for a minute. Then give it a splash of white wine, cook off the alcohol, and add the charred tomatoes."

"Yes, Chef." I knew to look up whenever Chef paused, to assure him I was paying attention. He held my gaze and continued in his robotic monotone.

"Cover with veg stock, stir in a few cloves of garlic confit and a glug of garlic oil, bring to a boil, and reduce to a simmer for about twenty minutes. You're essentially making a flavorful tomato sauce. Once the tomatoes have broken down, run them through your food mill, reduce, season, ice it down, and hold for service."

Tomato sauce, I wrote in my battered notebook.

"On pick up," he continued, using kitchen jargon for when you're getting a dish ready to serve to a customer, "roast the squash and eggplant in a hot pan, get come good color, deglaze with a little veg stock, hit it with your tomato sauce, reduce, and finish with a generous amount of chopped parsley and chiffonade basil and a pinch of chili flakes. Season, taste, and finish with extra virgin olive oil. It should be rich, sweet, savory, a little tart, a little smoky from the char, and just a bit of heat in the background."

I scribbled furiously.

"Got it?"

I nodded. I was quickly becoming fluent in "kitchenese," as Anthony Bourdain called it. I was learning how to follow rapid-fire instructions and commit them to memory, figuring out how to work quickly and efficiently.

I was becoming a chef.

Back at culinary school, many of my classmates had trouble with basic knife technique, complained loudly about getting small cuts, and were constantly talking back to our chef instructors. When I let our Culinary Fundamentals instructor, Chef Michael Whelan, know that I had landed a cooking job at DC Ranch, he told me to pay close attention to the other chefs in that kitchen and I would learn valuable lessons. He treated me differently after that conversation, asking me questions like "How was service last night?" It made me feel proud, like I'd earned some respect.

The cooks at the Country Club at DC Ranch were all very experienced. Tony, an obnoxious New Yorker, was in charge of the grill station. On my second day in the kitchen, he walked past my station, pinching my ass and making a smacking-kiss sound. It felt more like straight-up harassment than a genuine sexual overture, the kind of hazing I would come to find out is a feature in many professional kitchens, where the culture is built around the idea that only the strongest survive, that being sensitive is a weakness. I never told anyone about it because I was the new kid and I didn't want to cause any trouble, but from then on, I was cautious around Tony.

Joe was from the mean streets of Detroit, and he held down the garde manger (cold plates) station. He wore beat-up white running shoes and talked about work like he didn't give a fuck, but any time I asked him a question, he would light up, giving me pointers about specific knife cuts and vinaigrettes. Joe was passionate about salad greens, and he taught me to wash them in ice water to keep them fresh and crisp, especially during the summer.

"Nothing worse than getting a clump of dirt in your salad or appetizer," Joe barked one day as Tony walked by his station. "You don't wanna be like some fuckin' idiots who wash their greens like they wash their ass!"

When I first started at DC Ranch, Tony and Joe would ride me for being slow every day, saying stuff like "Craig's here, leaving a snail trail," and shouting at me to come get my shit and whip my station into shape.

As I grew more comfortable and efficient, I didn't need as many pointers and was yelled at much less. Compared to the guys I worked with, the students in my classes seemed slow and soft to me—their jokes were so clean and innocent. I secretly wondered if any of them could really hack it in a restaurant kitchen, where they'd have to work fast and organized under real pressure.

At the time, I didn't know enough about restaurants to understand that I was working in a particularly high-functioning kitchen, that many other restaurants didn't operate like DC Ranch, with fresh, quality ingredients and an herb garden outside, a pastry chef, and everything made from scratch. I realize now that I didn't fully appreciate what a great boss Chef Olson was, either, level-headed and fair.

I remember one very busy night, three servers stood around gossiping loudly while everyone on the line was cranking. All the chefs were annoyed, including Chef Olson, but instead of scolding them or making some biting, smart-ass remark, he turned to face them and, in a calm, firm voice, said, “I know you are enjoying your talk, but could you continue this conversation at another time?” Later in my career, I would see other chefs handle similar situations by cussing out the staff or humiliating them. But Chef Olson was a pro.

I sometimes regret that I was so afraid when I started working for him that I wasn’t more vocal about my ambitions. I wish I had asked him to explain the path to becoming a sous chef in his kitchen one day. I understand now that he had so much to teach me when it came to running a busy but always respectful kitchen.

✦ ✦ ✦ ✦

I fielded more than a dozen tickets for dry-aged steaks the first night I made ratatouille. In the middle of the Saturday dinner rush, I was running low on the diced baby eggplant that I’d gotten from Deidre.

“Chef, I’m almost finished with the eggplant, Chef!” I spoke loudly so I could be heard above the clatter and clang. “Only two more orders!”

Chef Olson stood down the line at the sauté station, plating a halibut special. Without hesitating, he responded, “Go ahead and substitute the eggplant with roasted button mushrooms.”

A couple of the waitstaff were standing within earshot and they echoed Chef’s orders like soldiers.

“Yes, Chef! Eggplant out, buttons now in the ratatouille!” (This was in the days before “Heard!” became a common shorthand refrain in restaurant kitchens.)

I turned back to my sauté pan, tossing a handful of squash pieces with the mushrooms we'd prepped for a different entrée. After deglazing the pan, I added the tomato paste.

"Oh, shit! This ain't no French dish!" I didn't mean to say it out loud. The simple veggies in my pan reminded me of something my mom might make. We ate a lot of squash in our house—my great-grandfather grew rows and rows in his garden, the leaves as big as my head—and, in the summer, my mom would fry it up in a pan with fresh tomatoes and corn.

Had Chef Olson not switched things up that night, I wouldn't have had my ratatouille eureka moment, but after the eggplant was eighty-sixed, I'd mentally subtracted all the other non-Native ingredients and replaced them with foods that were more familiar to me, subbing out the basil and parsley for sage and wild spinach, and replacing the white wine and olive oil with deer fat and spring water. Instead of the perky Mediterranean varietals of garlic and onions, I would swap in the scraggly wild onions and garlic that grew all over our Rez.

Who stole this shit from us first? I wondered, in the midst of the shouting and hiss of the dinner service. *After the Spanish took it from us and brought it to Spain, did they hand it over to their Italian homies? Did the French then just prance over and take credit for it?*

I chuckled to myself. *Was I the only person in the whole fucking world who saw the truth?* Take away the eggplant, and ratatouille was a mélange of squash and tomatoes, two elemental Indigenous foods.

THREE

UP THE GOLDEN ELEVATOR

With its plush carpet, ornate domed ceiling, and elaborate table settings, Mary Elaine's was the kind of restaurant that told you what it was all about before you even opened a menu.

The most celebrated fine-dining establishment in all of Phoenix was located on the top floor of the ultra-fancy Phoenician Resort, where the pool is tiled in mother-of-pearl. To get to the restaurant, you walked through the grand lobby and rode up a special gold elevator that was all mirrors. As soon as the doors opened, you were hit with a view of a huge chandelier hanging in front of a wall of windows framing spectacular views of the burnt-orange Sonoran Desert.

It was my day off and I had already knocked back four cups of coffee before leaving my small, two-bedroom apartment in South Scottsdale, which I'd moved into after finishing my second semester of culinary school. My brother had been patient with me, but I had definitely worn out my welcome stumbling home at all hours of the night. It was a relief when I had enough money in the bank to pay a security deposit on my own place, but even so, I remained restless, hungry for a new challenge.

I unzipped my backpack, popping a breath mint into my mouth. This wasn't my first time riding up the glittering elevator—I had dropped off my résumé a handful of times by now and was returning to apply for another position.

In 1999, the executive chef of Mary Elaine's, Alex Stratta, won the James Beard Award for the best chef in the country, cementing the restaurant's reputation as one of the top kitchens in the Southwest. Now, two years later, even with a new head chef, it was still a culinary destination. I knew it was a long shot to get a chef job here, but I thought they might hire me to scrub pots or jump on as a prep cook. Once my foot was in the door, I would show them that I was willing to do whatever it took to work my way up.

I'd been at the Country Club at DC Ranch for around three years by this point, going full time after receiving my Fundamentals Cook certification. I was grateful for Chef Olson and everything I had learned in his kitchen, but I couldn't help myself: I wanted to reach the mountaintop. The terms of my probation still didn't allow me to leave the state. DC Ranch was great, but Mary Elaine's was my Shaolin Temple—it was the closest I was going to get to California, New York, or France for now.

I had first heard about Mary Elaine's at the Phoenician from Chef Whelan, my favorite culinary school instructor, who had worked there as a line cook under both Alex Stratta and James Boyce, the chef who took over for him. Both of these men sat at the pinnacle of fine dining in the United States, and whenever Chef Whelan talked about his experiences in their kitchen, his eyes would glaze over.

Many of my classmates didn't like Chef Whelan because he was stern and structured, a tough critic, but I was fascinated by how he spoke directly, looking you straight in the eyes, and how easily he commanded a room. I liked how he took cooking so seriously, telling us stories about famous chefs, some of whom I recognized from watching *Great Chefs of the World*, explaining their lineage and how they'd moved up in the food world. He called Jean-Georges Vongerichten, Alain Ducasse, Jean-Louis Palladin, and Daniel Boulud "living legends" who were "changing the culinary landscape," which sounded pretty impressive. In my spare time, I gobbled up industry news online and read every food magazine I could get my hands on, eager to learn about the modern-day chefs continuing in this storied tradition. I could now rattle off the names of superstar chefs and their mentors and protégés. Before Mary Elaine's, James Boyce had worked as a sous chef at Le Cirque with Daniel Boulud, and Boulud had worked for top chefs in France before making his way to America and eventually opening his Manhattan flagship, Daniel.

The elevator pinged and the doors slid open silently. I stepped onto the plush carpet. The first time I'd come up to the fifth floor, I had frozen in place, feeling like an intruder, until a custodian came by to clean and took pity on me, pointing me to the kitchen. Now, I strode confidently across the hushed, empty dining room, CV in hand, and passed through the kitchen door, which blended discreetly into the back wall. I knew it was customary to submit your résumé through the front office, but I thought it was always preferable to hand it, in person, to the person in charge.

At this hour, the kitchen was empty and pristine, every surface gleaming. I closed my eyes, inhaling the smell of the finest ingredients—steak, butter, caviar, espresso beans, chocolate—mixed with freshly laundered linens, lemony dish soap, steam, copper, and the faint hint of high-end industrial cleaner. It was a scent that announced the seriousness of the place. *This is where luxury is created*, it communicated. *Welcome to the master's dojo.*

I opened my eyes and kept walking toward the chef's office, barely missing one of the sous chefs, who emerged from the walk-in carrying a tray of perfectly square beef short ribs.

"May I help you?" He looked at me with cold eyes that reminded me of a cop.

"I'm here to apply for a cook or prep position—"

He cut me off. "You have to apply with the HR department. We're closed."

He maneuvered around me, stiff and impatient.

"Use the staff elevator back there," he said, gesturing with his head. "Go all the way down to the basement and follow the signs."

"Yes, Chef," I replied.

I rode down the scuffed freight elevator, left my application with a chatty office worker, and exited the hotel through the loading dock.

Just like all the times before, I never got a callback.

+ + + +

On the home front, at least, things felt solid. Two years after I got to Phoenix, Kim moved to the city to be with me. We had kept things casual when I left Window Rock, but we still talked on the phone regularly. Kim and I had always shared a curiosity about the world beyond the Rez, and we both liked to daydream about all the places we hoped to visit in the future. I was drawn to her inquisitiveness and bright personality—she made me feel better about myself.

Shortly after I graduated from high school, my parents had moved back to Whiteriver when my mom won a seat on the tribal council. I didn't get back to the Navajo Nation much anymore, but in May 2000, I returned to attend Window Rock High's graduation ceremony. Kim and I got back together, and, after a few months of long distance, I asked her if she wanted to come live with me in the Scottsdale apartment. She enrolled at the same community college where I had once studied, planning to work toward a business degree, and found a job doing data entry for a medical company at night.

Kim turned our tiny apartment into a home, filling blank walls with photos of our families and friends and tacking up traditional Navajo rugs and Apache burden baskets. She had always been crafty, and in her free time, she started sewing handbags and quilts out of thrifted Pendleton blankets and shirts, which she sold at Native vendor events, powwows, conferences, or whenever she traveled home to the Rez. Even with my full-time kitchen job, we were barely scraping by, but we were happy.

Because of our schedules, we didn't see a lot of each other, but I found my own ways to show her how much I cared. Kim *loved* hazelnuts, and through trial and error, I figured out how to make perfect truffles, mixing chopped toasted hazelnuts into smooth chocolate ganache and coating the mixture in a thin layer of crisp, bittersweet chocolate. I would top each one with half of a perfectly toasted hazelnut. I'd make a big batch of these homemade chocolates on my night off while Kim was at her job, and leave them out for her on a plate scattered with rose petals and wrapped in red cellophane.

+ + + +

Early on in cooking school, we had been taught how to temper chocolate and make ganache, and, later, in pastry class, we were instructed on how to prepare éclairs, profiteroles, Mousse au Chocolat, and soufflé. What no one ever taught us about was the history of cacao, which, it turns out, is much more bitter than sweet.

Chef Whelan gave us an assignment in his Culinary Fundamentals class: Select a common kitchen ingredient and explore its origins and historical uses. I chose chocolate because my dad had a real sweet tooth—his favorite treat was a Snickers bar, which made his eyes light up like a kid's. He also stocked tubs of chocolate ice cream, which would disappear with astonishing speed.

Chocolate was a fixture of my childhood, but I had no clue it was a sacred Indigenous food. Now, I spent hours sitting in the community college library, reading about ancient cultures that, at that point in my life, I knew almost nothing about: the Olmecs, Mayans, and Aztecs.

Growing up in Apache and Navajo Land, I had internalized the message that Mexico was an entirely different world, and that Mexicans were our enemies. In school, we never explicitly learned about topics like colonization or indigeneity, a term that captures the unique experience of moving through the world with traditional Indigenous values and ways of knowing. No one had ever connected the dots for us, explaining the historical parallels or how the history of colonial violence across the Americas continued to impact Native people's lives in similar ways.

The cacao tree, I discovered in my research, is native to the rainforests of South America, including the Amazon. Archaeologists believe it was domesticated by the ancient Mokaya and Olmec societies of Central America and Mexico sometime around 2000 BC, and that the Mayans inherited their reverence for cacao from the Olmecs.

Shaped a little like a football, a cacao pod contains dozens of seeds—often called cacao beans—which are extracted from the shell, dried, and then roasted. The Mayans mixed cacao beans with water to prepare a fermented beverage that was doctored with spices and chilies to mask the bitter taste. They believed the drink had the power to open up people's hearts, and they used cacao for spiritual ceremonies as well as everyday meals.

In the Aztec civilization, which rose to dominance after the collapse of the Mayans, cacao became a symbol of power and wealth. Cacao beans were actually considered so valuable that they were widely used as a form of currency. According to one historian, Montezuma II, a fabled Aztec ruler, consumed gallons of a spiced cacao beverage called xocolatl every single day to boost his libido. Even centuries later, cacao remains an integral part of the traditional Indigenous diet of the Mixtec and Zapotec peoples in and around Oaxaca, used to make mole sauces and to create a foamy, mealy beverage called tejate (definitely an acquired taste).

When Cortés first arrived in Central America around 1519, he would have encountered Indigenous leaders like Montezuma drinking xocolatl. Like most Europeans, he had probably never heard of this treasured Indigenous cultivar before, and he certainly had no respect for the Aztecs' cosmology, no understanding of the food's cultural, medicinal, and spiritual value. He probably just thought it tasted strange.

Ultimately, Cortés's food preferences didn't matter. For the colonizers and conquistadors, power was equated with domination, property, and prestige. In cacao, Cortés would have seen an opportunity to extract a valuable commodity and gain notice from his higher-ups.

Cacao arrived in Spain somewhere in the first half of the sixteenth century, and, just as with tomatoes, it took time for the Europeans to treat this sacred plant as anything other than an exotic oddity. That started to change in the 1600s, when Spanish friars figured out how to "refine" cacao by mixing it with sugar and making what we now call milk chocolate. The concoction quickly became a sensation among Spanish and French royalty; in many ways, chocolate took off because it was rare and expensive, a gourmet ingredient that needed to be exported from faraway colonies and was exclusively available to the wealthy and powerful.

In the eighteenth century, things took an even darker turn. Seeking to capitalize on the demand, European nations set up cacao plantations throughout their colonies—including the Philippines, Brazil, and the Caribbean—and "imported" enslaved Africans to work them. In Mexico and other parts of the Spanish empire, Native farmers were now forced to grow and cultivate cacao as indentured laborers. A food once revered for opening hearts now broke Indigenous people's spirits and backs.

Today, the global chocolate industry is a booming business, raking in upward of $200 billion a year, but all of the top-grossing companies are based in the United States, Western Europe, Japan, and South Korea. I suspected that most of the chefs I worked with at DC Ranch had no clue that cacao originated in Mesoamerica. I was certain that none of them considered it sacred.

+ + + +

I got along okay with everybody in Chef Olson's kitchen, but I didn't think of anyone there as a close friend. I could see how inexperienced I was compared to the fifteen-year veterans and lifers I worked with, so I never said anything about applying to Mary Elaine's.

I didn't tell any of them about my growing interest in Indigenous food traditions, either, even though I continued to spend any free hour I could find in the library, tracing the foods native to the Americas back to their roots. The few times I casually mentioned a fascinating fact I had learned, I didn't sense much interest from the cooks around me. The only Native food reference they had was fry bread, which fit in with some of the other tired clichés they threw around, about teepees, casinos, and drunk Indians.

Truth be told, I was living up to the stereotype. Although I didn't hang out and party with my coworkers, I took pride in being able to drink more, and faster, than any of my friends, cousins, and skater friends. While most other people in my extended circle worked day jobs, I worked nights, weekends, and holidays, meaning I'd show up at eleven o'clock to parties that were already raging. I'd stay out all night drinking, regularly coming in to work hungover, but I was still young enough that I was able to easily shake it off. In the DC Ranch kitchen, I had developed a reputation for being quiet and serious, a workhorse.

Then in the fall of 2000, shortly after Kim moved in with me, I was driving home late and a policeman caught me swerving and making an improper turn. I was half a block away from our apartment building, and he tailed me. As soon as I pulled into my parking space, he walked over and knocked on my window, placing his hand on his gun. When I got out of the car, he started speaking loudly in Spanish. When I told him I couldn't understand him—that I was White Mountain Apache—he made a crack like, "That explains why you're drunk."

I raised my voice at him and he slammed me up against the car. We began wrestling. Once a second officer showed up, the two of them finally managed to pin me down. I was back in police custody, and this time, the judge sentenced me to ninety days in Maricopa County jail, aka Sheriff Joe Arpaio's notorious Tent City, a sprawling outdoor detention center that had made national headlines for its terrible, extreme conditions. After a few weeks, I qualified for the work-release program, and Chef Olson agreed to let me continue working at his restaurant on the condition that I used the time to write up a report about my goals as a chef.

Now, everyone at DC Ranch knew about my struggles and some of them, like Tony, started to give me shit. I didn't care what Tony thought—he was an idiot who acted all street smart but had no idea what my Rez buddies and I had been through—but I was ashamed about letting Chef Olson down. He had always been fair with me. The first time I had to leave work to report for a random drug test, I told him all the details of my probation. He never once used any of the information I shared against me.

Now, though, he made me pay my dues and re-earn his trust. Once I was released from jail, he assigned me to work in the country club's employee cafeteria, where there was a small salad and sandwich bar, a soup station, and a few chaffers for hot food. It was a major downgrade from cooking in the restaurant.

My shifts started at seven a.m. and I was expected to have the staff meals ready by ten, making sure that there was hot food available continuously until two p.m. It was my job to plan out the menus, transforming unused mise en place and extra inventory into varied and delicious offerings. Surplus potatoes, bacon, and roasted garlic, for example, might go into a potato-corn chowder, or I'd turn leftover mashed potatoes into crispy fried croquettes. I used leftover duck, beef, or lamb to make ragù and other hearty pasta dishes.

I enjoyed figuring out how to cut down on waste—not only did it teach me practical skills but it reinforced humility, an Apache virtue.

Working in the staff dining room also showed me the importance of interpersonal communication for a chef. The administrative staff and golf pros always wanted to chat, and Chef Olson would come in at nine each morning for a quick check-in. I had never seen him in his street clothes before, and my new position offered me a fresh perspective.

"Don't be too hard on yourself, Nephi," he'd advise me. "It's work, but it should also be fun."

Before working in the employee cafeteria, I hadn't realized that, by the time those of us on the dinner crew rolled in at one, Chef Olson and his sous had already been working for four-plus hours.

Finally, after a few months in the cafeteria, once Chef Olson saw that I was being consistent and reliable, he gave me the okay to jump back on the line. By that point, I was raring to work with the core kitchen team again, and I threw myself back into the restaurant production mode with renewed intensity and focus.

Unfortunately, in the fall of 2001, I was arrested for another DUI. My first call from jail was to Kim, who was angry. I knew she worried about me, but almost everyone we associated with partied—

among my friends, going to county jail was almost a normal thing. She had been pushing me for a while to cut back on my drinking because she was afraid I was going to lose my job.

"I told you things were headed in a bad direction," she said now, her voice cracking.

Luckily, I had established a good rapport with my probation officer, who got the court to agree to allow me to go to treatment instead of prison since I was only twenty-one and consistently employed. The White Mountain Apache Tribe's behavioral health office secured a spot for me at the Native American Rehabilitation Association, or NARA, in Portland, one of the first treatment centers in the country dedicated to Indigenous healing. It took a few days for the paperwork to come through, but once it did, I was released.

Before going home to see Kim and pack a bag, I took the bus over to DC Ranch. I had gotten word to Chef Olson about my situation, but I wanted to talk to him in person. It was eleven in the morning, between services, and we went to sit in the dining room solarium, this bright, calming room with whitewashed adobe walls and ten-foot-high windows looking out on a giant mesquite tree and shaded herb garden. We sat across from each other at one of the long oak tables where we'd have our staff meetings.

I told him that I had a drinking problem—something I'd never said before—and that I had arranged to go into rehab.

Chef's expression was serious.

"I talked to HR," he said.

I swallowed. *What would I do without a paycheck? How would Kim and I pay our rent?*

"We decided that if you went into treatment, we'd hold your

position for you. You're asking for help and you've been doing good work with us for a while now."

I started to thank him, but he cut me off.

"Here's the thing. You *must* successfully complete the program with documentation." I looked straight ahead, meeting Chef Olson's eyes. I saw the desert stretching out behind him, thinking of my friends and family out there in Apache and Navajo Land.

"And Nephi . . ."

I nodded.

"When you get to Portland, think about what you want, how you want your life to be. Think about all of this," he said, sweeping his hand across the beautiful dining room and its dramatic backdrop: the lush garden, the insanely green golf course with its multimillion-dollar homes, and the craggy McDowell Mountains beyond them.

"You've earned what you've got here, but your credit is running thin."

+ + + +

The NARA treatment center is located twenty-five minutes from downtown Portland up St. Helens Highway, past the industrial part of town, with its sprawling warehouses, railway yards, and steel bridges, and along the river, through thick, green forest.

Perched up on a steep hill, the center looked to me like a school—because it once was one. A large gymnasium and cafeteria took up most of the building, and the first thing I saw when I got out of the van was a faded, five-foot totem pole.

Inside, the smell of old books and cafeteria food hit me, bringing to mind my junior high school in Fort Defiance. A happy Native woman sat behind the reception desk, greeting me warmly before searching my bags and checking me in. I fixed my eyes on the massive dream catcher hanging behind her, along with different artwork that had been neatly taped to the wall.

The men and women who were residents all slept in converted classrooms; in addition to the administrative and clinical counselors' offices, a few rooms had been set aside as family units. The whole place gave off a boarding school vibe, but in a good way. You saw Natives from all over the Pacific Northwest and Southwest walking around together and chatting in the shabby dayroom. During my time there, I met people from Tacoma, Spokane, and Warm Springs and members of the Puyallup, Umatilla, and Yakama tribes. There were a few residents from Navajo Land, but, as far as I could tell, I was the only White Mountain Apache.

The team leader when I arrived was a resident named Timothy, a tall Nez Perce guy with long black hair tied in a ponytail.

"Nephi, right?" Timothy flashed me a big smile, shaking my hand enthusiastically. "A down-south Native, aye?"

Timothy walked me around the building, introducing me to several residents, who all greeted me like a friend. Then, he showed me to my bunk in one of the men's rooms.

"Someone will be around to get you for dinner in an hour and a half. Missy, the cook, will bark at you if you are late," he said with a chuckle.

By my second week at NARA, I was in a groove. I felt comfortable surrounded by all these Natives, many of whom had arrived straight from the streets of Portland. Whether they had come from a city or the Rez, everyone around me had been through similar struggles. Even in the lush, beautiful landscapes of the Northwest—with their seemingly endless natural resources—shit was hard. During our talking circles, the other residents opened up about their childhoods, their parents, their children, and the people in their lives who had died. They spoke honestly about their experiences with addiction.

In our free time, we'd throw a football around in the old baseball field or sit outside at the picnic tables by the fire pit. Rehab is a place where people are searching and desperate for change—everyone is open to making new friends and talking about their lives. One of the questions people asked each other a lot at NARA was whether you still had your language, whether you spoke it. Like me, so many of the residents were confused and angry about everything that they and their community had lost, in terms of land and ceremonies and kinship. I started to realize that we, as White Mountain Apache and Navajo people, had managed to keep much of our cultures intact, all things considered. That made me feel grateful. Although I didn't have the words to describe it as such then, being in a program designed specifically for Natives was my first encounter with Indigenous resistance. I remember this half-Native, half-white guy named Jimmy talking about the importance of creating safe urban spaces in the "Native wasteland," as he called the cities.

Once, after a particularly intense session with my counselor, Pam, I decided to check out the men's sweat lodge, which sat behind the treatment center along a walking path. I had never been in a sweat lodge before, and as I walked down the path in shorts and a T-shirt, a towel wrapped around my neck, I felt curious and a little nervous.

I reached a giant pile of wood and an even larger pile of lava rocks that were about the size of volleyballs. Some were cracked and ashy, while others obviously had not been used in the fire yet.

The sweat lodge at NARA was Lakota-style. I joined the line of men waiting to get into the four-by-eight-foot structure constructed of branches and canvas; when it was my turn, I crouched down and pushed through the blankets hanging across the low, arched opening. It was pitch black inside, and as water was being splashed onto the pile of red-hot stones in the center, the whole room hissed. I got down on my hands and knees and crawled forward, finding a spot to sit, willing my dizziness and anxiety to pass.

"Permission to speak," said a disembodied voice once everyone was settled inside. I instantly recognized his accent.

"I want to sing an Apache song for my young brother that's new here. I know his family and the neighborhood he comes from."

It sounded like the speaker was sitting directly across from me.

"I have not been home in over twelve years," he continued, "and I don't have the chance to speak my language much anymore, so I want to sing an Apache song. Is that okay with you, brothers?"

A chorus of voices responded positively.

"Aho!"

"Yes, brother."

He said a short prayer and then he began singing in Apache. I closed my eyes, letting the drumbeat and the lyrics reverberate inside me, feeling all of my discomfort melt away as pictures of home flashed across my inner landscape.

I saw the beautiful mountains. The overgrown river. The streets of Whiskey Flats. The scraggly apple tree in our front yard.

In the murky darkness, every image was clear as day.

The man, whose name I would later learn was Carson, was singing the Horse Song, which I recognized from the dozens of ceremonies I had participated in since as far back as I can remember. Emotion crashed over me in waves. I saw a group of Apache Crown Dancers moving around a roaring fire. Through the smoke, I saw the faces of what I knew were my unborn children and, next to them, my mother and father, their faces shining.

It was overwhelming. When I opened my eyes, these complicated feelings of home didn't dissipate. Past, future, present—they were all the same. This was my reality: shame laced with hope, a never-ending chain of love and pain.

Tears rolled down my face as Carson's song came to an end. All of the men let out wild war cries and victory whoops, and I joined them, my heart beating mightily.

One of the men opened the door now, releasing the steam and softening the darkness. I looked around, seeing all these Native dudes, red like lobsters. Everyone started filing out one by one, and I took advantage of the extra space to lie down and soak up the last of the steam.

As they exited, I heard many of the men thanking Carson and giving him shit for not letting on until now that he could really sing. I watched Carson carefully as he ducked out the door, turning a clockwise circle once he stepped into the mild afternoon. I got up and did the same, following our traditional protocol and marking my respect for Mother Earth, the four directions, and all of creation.

I stretched my neck, admiring the tall pine trees and the floating embers dancing toward the wide sky. For an instant, I thought I was back in Whiteriver.

Carson approached me, his expression warm, and introduced himself in English before launching into our mother tongue.

"I can't speak Apache that much, just a little bit," I said, passing a towel across my face. "But I wanted to thank you for welcoming me in like this."

Carson busted into a huge grin. "Yaa-heeeey, Chizzie is your dad, huh? Whiskey Flats, huh?"

I nodded, grateful to feel understood. Carson peppered me with questions about the Rez, wanting to know what had changed, who was on the tribal council, whether there'd been any recent forest fires.

I immediately felt comfortable with Carson—he knew my people and *exactly* where I was from. As we walked together back to the main building and sweat continued to pour out of me, I told him about my life, the words coming fast and fluid. I talked about culinary school, about the accident and my arrest and the subsequent probation violations.

"This is my first time in rehab," I admitted.

Carson clapped a hand on my shoulder. "Kaa-heey, Nephi, I hope you can stay sober . . . you are from a good family."

I know that he meant it as encouragement, but as usual, that observation only reminded me of what a fuckup I'd become. My throat tightened and I felt something shut down inside me.

✦ ✦ ✦ ✦

I was twenty-one during my time at NARA, young and cocky. I believed that I could stay sober if I chose to, but I couldn't imagine my life without Heineken or stinky green bud. I just had to cut back and ride out my probation, I told myself.

When I got back to Phoenix after my forty-five days in Portland were up, I was determined to show my probation officer, Chef Olson, and Kim that I was doing better—and for three whole months, I didn't touch alcohol or weed. But even with all the constructive counseling sessions and groups I'd participated in at NARA, I was still steeped in shame, especially now that my alcoholism was out in the open with family and friends. I hadn't truly surrendered to the idea that I was an addict in recovery—I was still walking the tightrope, justifying having an occasional beer with my friends. Mostly, I was focused on getting everyone off my back and staying out of prison, so I just got smarter about partying, going hard on those nights when I didn't have to work the next day.

All the chefs at DC Ranch knew I had gone through rehab, and they'd make jokes about it, which irritated me. The only person who never brought it up was our new sous chef Rusty, who barely spoke to me at all.

Rusty had been hired at the beginning of 2001, after our previous sous chef, Michael, had quit. He was a self-proclaimed "dirty southern boy"—and a mean cook. He was also just plain mean, a vulgar chain-smoker with a raspy voice who liked to go on and on about his favorite music, including the Ramones, Black Flag, the Dead Kennedys, and the Red Hot Chili Peppers, although—he made a point of saying each time he mentioned them—he only liked the band when they were on heroin. The only time Rusty seemed happy was when he talked about the food he'd grown up with in South Carolina; he'd get starry-eyed talking about she-crab soup, smoky Tasso ham, peaches, and grits. Rusty was quick to cuss out the other cooks in the kitchen, pointing out that they didn't know shit. I remember overhearing him telling one of the other chefs that he thought the culinary scene in Phoenix was fake as fuck.

"Except for Mary Elaine's," he added, which I tucked away as yet more confirmation that the restaurant was truly the best.

I remained fascinated by the lineage of classical French cuisine, as well as the fact that the kitchen I worked in was organized according to a centuries-old tradition, Georges Auguste Escoffier's *brigade de cuisine*. One day, browsing through one of my favorite Phoenix thrift stores, I found a copy of *Great Chefs of France* by Anthony Blake and Quentin Crewe, which instantly became a favorite book of mine. I'd lie on our couch, flipping through the pages of the 1978 classic, reading about characters like Alain Chapel, whose signature dish was a truffle-stuffed chicken cooked in a pork bladder, and who once scoffed that America didn't have a food "tradition," and Pierre Troisgros, who was an early adopter of the nonstick pan.

This culinary lineage was exclusive and intimidating, full of tough guys commanding respect, just like in *Goodfellas*. I hadn't yet grasped that the whole notion of "classical" cuisine was steeped in a colonial mindset or that Escoffier's brigade system was classist and sexist. I just knew that I wanted in.

One night in November, not long after I came back from Portland, Chef Rusty and I were assigned to cater a party for eighty people in one of the multimillion-dollar homes by the country club. It was just the two of us working the event, and after the service was over, he went out for a smoke break.

I pushed open the exit door and asked if I could join him.

"I don't give a fuck" was his predictable answer.

I pulled up a milk crate, looking out beyond tall and bulbous cactuses to the lights of Scottsdale and Paradise Valley. The occasional burst of laughter or drunken chatter echoed around us, but mostly it was quiet. I unzipped my backpack and grabbed Thomas Keller's *The French Laundry Cookbook*, which I'd brought with me in case I had any downtime. Like most of the cooks I knew, I'd bought the book when it first came out in 1999, and my copy was dog-eared and spattered. I opened the book to the About the Chef page, where there was a photograph of Chef Keller hunched over the pass, and another picture of his hands slicing what looked like veal sweetbreads, the sleeves of his chef's coat as gleaming white as the pearl-handled slicer he was using.

"Chef, you got this book?"

Rusty turned his head slowly. "Yeah," he replied flatly.

"It's fucking badass, huh?"

I flipped through the pages to my favorite recipe, Fish and Chips, with its photo of two perfectly cooked fillets of red mullet, palette d'ail doux, and a few gorgeous parsley leaves topped with light golden fried garlic chips, all plated on top of a vibrant green parsley puree.

"You think you can cook like this, Chef?" I flipped the book around.

For the first time that evening, Rusty smiled, revealing a row of crooked, nicotine-stained teeth.

"Shit, if you want to learn to cook like that, you have to work with the best and cook with guys that cook like that *every day*. We do fine food here, but you're not gonna learn that"—Rusty pointed at the book—"working here."

"Man, I wanna train to cook like this." I took a deep breath. "I know I can."

It was the most honest I'd ever been with anyone about my dream.

"I've applied to Mary Elaine's twice a year since culinary school, you know?" The words kept popping out.

Rusty crushed his third cigarette under the toe of his black clog.

"Put the fucking book away, let's start breaking down," he said, walking inside.

I followed him and we packed up all the equipment and leftover food in silence, carrying it to the catering truck.

Rusty drove us back to the loading dock at the Country Club, and after we unpacked our gear, I started organizing my station for the next day. I was cleaning my knives when Rusty spoke to me again.

"You really want to learn to cook like that?"

"Fuck, yeah!" I said, grinning.

He hit me with an intense stare.

"I really do," I said, adopting a serious tone.

Rusty turned around, swinging his backpack over his shoulder.

"I'll make a call," he muttered over his shoulder.

Two days later, after a busy night on the line, Rusty walked over and handed me a crumpled Post-it note.

"Call this number. I got you a stage," he said, using kitchen-speak for a short, unpaid stint apprenticing in a fine-dining kitchen.

"Holy fuck." I was in shock. Rusty walked away before I managed to thank him.

\+ + + +

In mid-November, I arrived for my gig as a stagier at ten a.m., dressed in my freshly laundered chef's whites. This time around, the kitchen was full when I got there, although still strangely silent. All of the chefs were bent over their stations, working intensely. The only sounds were the whirring of the exhaust hoods and the occasional clanking of pots, pans, and tools.

The first station next to the door was the meat station, and one of the cooks there looked up from the saucepot he was stirring.

"Nephi?" I recognized his soft voice from our brief phone call. It was Rusty's friend Eric, who had hooked me up with the gig. He was barely taller than me, but his eyes pierced right through me.

"Yes, Chef." I tried to keep the nervousness out of my voice. I knew from Rusty that Eric had worked at the French Laundry before coming to Mary Elaine's—he was among the best of the best.

"You're going to work with me today," he said. "Let me show you around and then we'll get you set up and started right away."

Eric introduced me to all the other cooks and chefs on the line, although there was no way I was going to remember anyone's names. It was the biggest kitchen team I had ever seen. At DC Ranch, we adhered to an "American version" of the classic kitchen hierarchy—we didn't have enough people to run a full-fledged brigade system, and junior cooks like me were referred to as line cooks, as opposed to the classic French term *chefs de partie*, which I preferred. I thought it connoted a more disciplined mindset. A line cook is definitely skilled, but in a more American way, working for a paycheck.

At Mary Elaine's, every station on the line was staffed by at least two chefs. Eric was the *saucier*, in charge of cooking the meat and making the sauces. Under him was the *entremetier*, who prepared the accompanying vegetables and starches and all the garnishes. For this shift, that would be me.

Over on the fish station, a *poissonnier* oversaw the cooking of the fish and another *entremetier* supported him. Same deal on the hot apps station. The garde manger station, where cold appetizers were assembled, had two *entremetiers* because composing dishes like salads could be an involved and intricate process.

The last station Eric took me to was the pastry station, where the *chef de partie* was extremely tough-looking, stubbled, and with a sleeve of tattoos on both arms. (This was back in the day, before every culinary student, line cook, and chef had arm tattoos.) There were three *entremetiers* working under him and one of them was breaking up the biggest bar of chocolate I had ever seen.

In the back of the kitchen, next to the meat and fish coolers, was a long, stainless steel counter where the sous chef was cutting and portioning all the fish. I peeked into an open cooler and spotted glistening treasure: Dover sole, skate wing, scallops, salmon, daurade, red mullet, Loup de Mer, and black bass. All of it was stored just like the description in the *French Laundry* cookbook—the fish nestled next to each other in crushed ice, lined up in the direction they swim—head up, tail down—so as not to damage the flesh.

As we were standing there, an extremely tall man who looked like Mr. Clean in a chef's uniform came up to us. This was Bradford Thompson, who had taken over as Mary Elaine's executive chef when Boyce left.

"Nephi, right?" He nodded at me.

Before I could answer, Eric flashed me a big smile like we were good buddies. "Yeah, I'm just showing him around and he's gonna hop on my station."

"You're in good hands. Just follow his lead," Chef said, nodding at Eric.

As soon as Chef Thompson walked away, Eric's expression chilled again.

"Let's go," he said, leading me to the produce walk-in, where we loaded a small cart with baby turnips; baby carrots; English peas; a container of arborio rice containing black truffles; bunches of pristine baby spinach and chard; carrots, celery, and onion for mirepoix; and many clear containers of stock and broth.

We rolled the cart over to the meat cooler, where Eric asked the sous chef if he'd had a chance to portion the foie. Without looking up from the fillets he was slicing, he replied, "Up on the second shelf from the bottom, next to the veal."

We placed the Cryovaced packages on top of the vegetables. I had never seen so much foie gras in one place. Eric also handed me stacks of veal, Kobe beef, duck, and bison tenderloins, which I carefully placed on the cart.

We took all these ingredients back to our station and my work began. I turned baby turnips with a paring knife, shelled English peas, washed greens, peeled carrots, and rough-chopped chard. At every juncture, Eric snapped at me, correcting my knife cuts. It seemed like every single thing I did was wrong, that there was a cleaner, faster way to do it. At one point, Eric snatched up the baby carrots I was peeling and banged a half sheet pan down in front of me.

"Don't peel anything on your cutting board," he snapped. "You need to keep it as clean as possible."

I was frustrated, but I made a point not to show it, responding, "Yes, Chef," or "No, Chef," or "Right away, Chef," or "Thank you for showing me another way, Chef." Thankfully, time flew by, and soon the service captains and servers began to arrive, all dressed in Armani suits and tuxedos, their movements efficient and graceful.

At three p.m. on the dot, the stovetops all around me ignited, the flames making a synchronized *whoosh*. Instantly, the kitchen filled with the sweet, robust smell of lobsters roasting and simmering, and brandy and fennel being flambéed on the fish station. The lobster bisque for that night was being made, its smell mingling with the intoxicating aroma of a bouquet garni being deglazed with white wine.

The hours ticked by, and we were almost ready for dinner service. Eric kept telling me to ask questions, but I was too intimidated. Finally, before the servers started coming in with orders, I lifted my head and looked around.

That night, one of our meat specials was a reinterpretation of a classical French dish, Tournedos Rossini, using bison in place of beef. One station over, they were using Quinault River sockeye from the Pacific Northwest for a classic salmon roulade. Bison and salmon were so sacred to Native American peoples that entire ceremonies and lifeways revolved around them. The tomatoes that were being blanched, shocked, peeled, concassed, sliced into petals, diced into perfect diamonds, pureed for house-made tomato paste, and slowly cured for tomato confit; the bag of "stone-ground," "artisanal" dried corn being used for polenta; the beans in the cassoulet; the squash, the chilies, even the oysters—I recognized that all of these were Indigenous cultivars nurtured through Indigenous agriculture and science, through prayer and ceremony. I could smell the gorgeous, sacred smell of baked chocolate wafting down from the pastry station at the end of the line.

Native foods were all over the menu at one of the finest French kitchens in America, even if they weren't being recognized or honored. I felt them egging me on, encouraging me to trust in my power as a Native cook, in my intuitive cultural knowledge.

Yeah, we're here, the beans and corn were telling me. *Just go for it.*

I felt a lump in my throat, but I pulled myself together and kept cranking.

That same night, at the end of my stage shift, Chef Thompson pulled me into the dining room and offered me a permanent job.

+ + + +

About four months after I started at Mary Elaine's, Kim called me into our bedroom. Her tone was serious.

She was sitting on our bed, frowning, her eyebrows raised like maybe I'd done something wrong. Suddenly, she whipped her hand out from behind her back—she was holding a plastic contraption that looked like a cheap kitchen thermometer.

"I'mmm prrregnant!" She drew out the words, her eyes twinkling.

"Oh, shit." I flopped down next to her, taking the pregnancy test from her and examining the emphatic, baby blue plus sign. I felt a rush of nervous energy, like that time I tried to ollie the "roof gap" between two classroom trailers at Window Rock Elementary, landing it on my third try.

"Do these things really work?" I made an effort to keep my tone light.

Kim playfully punched at my stomach, but I caught her hand, pulling her in for a hug.

"I tested three times!" Kim was blushing now. I knew how much she wanted to be a mother—it was something we had talked about often. We spent the rest of the afternoon in bed, laughing, kissing, and joking about what we thought was the most likely conception date. We agreed to wait until she was twelve weeks along before we started telling people.

I walked around the next few days in a daze. On the one hand, I was excited about the idea of being a dad, of teaching my child how to skate and cook. I couldn't wait for Kim and me to show them all our favorite places in both Apache Land and Navajo Land.

On the other hand, I was absolutely terrified. I had taken a one-dollar pay cut when I moved from DC Ranch to Mary Elaine's, and once the baby came, Kim would have to quit her night job. I had no idea how I was going to pay all the bills and help raise a newborn making ten bucks an hour.

My low self-esteem kicked into overdrive, cycling through every variation of "you're not good enough, Nephi." I had a criminal record. I was on probation. I wasn't any closer to becoming a sous chef. I wasn't half the man my own father was. Despite the fact that I was working in this fancy kitchen, I remained an irresponsible loser.

I hadn't had a drink since starting at Mary Elaine's, but my main motivation was getting the system off my back. I was tired of being on probation, submitting to random drug tests, having surveillance officers show up unannounced to search our apartment, and having to attend mandatory AA meetings.

No one at work knew about any of this. I was the first Native American most of the people at Mary Elaine's had ever met, and there was no way I was going to tell them about my struggles with alcoholism and staying sober.

Working underneath Eric was, by far, the hardest part of the job. He'd been hazing me since day one. I'd arrived for my first shift as a formal employee feeling proud, anxious, and ready. The night before, I had cleaned all the tools in my large black craftsman toolbox covered in skateboarding stickers, which I had carried with me to DC Ranch every day. As soon as I walked into the kitchen, Eric looked me up and down.

"Is that your toolbox?" he asked, his voice a monotone.

I nodded.

"Can I see it?"

"Yes, Chef," I said, feeling glad that I had meticulously sharpened each and every one of my knives.

He placed my toolbox on the counter and rummaged around, taking out my eight-inch chef's knife, my small black paring knife, my vegetable peeler, and my knife steel and placing them on the cutting board.

"This is all you'll need," he said, looking me dead in the eyes as he dropped my toolbox in the trash.

"Let's go," he commanded, brushing past me.

I was so shocked that I almost laughed. Instead, I reached into the garbage can and got my box out, hiding it under the prep counters at the back of the kitchen before heading to meet Eric at the meat coolers.

That set the tone for all our interactions. I couldn't tell if he was just trying to toughen me up or if he actually hated me. Not a single shift went by without him criticizing my technique, scraping my prep work into the trash, or making some mean, demoralizing comment.

"Ever hear of affirmative action?" he hissed as I was struggling to get my station set up one afternoon. "That's how you got in here."

A few weeks later, I was kneading the chickpea dough for the half-dollar-size Swiss chard tarts we served as a side dish, struggling to get the consistency right, when Eric approached. He had already finished his prep, and his voice was upbeat.

"What are you going to do when you fail here? Do you have a backup plan?" Eric kept his voice low in case Chef Thompson happened to walk by. "Willard over there has a bachelor's degree to fall back on," he said. "Do you even have anything in your fucking life besides this? Because you suck right now."

Like me, the other chefs in the kitchen were impressed by Eric's résumé; even when they overheard him saying something demeaning, they didn't say anything. Of course, Eric was never cruel or vulgar when Chef Thompson came around, nor toward the other sous chefs or the service captains. He was especially friendly with our sommelier, who he buttered up to for free drinks.

Even with all the abuse, Eric was teaching me a lot. I was becoming a stronger, faster, more skilled and disciplined chef under his watch. Looking back, I know that I should never have put up with all the toxic shit he did to me, but at the time, I thought it was something I needed to live with if I wanted to move up to the next level, to a restaurant like the French Laundry or Daniel. I never once went to HR or to Chef Thompson, not even when I started losing my hair from the stress. I just covered the bald spot on the back of my head with a beanie, even at home, taking it off only when I came into work, where we were all required to wear black surgical caps.

We were working with the best ingredients, plating exquisite food on expensive Wedgwood china. Many of the chefs in our kitchen had come from the most revered restaurants in the country—places like Lespinasse, Café Boulud, the Inn at Little Washington, and, yes, also Daniel and the French Laundry—and one of the twelve master sommeliers in the country at the time was in charge of our wine list.

As someone who grew up on martial arts movies, I knew that becoming the best required pain and sacrifice, but it was sometimes hard to reconcile all the glamour and luxury of this high-end kitchen with the cuts, burns, stitches, severed digits, and cauterized wounds, with the twenty-hour workdays and the casual racism.

It was a little like how I felt about making truffles for Kim now that I knew all about chocolate's origins. It was crazy to me that a food with such an intense, bloody history had somehow become a symbol of romantic love.

FOUR

DOWN FROM THE ROOFTOP

In November 2003, exactly a year after I started at Mary Elaine's, I arrived for the dinner shift fifteen minutes early with a copy of a flyer I had designed rolled up carefully in my backpack.

NACA Promotional Conference, Dec. 10, 4:00 pm, read the text across the top and, in smaller letters, *We wish to discuss the objective and mission of the Native American Culinary Association*. Underneath that headline, I had used a couple of artsy black-and-white pictures I'd taken with my dad's 35mm manual Canon—a stack of saucepans and chefs' hands passing plates in the kitchen during a busy shift—along with a photograph of my dad wearing a cowboy hat with his guitar and a harmonica holder around his neck. A second line of text, in bold letters, proclaimed, *Entertainment by Vincent Craig* and *THIS EVENT IS FREE. NO COVER CHARGE.*

The idea for the Native American Culinary Association had first come to me while I was locked up in Tent City back in the DC Ranch days, fall 2000. As part of Maricopa County's work-release program, I was allowed to leave five times a week to work at the restaurant, but the rest of the time, I desperately sought out ways to keep myself occupied—boredom and despair hovered over the jail's khaki tents, as relentless as the Arizona sun.

As a teenager, I had become known as a tagger on the Rez, so I started passing my time scrawling random phrases on the concrete slab in front of my bunk with the stubby golf pencils the jail distributed to inmates: *Chef Tech 2000*, *Aerosol Madness*, *Chef Technique*, *Fuck the Cops*, *Skate & Destroy*. Making graffiti made me feel calmer, like I was emptying my brain. Chef Olson had given me an assignment—an essay that explained what it was I wanted to get out of being a chef and what I wanted to do with my life—and I needed to focus, but I was finding it difficult to do. After a while, though, my assignment started to creep into my tags.

Native Chef, I scribbled. Then: *Native American Gastronome*, *Apache Knife Skills*, *Native Chef Crew*, *Native American Culinary Association*.

My hand froze. I tried again, jotting down the acronym. *NACA. NACA Chef Tech 2000.* I shaded each letter carefully.

I'm gonna start some shit with this, I thought to myself.

I wrote it down again. *Native American Culinary Association.* I sketched an image to go with the words—two chef's knives overlaid with an upside-down eagle feather in the center of a simple feathered hoop.

It was late and chilly, but it felt like I was on to something. I set the notepad down, gazing out past the double chain-link fence and razor wire.

During my time at DC Ranch, I had learned about different culinary organizations like the James Beard Foundation, the International Association of Culinary Professionals (IACP), the American

Culinary Federation (ACF), and the Chaîne de Rôtisseurs, an international gastronomy association where Chef Olson was a member. I yearned to be a part of something like that, but none of these groups seemed like they were for me.

I thought about my dad's song "Custer," a strike back to Hank Williams's "Kaw-Liga," a track about a lovesick wooden Indian standing outside a white man's store. "Custer" turned that image on its head, imagining the general who led the U.S. Army's murderous campaign against the Great Plains tribes as a statue stationed outside the Bureau of Indian Affairs. Whenever my dad performed the number, his fans went crazy, appreciating the idea of history going a different way—with the Natives holding their ground and the heartless general getting his comeuppance.

A journalist once asked Dad what had inspired his remake, which follows the cadence of the original with stylish precision, and my father had replied, "Because we need an Indian one."

I looked up at the sky, tinted a dirty orange thanks to the smog and the jail's floodlights.

"We need an Indun wun!" I said quietly, channeling my father's Navajo accent.

Now, three years later, my lock-up graffiti was becoming a reality. I'd met with the staff at Mesa Community College's Native American Student Resource Center, getting them to agree to host the inaugural NACA event in late November. I'd distributed my promotional posters at all the Native hubs around the Phoenix-Scottsdale area—the Indian Health Service hospital, the Native American arts and crafts store called Drumbeat, and the Fry Bread House on Seventh Ave.—but I wasn't sure how my idea would land in the confines of my very white workplace.

I poked my head into Chef Thompson's office, eager to connect with him before the other chefs de partie rolled in.

"Morning, Chef." I handed him the flyer, watching as he eased the rubber band off. "I wanted to let you know about an event I'm organizing at the end of November."

Chef Thompson scanned the page, a smile creeping across his long face.

"This is fucking cool." He came out from behind his desk and tacked the flyer up on his corkboard among staff schedules and wine lists.

By this point, several of my coworkers had arrived and they stopped to check out what Chef had pinned up. I was proud to see my homespun flyer hanging in this world-class kitchen, a mashup of my fine-dining ambitions and my passion for Native foods. Over the next few weeks, a few chefs asked me questions about what I meant by "Native American cuisine," and a couple even expressed interest in attending my event, although not one of them actually made it. I never expected them to and I didn't really care. This was about reaching out to the Native community in the Phoenix area.

✦ ✦ ✦ ✦

A few days later, on my afternoon off, Kim and I rushed to the Indian Health Service hospital in Phoenix. Once we'd checked in, I found a pay phone and called Mary Elaine's to say I wouldn't be coming in for my shift the next day—our baby was on his way.

Ari Carter Craig was born at 6:42 p.m. on a cool October evening in 2003.

After placing him on Kim's chest, the delivery room nurses

passed my son to me and told me to bring him over to the scale, which looked a lot like the one I used to weigh fillets of meat in the kitchen.

I unwrapped Ari from his blue-striped blanket, gently stroking his tiny hands, which were clenched in tight, red fists. When I placed my pointer finger in his right palm, he squeezed it, looking up at me with mysterious black eyes. It's something I will never, ever forget: being seen as a father for the first time. When the nurses and doctors were done with their measurements, I picked Ari up again, holding him close to my body.

"Kaw heeey, Dagotee Yá'át'ééh. Shi'mé'zhaazhé, nił gozhóó née, shił gozhóó . . ." I whispered tender words in both Navajo and Apache. "*It's me, little son. Your dad is here. I am happy.*"

While the nurses attended to Kim, I wheeled Ari to our recovery room, where we'd be spending the night. Approaching the swinging double doors leading to the waiting area, I caught sight of my mom and dad, my cousin-sister Kyra, and my younger brother through the window. As soon as my family members saw me, their faces lit up. Everyone huddled around us to get a good look at the baby.

I locked eyes with my dad, who was standing off to the side. I could see the big, tight-lipped grin beneath his bushy mustache—he was quietly shedding tears. I had joined him in the sacred circle of fatherhood. There was so much I didn't know. I had big shoes to fill.

\+ + + +

"Anyone know why squash is so nutritious?" I held up the two halves of the butternut I'd just hacked in half on the cutting board in front of me. The flesh was the color of light terra-cotta, the cavity packed with small white seeds. "Anyone want to guess?"

"'Cuz my mom says so?"

I squinted into the auditorium, trying to identify the smart-ass who had spoken, a kindred spirit. I couldn't believe I had filled the room with more than two hundred Natives from all over the city, although I suspected that many of them were there either for the free entertainment or the free food—with an assist from various relatives, my mother had prepared several large pots of stew and big stacks of fry bread.

I'd actually done it, pulling off the first-ever gathering of the Native American Culinary Association just a few weeks after my little boy's birth. It was a Monday, my day off, and I stood in front of the audience in my starched-white Mary Elaine's chef's coat, which was embroidered with a thick circular logo of a golden phoenix rising from the ashes. Chef had given me permission to wear it outside of work; it showed anyone who knew what was up that I was legit.

"Actually, it's because the squash *is* a momma." I looked down into the front row, where Kim sat cradling our newborn son in a fabric pouch. She looked tired but happy.

"These are all the squash's babies"—I pointed at the stringy innards with the tip of my chef's knife—"and she's carrying all the nutrients they need so that, one day, they, too, can grow into big, healthy squashes."

In the months leading up to the NACA event, I'd learned as much as I could about squash, one of the so-called Three Sisters crops. The fruit's English name—squash—originated with the language of the Narragansett people, the Native inhabitants of modern-day Rhode Island, whose word *askutasquash* translates into *eaten uncooked.* Based on archaeological evidence, some experts suspect that squash is one of the most ancient cultivars in the world, grown in various parts of the Americas more than ten thousand years ago.

The word *squash* is used as an umbrella term for a wide swath of plants, obscuring the fact that each varietal is a wonder unto itself—different in shape, size, color, flavor, and growing season. Here was another point of connection, I realized, between this versatile fruit and the Indigenous farmers who had cultivated it for millennia. By lumping us all into one group—Indians—European settlers had essentially erased the impressive, rich diversity of North America's Native inhabitants.

I remember reading on the Library of Congress website that "Virginia and New England settlers were not very impressed by the Indians' squash until they had to survive the harsh winter, at which point they adopted squash and pumpkins as staples."

Racist dumbasses, I responded in my head. Of course, the colonizers' first reaction was to assume we didn't know what we were doing, to label one of our staple foods a dud.

"I work as a chef at Mary Elaine's at the Phoenician, which is considered one of the best restaurants in the country right now," I continued, cubing the butternut squash to keep my hands busy.

At the back of the room, one of my skater friends let out a war cry, making the people around him chuckle.

"Most of the people I work with don't know anything about us or our foods. Some of them just don't care, but others will occasionally ask me questions about Native foods like I have all the answers."

I swept my gaze across the room, excited to see so many brown faces.

"*I* don't, but I think that, collectively, as Natives, we have the answers. I want to create a forum for us to share our wisdom around traditional foodways. I want us to remember that Native foods matter, that they're an essential part of our culture."

I paused, nodding at my father, who was sitting below me with Kim and Ari, letting him know it was almost time for him to take the stage.

"I'm tired of all these white chefs putting out corny-ass interpretations of Native cuisine, like a dessert with a stenciled cocoa-powder coyote howling at the moon."

A few more audience members whooped.

"By building a network of Native food practitioners all around the country, we can start to circulate knowledge and to gain a true understanding of how powerful our foods are." I tapped the winter squash in front of me again. "We carry all kinds of traditions and beliefs that could help us and benefit the whole world. We are the seeds that our ancestors planted."

After I wrapped up my presentation, I jumped off the stage to help my mom and aunties serve a casual dinner. After twenty minutes or so, I asked everyone to return to their seats for my dad's performance.

I stood at the back of the darkened auditorium, watching him charm the audience, as usual. He performed his song "Rita," about a boy, his crush, and a candy bar, followed by "Thank God for Polyester," the autobiographical account of a weight-conscious Navajo man cooking Spam and eggs in butter for himself despite knowing better. He made everyone laugh riffing about how, during the sixties, his uncle Charlie would wipe fry bread grease into his hair to tame his scraggly mane and big lamb-chop sideburns. He also told a story about naming each one of his family's sheep even though he knew they'd eventually end up in a pot, causing a few of the older women to cluck.

It was amazing to be in this roomful of Natives laughing and eating together. I let the emotions of the evening wash over me. For the first time ever, I was starting to feel like I might be capable of following in my parents' footsteps, making a name for myself as a respected professional and being a positive, constructive force in our Native community. I was happy—and exhausted. I couldn't wait to go back to our cozy apartment, tucking up in bed with Ari and Kim.

+ + + +

Working a station in a bustling kitchen is a lot like skateboarding. You have to be focused and thoughtless at the same time—if you start to overthink it, assessing and critiquing your work, you'll get wrecked. The trick is to visualize the dishes you're making and then give yourself over to the flow, teetering right at the edge of chaos. One night in early December, in the middle of one of these wild-ride shifts, Chef Thompson barked, "Order in. Eight VIP tastings for the Chef's Table."

After twelve months on the job, I was overseeing the busiest station in Mary Elaine's kitchen and mentoring my own *entremetier*, a new hire named Steven. Without hesitating, I called back, "Yes, Chef. Firing eight VIP tastings," my hands springing into action and separating out eight perfect portions of the foie gras, Kobe beef, duck confit, lamb racks, and trussed veal tenderloin. Between us,

Steven and I had eleven burners going, caramelizing the exquisite Japanese beef and glazing multiple pans of delicate baby vegetables with emulsified chicken stock, butter, and fine herbs.

Despite the sizzle of the flames, the steam, and the metallic clank of the All-Clad pans moving against the ranges, everything was perfectly in control. I snuck a look down the line at the rest of the team. Every person in the kitchen had a determined but calm look on their face. The sous chefs were directing traffic, and the tuxedoed waitstaff and service captains communicated back and forth with Chef Thompson.

For a moment, time seemed to freeze. I clearly remember the slow-motion intensity of the fire and steel, the firm voices and precise movements, everyone working in tandem. It was poetry in motion.

Minutes and hours melted away, and toward the end of the evening, as the action on my station slowed down and the pastry chefs got busy, Chef Thompson announced, "Guests in the kitchen," letting the staff know that we should clean up our stations, stand at attention, and adjust our uniforms if needed. He was inviting someone important into our temple.

I was organizing my ninth pan of mise en place on the crushed ice at my station when I heard a familiar voice boom, "NEPHI CRAIG." I looked up to see Chef Whelan—the culinary school instructor who'd first told me about Mary Elaine's—standing across the counter from me. He looked sharp in a three-piece suit.

"Of all the people . . ." Chef Whelan looked stunned and a little amused. "I never thought I would see *you* here!"

I grinned. "I made it, Chef."

Chef Whelan introduced his wife, who was standing beside him, elegant in her green dress.

"It was busy tonight, Chef. Every station was cranking." I motioned down the line, palm up, fingers together; we were trained to never point in the kitchen. "How'd we do? How was your meal?"

"Everything was perfect, fantastic, delicious, stellar." Chef Whelan had always liked piling on the adjectives, especially when he was talking about restaurants he admired. He reached over, gently placing a hand on my shoulder. "Great work, Nephi. Keep it up, keep pushing!"

It was one of my proudest moments as a chef up to that point. My old teacher had come to celebrate a special occasion with his loved ones and been wowed by the meal I'd been part of creating. As someone who had once worked in this same kitchen, he got the rigor and sacrifice required of us. He understood what it meant for me to be working the meat station.

Suddenly, my dream of landing at a restaurant like Daniel in New York or the French Laundry in Napa didn't seem so far-fetched. As I made my way home that night, I hoped that little Ari might be awake for a late-night feeding. My favorite thing was to unwrap him from his baby blanket, lay him on my chest, and take off his little socks so I could see him stretch out his tiny toes. Maybe if I put in a few more years at Mary Elaine's, I thought, I'd move to New York with my little family. I knew Chef Olson, who was still holding it down at DC Ranch, would give me a good reference and now Chef Thompson would, too.

I had Christmas Day off, so Kim and I celebrated in our apartment with both of our families. Everyone showered Ari with gifts, which was very helpful since we were living paycheck to paycheck. There were toys, but also socks, burp cloths, blankets, diapers, and a baby bouncer. I bought him a pair of tiny leather moccasins that I have to this day, laced together and pinned to the wall with a thumbtack.

New Year's Eve fell on a Wednesday that year, and the dinner service passed in a blur, course after course, seating after seating, one intricately composed plate after another—a Kobe strip loin with red wine sauce and chanterelle mushrooms, served with a side of creamy-rich buttered gomiti pasta with mushroom cream and black truffles; an extravagant rack of herb-crusted Colorado lamb, served with cured tomato and lamb's neck tortellini, perfect crescent moons of flavor that we cooked in a bamboo steamer.

Ingredients that had once baffled me had become quite familiar. I no longer found all this opulence and luxury intimidating. I had worked so hard since coming to Mary Elaine's that some of the mystique had eroded away. I'd realized that exquisite food was produced by normal, flawed humans who could be petty and sometimes made mistakes. Just like with skateboarding, you developed your skills by putting in the time and not getting discouraged when things went sideways.

After serving the last seating of the night an array of intricate petits fours and mignardise—the final course of the special ten-course tasting menu that we'd been preparing for for weeks—the entire culinary team, along with a few servers, climbed to the roof to celebrate. Alfredo, the head server, carried eight champagne flutes upside down between his fingers as he scampered up the fire escape. Others followed with more bottles and glassware.

As the clock ticked toward midnight, we counted down, and as soon as fireworks and gunshots went off all across the city, people popped open the bubbly. When one of the servers handed me a glass, I instinctively turned to pass it on to the person next to me.

It's just a glass of champagne, my brain protested. I hesitated. *Despite all the obstacles, I'm standing here. I fucking deserve it. It's not a big deal.*

I looked around. Not a single person I worked with knew about my struggles—no one was going to judge me.

I took a big swig. The champagne was crisp and perfectly chilled. As 2003 slid into 2004, the alcohol hit. Climbing down the fire escape to finish cleaning up my station, I finally felt like part of the team, laughing and rowdy. I felt like myself.

Maybe working under this kind of pressure has given me the strength to control my drinking, I thought to myself. *Maybe everything's going to be okay.*

But the truth was that there was this caged dragon inside me and I'd opened the gate a crack—it was just a matter of time before the creature realized it was free.

\+ + + +

Six weeks into 2004, at the tail end of a two-day bender that corresponded with my days off, I was arrested for another DUI. I don't remember anything about that particular Monday night. When I was fucked up like that, days and nights sloshed together, everything fuzzy—details and faces and conversations. The one constant was the nasty taste in my mouth, which I masked with strong coffee. Apparently, I had thrown punches at the officers who arrested me; when I came to in a cell at the Scottsdale city jail the next morning, I used the pay phone in the hallway to contact Kim and ask her to call work for me. The two of us had been on shaky ground since New Year's Eve—she hated that I was back to drinking heavily, downing beers and whiskey in the apartment after she'd gone to sleep, thinking that I was being sneaky stashing liters of Bacardi and J&B whiskey under the sink, behind the couch, and under the dumpster outside. I'd get wasted most nights, making a complete mess trying to make a sandwich or cook spaghetti. One night, I was so far gone that I fell into the refrigerator, cracking the glass shelves, breaking a whole carton of eggs and spilling cartons of milk and juice. There was blood and shattered glass all over the floor. I remember trying to stand up and Kim grabbing my arm and dragging me away from the mess. Ari was wailing in the bedroom. That was the first time Kim left the apartment; when I woke up the next day, I found a note on the fridge that read *Clean your disgusting mess. You ruined all our food*, with a broken heart drawn next to it.

"What do you want me to say?" Kim's tone was all business. She was sick of my ass.

"Tell Chef I got pulled over and I'm in trouble. That I'm in a jail downtown. I'm not sure how long they'll keep me here. I'll let you know as soon as I find out."

When I called Kim back two hours later, she said that Chef Thompson had listened quietly as she recounted what had happened. I pictured him sitting in his office, savoring the calm of an empty kitchen.

"He sounded genuinely sad." Kim sighed. After a bit, she continued. "He wanted me to tell you he'd be happy to write a letter for the court. He said he could vouch for you, tell the judge what a good employee you are."

My eyes stung, so I turned to face the wall.

"Tell him thanks, but that's not necessary. It was my fault, and I'm gonna take the consequences. I'll keep you posted." I had disappointed every single person who mattered—somehow, my boss's kindness made my situation even more humiliating. He was supporting the fake-ass square I'd been pretending to be.

I'm not sure what Chef Thompson told the staff, but when I showed up at work five days later—after being released and reinstated on probation—no one gave me any trouble. I was thankful for that, although it didn't stop my downward spiral. Within a week, I showed up at Mary Elaine's still buzzed from the night before. I hid it enough to get through our shift meeting, standing outside the circle, breathing slowly in and out of my nose, but once I started sneaking shots of whiskey from a bottle I'd stashed under my station, it was impossible to ignore how far gone I was.

Someone must have alerted Chef Thompson, because he called me into his office, instructing me to call Kim and have her come pick me up. Even worse, Chef had my former supervisor, Eric, escort me out of the building.

"Get his ass home," he said as soon as Kim drove up.

Her eyes were red and puffy—I could tell she'd been crying—and Ari was fussing in his car seat, but I got in the car without saying a word, yanking my seat belt across my body and looking straight ahead with my hands wrapped around my backpack. I'd put the bottle back in there when Chef called me into his office.

"Let's go," I mumbled.

Kim had been angry with me for weeks—I couldn't handle her disappointment on top of mine. We barely exchanged a word.

As soon as we got back to the apartment, I finished what I'd started, emptying the whiskey and whatever other alcohol was in the house and passing out cold.

When I woke up the next morning, Kim and Ari were gone. I

knew the drill, she'd had enough, driving home to the Rez to stay with her family.

I checked my cell phone, shocked at the number of voicemails I'd received. Coworkers that I had always assumed hated me sounded genuinely worried, offering help and asking me to call them back. I didn't respond to any of them.

I'd hidden my struggles for so long, keeping my head down and working neatly and efficiently, never getting rattled. Working at Mary Elaine's, I had achieved something nobody from my White Mountain Apache or Navajo tribes had ever done before. I had been a ninja in a chef's coat.

But now the true me had been revealed. That pressure-cooker kitchen didn't break me, Eric didn't break me—*I* broke me. That simple truth was so shameful and painful that it physically hurt. I slid to the floor, leaning back against the dingy wall and surveying the counter littered with empties and dirty dishes.

I had spent a year gritting my teeth, determined to act like a responsible adult and do right by the three primary relationships in my life. But now I had failed Kim and Ari and shit on the team who had helped me get to the top of my game. I felt my heart breaking, so I stood up and grabbed another Bacardi bottle from the freezer.

+ + + +

By the fall of 2004, I was back in Tent City. I had violated my probation with another DUI, receiving a three-month sentence, and, this time, because I was unemployed, I didn't qualify for the work-release program. I felt like I was moving backward.

Like at every other jail, the prisoners in Tent City grouped themselves by racial affiliation—the whites were called the Peckerwoods or Woods, the Mexicans were the Piasas or Chicanos, and the Black prisoners were the Kinfolk or, simply, the Blacks. The Asians tended to be such a small population that they had to choose who they were going to roll with, which was usually the Chicanos. The leader of each group was referred to as the Head.

We Natives were known as the Chiefs—and somehow, we sat close to the top of the jail's fucked-up, racist totem pole. On my very first day, a lanky young guy with a sleeve of tattoos and a long scar that ran from his ear down his whole neck came to find me. He told me his name was Rudy and that I should follow him so he could introduce me to Harry, the Head of the Chiefs.

Rudy walked three steps ahead of me, spitting do's and don'ts. Don't go here, don't go there. Eat here, not there. Don't drink from that fountain, don't use this side of the shower, don't walk on this path, don't accept shit from anyone that's not a Chief. If I had beef with someone and wanted to fuck them up, I needed to make sure to get permission first.

In the courtyard, we approached a table where a group of older Native men were sitting on benches. Only one of them had a chair, this tall guy with shaggy, overgrown hair and real leathery skin like he'd been out in the sun his whole life. He had a little gut, but you could tell just by looking at him that he was a working man. He looked like some dude you'd see at the rodeo or carrying heavy loads at the flea market in Gallup, or like the guys I'd met working construction. I immediately recognized him as Navajo, which was confirmed by his accent.

"What's your name?" he asked me, his eyes narrowed in slits. "What's your tribe and what are you in for?"

"I'm Nephi Craig." I looked him straight in the eyes like my father had taught me. "I'm White Mountain Apache and Navajo, and I got arrested for a felony DUI and violated my probation a bunch." I'm ashamed now to think of the cocky pride in my voice.

Harry sized me up. "Craig, huh? Any relation to the singer Vincent?" I could tell by his voice that he was joking around. There may not be many of us, but we do know that not all Natives know each other.

"Yeah, man!" I smiled. "Vincent Craig's my *dad*."

Harry's eyes lit up. He suddenly looked a lot less intimidating. "Ayyyyyeeee, Izzziiit? That's crazy!"

He chuckled out loud and spoke to the two old-timers sitting next to him in Navajo. When he turned to look at me again, he motioned for me to grab a chair from the table behind me and sit down.

"We'll get you some items," he informed me, using jail-speak for snacks from the commissary. "Do you need socks or anything else?"

I shook my head.

"Okay, we'll make sure the brothers know who you are. Your dad is a good man and we love his music."

A few days later, I received my work assignment. Up until that point, I had managed to avoid cooking duty while incarcerated, which seemed like a blessing given the quality of the food, but now I would report to the Durango Kitchen, the main facility for all the Maricopa County jails. The detention officers who briefed us explained that we would be responsible for feeding approximately 7,800 men and women each day.

When we got to the spot, I was pleased to see that Harry and some of the other old-timers from his table also worked in the kitchen and that we Chiefs had the best gig, manning the "Hot Cook" area where we turned thousands of pounds of donated, almost-expired food into warm meals, using a dozen hundred-fifty-gallon, industrial steam kettles in two rows of six that faced each other.

Most days, we'd work with expired "Italian meatballs" or four-foot logs of leftover processed "turkey" that were rumored to actually be emu meat. On a good day, we'd get boxes of old produce: carrots, celery, potatoes, apples. Harry was especially happy when we received a delivery of frozen squash pieces. If we needed additional ingredients, we had to ask the guards and they'd radio the request in—inmates from other parts of the kitchen would show up in their blue hairnets and big, black waterproof kitchen boots pushing a cart with whatever we'd asked for. Often, they just showed up with random pallets of food and we had to turn it into some crazy goulash.

I got along well with the other cooks, especially the older Natives. I became a member of Harry's inner circle—the big, muscular Navajo who was twice as big as my actual father treated me like his son, always making sure to assign me one of the vats closest to his. We'd all stand there, stirring our big-ass bubbling pots with a five-foot stainless steel spatula we called a boat paddle, and wiping the sweat off our faces. While we worked, Harry talked to me about my dad's songs and told me stories about his own kids, his multiple divorces, and working in the rodeo. I shared what I knew about various Native foods and demonstrated techniques I'd learned in culinary school and restaurant kitchens.

On one of our first days working side by side, Harry put me in charge of making soup out of precut, frozen butternut squash. He watched carefully as I stirred half a bottle of cheap corn syrup into my kettle.

"It'll accentuate the sweetness."

Harry nodded. I could tell he was impressed with my knowledge.

"We'll need two of those twenty-pound bags of diced onions," I said to one of the other cooks nearby, gesturing over at the pallet jack parked at the end of the Hot Cook row. "Ask the guards if there's any frozen apples, corn, or potatoes. I'll take them, too."

"So you have been cooking since you were little, huh?"

I nodded, slicing open the bags of frozen vegetables with a knife that was chained to the big prep table.

"I liked to cook outside," Harry continued. "We took over the Hot Cook area because the Woods were messy and disrespectful. They complained about having to clean up, and some of them got caught spitting in the food."

Harry winced. I handed him a flimsy plastic spoon to taste the base of my soup. He closed his eyes as he sipped the thick orange liquid.

"Tastes good. We should trade the bakers some Honey Buns for flour and make some fry bread." Harry chuckled. "Wish we had a pallet of mutton bones and meat for your stew."

He wiped his hands on his black-and-white-striped jumpsuit.

"Man, squash always reminds me of the Rez . . . especially pumpkins and those big green ones, I think they're called cupboards or something. My family grew squash sometimes, but mostly people just gave them to us or we bought from neighbors."

I smiled. "Yeah, squashes are amazing."

As my soup simmered, I talked to Harry about how long before the whole nose-to-tail trend had become the big thing in modern cooking, Indigenous peoples all across the continent had made use of every part of this ancient cultivar.

"They made water dippers and storage containers from the hard shells of winter squashes and used strips of dried squash to weave mats. They ate summer squashes raw and used winter squashes in cooked dishes. They roasted seeds for snacking but also saved them for trade and planting. Have you ever eaten squash flowers?"

Harry shook his head.

"I bet your ancestors did," I said. "They're beautiful. I like to shred them up with my fingers and sprinkle them on a salad."

In many ways, I told Harry, squash is the most Indigenous of foods—tough and resilient, substantial but never fussy or fancy.

Harry laughed, not the cynical, smart-ass "heh-heh-heh" that came with a side-eye glance and reminded me of Paulie Walnuts on *The Sopranos*, but his loud belly laugh, head tilted back, eyes scrunched, that came after an exclamation of "Ayyyeeee!" I loved that laugh, which let you know he was straight out of the Rez.

I told him that, even though most people know them by their Anglicized names, most squash varieties people eat today were cultivated by Native Americans long before the Europeans' arrival.

"Crookneck squashes, butternuts, and pumpkins all originated with Natives on the East Coast. So did pattypans, even though that's not their real name. White people called them that because they looked like scalloped cake pans."

"We call squash beł'kaan in Navajo," Harry offered.

"That's similar to the Apache name," I replied.

I told Harry how I'd discovered many cool squash varieties, like delicata, turban, and kabocha, during my very first restaurant job, at the Country Club at DC Ranch.

"One day, my boss brought in these giant, ridged, khaki-colored squashes that I remember seeing at every roadside farmstand in Gallup, Shiprock, and Chinle," I said. "When I called it Navajo squash, the sous chef tried to correct me."

I imitated his high, nasally voice. "It's called Hubbard squash."

I told Harry how Michael had instructed me to use a house knife to split the squash open, because it could break the blade.

"I pulled a beaten-up cleaver from the drawer, thinking, 'Gey-aaahhh, dis Navajo squash can break German steel?'" I did my best Navajo accent for Harry. "I always knew Native foods were powerful."

During another long conversation, I told Harry the entire story of Mary Elaine's. The Head of the Chiefs had listened attentively, asking questions about the kitchen there—how it was the same or different from "our" kitchen, and whether there were any dishes off the restaurant's menu I thought we could re-create. When I got to the part about the champagne and my bender and losing this job that I'd loved so much, Harry got a solemn look on his face.

"Man, I did something like that more than once. This one time, I had a goooood, high-paying job as a welder. My ex-wife and family were so proud of me. I became a foreman, bought a truck, but then I blacked out one night, beat up a good friend of mine, and got arrested. I lost everything overnight. I know what that's like."

Harry shook his head. "You're still young, though."

I could tell we were both feeling upset, thinking about our failures, so I quickly changed the topic, explaining to Harry about my work with NACA.

During every shift, Harry—a big, tough motherfucker who had been in and out of jail his whole adult life, a man who inspired fear on the yard where the inmates congregated and worked out—would walk down our Hot Cook row, stopping to bless each kettle of food. It was so unexpected, to see him bow his head reverently over the slop we were preparing, and he must have caught me looking surprised as I watched him.

"My grandma raised me." Those four words hinted at so much: joy, love, and character-building lessons, but also tragedy, loss, and a heart-breaking rupture.

"I always bless my food no matter what, just the way I was taught." Harry picked up his boat paddle and returned to stirring his massive pot of Mystery Meat Goulash, a mixture of bagged diced "beef," hundreds of pounds of frozen breakfast potatoes, and the kind of frozen vegetable medley you get in a school cafeteria, all thickened with the roux I taught Harry to make using vegetable oil or lard and the all-purpose flour we got from the prison bakers in exchange for commissary items like chips, tuna packs, and plastic-wrapped pastries.

Beyond the chain-link fence that separated the Hot Cook team from the rest of the prisoner workers, there was a mess of clanging, curses, and shouts, but the silence between us felt thick and safe.

Harry shook his head, returning to the present. "We need your NAFA." He'd remembered my organization as the Native American Food Association. I didn't correct him.

"We need a reason to feel proud, to feel optimistic. A lot of our culture is in our foods. We need to remember these things if we want to survive."

After I was released, I never saw Harry again, but I still think about him from time to time.

I finally left Tent City after three months, feeling resolved to continue the work I was doing with Native foods. One day, I hoped to make the Chiefs' head cook very proud.

FIVE

ALL OVER THE MAP

After I was released from Tent City in the winter of 2004, Kim and I patched things up, moving into a cheap trailer park in Mesa before the start of the new year. It meant a lot, how much Kim believed in me. It was the two of us and Ari together, through good and bad, and I wanted to show her that I could be a responsible father. Now that Ari was one and eating solids, I took morning duty, waking up each day at six and scooping him up from his crib.

"Good morning. Let's go kick it in the kitchen and let Momma sleep," I'd whisper, my mouth close to his downy ear. "Are you hungry, son?"

I'd place Ari in the sturdy vintage high chair with chrome legs that we'd bought at Desert Industries, our favorite thrift store in Mesa, and, without fail, he would hit me with the big, bashful smile he'd inherited from his mother. I'd sit there, quietly feeding him spoonfuls of mush, wondering how many times my own father had done this for me. Once Kim woke up, I'd make her breakfast, too, usually a ham-and-cheese omelet with a sprinkle of red chili flakes.

I remember one day she picked up a jar of the baby food I'd bought on sale the previous week and joked that, even though it was labeled as sweet potatoes, she couldn't pronounce half the ingredients.

"You should make some baby food," she said, pouring herself a big mug of coffee.

She was right, but I couldn't make it happen. Groceries were expensive and I spent each day hustling for work.

In between short-term restaurant gigs, I threw myself into growing NACA, updating the organization's website and blog, sending out newsletters, and giving free cooking demonstrations at farmers' markets across the Phoenix metropolitan area.

Around this time, someone who had attended the first NACA event reached out to ask if I would conduct a healthy-cooking workshop for diabetes management at the Salt River Rez, located just fifteen miles outside downtown Phoenix and home to nearly eleven thousand members of the Pima and Maricopa tribes. I agreed, teaching participants basic knife skills and how to blanch and shock vegetables like asparagus, broccoli, and carrots as prep for a few days' worth of meals. I made $250 for the one-hour event, which seemed like a lot to me, although in hindsight, I hadn't accounted for the cost of transportation and the labor of sourcing ingredients. I used my earnings to buy a toy car for Ari and to print out more NACA flyers. I even took Kim out to dinner at the Olive Garden while our friends babysat. It was one of those rare times when I'd felt like things just might turn out okay.

I started getting more and more requests from different Native organizations, so I bought myself a full uniform, including a coat with cloth buttons and a long bistro apron like the one we wore at Mary Elaine's. I even shelled out sixty bucks to have the coat embroidered with the words NEPHI CRAIG, NACA CHEF & FOUNDER in black. I picked it up from the store with Kim.

"Look at Dad," she cooed at Ari in his blue stroller. "Doesn't he look shaaaarp?"

I wore my personalized coat to every NACA event from that day forward. One of the realizations that had come to me when I'd lost my toehold and tumbled from the mountain of fine dining was that my work around Native foods extended far beyond the professional food world. Talking to Indigenous people about traditional ingredients and foodways was actually a public health service.

I believed I could get people excited to make healthier food choices by focusing on the history of Indigenous people's eating habits, specifically how what they ate before and after contact with the colonizers was radically different. Instead of focusing on the dire consequences of consuming too many processed foods, I could frame nutritional recommendations like "eat more fruits and vegetables" or "eat less sugar, white flour, and oily foods like fry bread" as a form of cultural revitalization. I'd put a positive spin on a plant- and nutrient-rich diet—it was a way to connect with and honor our ancestors' wisdom.

Many of the groups that hired me through NACA requested that I speak about health-related topics. That's where the funds were at, I realized.

I knew I needed to deepen my knowledge base, so when I received an email from a White Mountain Apache tribal employee about scholarships to attend the two-week-long Winter Institute at the Johns Hopkins Bloomberg School of Public Health, I sent in an application. I was selected, and in January 2005, I flew out to Baltimore during a deep freeze.

The energy and enthusiasm of the other students at the Winter Institute was infectious—enough to make heady topics like epidemiology and biostatistics really engaging. I learned so much from our instructors, particularly the representatives from the Johns Hopkins Center for Indigenous Health. (A few years later, I would go down a wormhole, educating myself about Johns Hopkins' questionable relationship with the White Mountain Apache Tribe and the Navajo Nation. Public health researchers from the university had conducted a four-decades-long research project on respiratory syncytial virus [RSV] and infant health and mortality in our communities that resulted in the invention of Pedialyte, a medical breakthrough worth billions upon billions of dollars. None of which benefited our tribes directly.) I wished I could drop everything and study at the university full time, but with my criminal record and the financial pressures bearing down on our family, the idea wasn't realistic. Instead, I would use everything I'd learned in my work with NACA.

I developed an introductory workshop called Understanding Native American Cuisine, a broad overview of the history of Indigenous cultivars and the transition from precontact to post-contact diets, which usually included a cooking demonstration of some kind. My goal then—as it is now—was to help people feel more confident and excited about cooking. I avoided explicitly using the phrase *healthy eating*, which can feel punitive to many people, instead emphasizing skill development: knife cuts, kitchen organization, culinary technique. I researched all the Native American health agencies, diabetes centers, tribal council offices, and school districts in Arizona, sending them an introductory email about NACA and different educational offerings.

Around this time, I also started a passion project, researching the Indian boarding school experience and how it related to food. Like many Native Americans, I learned about the boarding schools through a family member's experience. My great-grandfather's story, along with my dad's songs, made this terrible history seem very close. I knew that Joseph Carley Ivins's passion for farming and growing his own food had to do with the deprivations of his childhood, and I was curious to know more about the impact of places like the Carlisle Indian Industrial School on Native youths' relationship to what they ate.

The conversation around boarding school abuses was gaining more attention on a national level, but I still hadn't heard much discussion about the culinary violence waged against Native children—the malnourishment and starvation as well as the malicious cultural shaming, messages along the lines of "your sacred corn isn't sacred, it's food for pigs." I reached out to Carlisle's archival department asking if they would send me any food-related materials, sending a check for ninety dollars. A few weeks later, I received a thick manila envelope stuffed with documents including cafeteria menus, letters, journal entries, school assignments, and photographs.

I sat at the high countertop in our trailer, looking through the photocopies while keeping an eye on Ari, who was playing with blocks on the living room carpet. I felt sadness pool deep in my stomach as I sifted through students' drawings of corn, buffalo, and deer and read letters in which they pined for favorite meals. Each document offered a window into what these children had been robbed of—and their longing for home. I was particularly moved by all the old photographs of these brown kids sitting at long tables with pained, serious expressions on their faces, their black hair lopped off and their uniforms stiff.

The printed menus for Carlisle's Easter and Christmas dinners showed how Christian holidays were shoved down students' throats, replacing Indigenous ceremonies and traditions. Instead of sitting around a roaring fire and eating traditional dishes cooked in a communal pot—and the kinds of plant-based dishes many of these kids had grown up with—Carlisle residents were served baked ham and other meat-potatoes-and-gravy fare. Lesson plans promoted the bogus story of Thanksgiving, how pilgrims and Indians sat down together merrily in the spirit of gratitude, and how the "traditional" use for pumpkin was baked into a pie.

When I read accounts from boarding school survivors, what struck me was how so many of these young Natives struggled to integrate back into their communities, feeling like they no longer belonged. Many of them expressed feeling ashamed about where their families lived, using words like *dirty* and *backward* and *desolate*, while others wrote of being teased and abused because they talked like white people. Many boarding school survivors felt so adrift in their ancestral homelands—emotional refugees—that they ended up moving to the city, only exacerbating their feelings of isolation. As a chef who didn't really fit into the culinary tradition I had trained in, and whose profession made me an anomaly on the Rez, I felt their loneliness deep in my bones.

My deep dive into the culinary environment also deepened my respect for Grandpa Ivins. He had encountered colonial violence as a young boy ripped away from his family and somehow managed to resist the crushing messages that his people were inferior and defective, finding his way home and filling his beautiful garden with Indigenous plants.

+ + + +

Right after losing my job at Mary Elaine's, I had put together an ambitious five-year plan for NACA. As soon as my probation was up and I could travel freely, I'd spend a few years traveling to as many Native American reservations as I could doing research and development. By year three, I would launch a fundraising campaign, seeking to formally establish NACA as a Rez-based institute, ideally located on White Mountain Apache land. I envisioned the NACA Institute as a place to train emerging culinary talent and I hoped to eventually open a five-star restaurant focused on Native American cuisine. (This was before the arrival of Michelin in the States.)

My plans looked great on paper, but the reality of independent contract work was incredibly difficult. My sporadic, unpredictable income was a source of stress at home, and each time I took a more traditional job—cooking for a catering company or working as a line cook at the decent Italian restaurant that was walking distance from home—I'd quickly get disillusioned by the caliber of the food and quit.

In the summer of 2005, though, my profile got a boost when a journalist reached out to interview me for *Native People's Magazine*'s Spirit of the Harvest section, which featured recipes from all over Native America. I talked about how my mother would cook us wild asparagus she'd harvested Downbelow, how my Navajo grandma loved cooking mutton, and how both our tribes loved piñons, and I put those inspirations together into a dish of rack of lamb served with roasted pencil asparagus and pine nuts.

The publicity led to even more invitations. Everywhere I went, I took my eagle plume and pollen with me for protection. I spoke in Native communities all across Arizona, California, Oregon, Washington, and New Mexico, and also in Utah, Colorado, and Idaho, always making sure to clear the out-of-state trips with my probation officer. I started making connections with other Native American chefs, including Walter Whitewater and Lois Ellen Frank, who had just published a book called *Foods of the Southwest Indian Nations*. The three of us were hired to cook together for a benefit for Tohono O'odham Community Action (TOCA), an organization started to revitalize agriculture among this Native community in the Sonoran Desert, and I found both Lois and Walt deeply charismatic. As we prepped passed appetizers and a six-course tasting menu, we talked about our shared vision of helping to inspire a new generation of Native cooks.

By the end of 2005, I had scraped together enough money to pay off the remainder of the $29,000 restitution fee for my car accident back in '98, qualifying for termination of my probation. I could finally come and go without getting permission from anyone, taking my chef skills on the road just like I'd once dreamed. I was ready to leave Arizona, to put some distance between me and the shame of fucking it up at Mary Elaine's, so I started to reach out to various chefs I had met through NACA to see if they were hiring, including Fernando Divina, the head chef at Cave B Inn and Winery in Quincy, Washington, and the coauthor of the James Beard Award–winning cookbook *Foods of the Americas*. My parents had bought a copy of his book for me at the TOCA event, where they were my guests, and had him sign it. It mortified me that he had written, "With sobriety comes great success!" *What had my parents told him?*

The good news was that Chef Divina not only remembered me but offered me an open chef de partie position in his kitchen.

Kim and I were going through another rough patch and she had moved back to Navajo Land with Ari so she could take classes at the UNM campus in Gallup, thirty minutes from where her parents lived. I was back in Whiskey Flats, at my parents' house, selling food from a tailgate in between NACA gigs. I saw my boy most weekends, and I sent Kim extra cash whenever I was able. As soon as I hung up with Chef Divina, I called Kim to let her know about my job at Cave B.

"How are you going to get there, Nephi?" Kim sounded tired. "You don't even have a driver's license right now."

"Whatever. I'm gonna catch a Greyhound. I'm just taking some clothes and my knives. "I'll send you and Ari more money as soon as I can," I hurried to add.

The phone was silent for a long time. I could hear Kim sniffling. She was crying.

"Oh, Nephi, you're so crazy," she said finally.

I was about to say something mean, but she continued.

"Ari needs you. And I still love you."

Something cracked inside me.

"I still love you, too," I mumbled, "but I failed you and I failed Ari. This cooking thing is all I have left. I'm just gonna go."

Tears rolled down my cheeks. We'd already been through so much and now I was going to be out of the picture, living thirteen hundred miles away in Washington.

"You and Ari could come with me." I hadn't realized I'd been thinking it until I blurted it out.

"I can't just pick up and leave!" Kim sounded angry now. "You're only thinking of yourself, as usual. I'm glad you're finally getting what you wanted."

I hung up the phone and went out to sit in my parents' backyard. It was just me and my knives now. I'd spend a couple years in Quincy and then move on to Seattle or the French Laundry or even France. I called up my drinking and drug friends and told them I was leaving for Washington state in a couple of weeks and wanted to celebrate. We partied for four days straight—I spent all the money I had been planning to send to Kim before I left.

When I finally came home again, my mom said that Kim had been trying to reach me. I called her back and she picked up right away.

"I wanted to tell you that, um, I want to come with you." Kim sounded unsure, like she was trying to convince herself. "Maybe it will be good for us to be out there as a family, just us."

"Skoden," I said, busting out the Native slang for *Let's go, then.* "I'll chill out on the drinking. I think if you and Ari are around, I might do a little better." I felt so sick in that moment that I fully intended to leave the booze alone even if I had never managed to really abstain for more than a couple of weeks, apart from that one standout year at Mary Elaine's.

A few days later, Kim, Ari, and I packed everything we could into our little Honda Civic. During that long, long drive, we didn't talk about anything negative. We wanted to pretend everything was okay, that we were a happy family setting off on an adventure.

As it turned out, this entire chapter was like rearranging the deck chairs on the *Titanic*. Even though working there was great, I lasted less than a year at Cave B. The winery, where the restaurant was located, sat on a bluff overlooking the monumental Columbia River and the surrounding farms. Chef Divina had a huge vegetable and herb garden, where I saw red amaranth growing for the first time, and his menu was simple, heavy on locally sourced ingredients. It was a beautiful, bountiful place, but I was not right with myself. I kept drinking and smoking, trying to shake off the chip on my shoulder. No other restaurant could compare to Mary Elaine's. I was jaded, with one foot out the door both at work and at home.

Things came to a head one day after I emerged from a blackout in the bathroom of our small, one-story house. There was glass everywhere and my knuckles were encrusted with blood. I stumbled into the kitchen, where I found a note on the counter: *We came home and found you on the floor. You broke the bathroom mirror. Not going to live like this anymore. We're driving back to Arizona.*

I surveyed the damage. There was blood all over the sink and I'd written *FUCK YOU* in my own blood on the second mirror, the one I hadn't slammed my fist into. There was a trail of blood leading to the living room and an empty bottle of Bacardi on the kitchen floor. I didn't remember any of it. Kim must have been terrified when she saw what I'd done.

It was the end of 2006. For a few weeks, I slunk around Moses Lake getting high and drunk, ignoring calls from work and draining my savings.

Finally, I bought a one-way plane ticket back to Phoenix, packing my laptop, knife roll, and some clothes in a duffel bag, and abandoning the rest of our stuff. Once again, I had destroyed everything. Once again, I was on my own.

+ + + +

Things were rough when I got back to Arizona. I moved into a dilapidated trailer in Mesa, working odd prep jobs, drinking, partying, and couch-surfing. I hawked the furniture I'd driven back to Washington with my father, who took pity on me, to retrieve. I sold my belongings piece by piece, until there was almost nothing left.

Pretty much the only time I didn't feel like a worthless piece of shit was when I was cooking. I might have been a terrible partner and parent, but in the kitchen, I was highly skilled. Putting on my chef's coat was a way to escape from the messes I'd created and feel like my life was in order. It was a relief whenever I was able to pick up contract work because it meant that at least I could support my little family with some money.

In March 2007, I received an invitation from the Intertribal Agriculture Council to travel to London and produce tasting dinners showcasing Native American products like buffalo meat and bison jerky, chokeberry syrup and fry bread mixes, wild-caught salmon, and beans and chilies from all over the Southwest.

I had never left the country before, and I wasn't a confident traveler. I spent most of my week in England in the industrial kitchen at the Excel conference center and exhibition hall. The only exploring I did was finding a pub to get shitfaced in each night.

But a month later, I boarded another plane, this time for a much more memorable trip. I had been invited to São Paulo by the organizers of the Shared Indigenous Heritage Festival, a weeklong celebration of Brazil's Native inhabitants and their cultural traditions. My first morning in Brazil, my guide Lucas, a native Paulista who worked as a chef and instructor at Senac University and dreamed of making it to the United States, picked me up at my hotel in the city center at six in the morning with a takeaway cup of strong coffee. He wanted to show me CEAGESP, the largest fresh-produce market in South America, where all the local chefs, store owners, and restaurant and hotel people shopped.

Driving through the drizzly, quiet streets in his little yellow hatchback, we passed neighborhoods of walled mansions located right next to sprawling favelas with shacks constructed from plywood, burlap, cardboard, and metal scraps. It was like leaving Whiteriver, driving off the Rez and into the neighboring white towns of Show Low and Pinetop-Lakeside, with their gated "communities," golf courses, and air-conditioned supermarkets.

I sipped my coffee, willing the caffeine to beat down the jet lag. "Is it true Americans are targeted and kidnapped in São Paulo?"

"People disappear every day in this city. It can be a very dangerous place, especially if you get lost or you get mixed up with the drugs and the criminals." Lucas grinned. "But for you, Chef, walking around will be pretty safe because you look like you're from here. You just need to stay where there are lights and people. The media likes to make it look worse than it really is."

I nodded. Being from the Rez, I felt confident about my street smarts. I also knew that outsiders often paint a warped, negative picture of places and cultures they don't understand.

"I have a question, Chef." The evening before, when he'd greeted me at the airport carrying a sign with *CHEF CRAIG* in big, blocky letters, I'd immediately told Lucas to call me Nephi, but kitchen lingo is a hard habit to break. "What is 'WesternApacheRacket-Bread'?" He enunciated the words carefully, his musical Portuguese blending them together.

"It's one of five simple Apache breads we make. It goes really well with the Apache Acorn Stew we're serving." The week before my arrival, I'd sent the festival organizers menus for the various events that I was cooking for. Bundi'tunneh, aka Apache Racket Bread, aka bubble bread, aka donkey bread, aka outside bread, is a simple flatbread prepared from a dough made of Blue Bird flour, baking powder, salt, and water and cooked over white-hot coals. When made just right, Bundi'tunneh is lightly charred and crunchy on the outside and soft and fluffy inside; its smoky flavor complements anything you serve it with, from roasted deer to squash soup. I've always loved using Racket Bread to scoop up sliced yellow hots, Apaches' fresh chili of choice.

"Apaches use a special tool to cook bread over hot coals." I patted my backpack, which sat between my feet. "I have one with me. We attach a steel hoop to a long metal handle and weave wires across it to form a crosshatch pattern. It functions like a handheld grill."

Lucas laughed. "We had a hard time figuring out the translation . . . and then when you emailed us a picture of a tennis racket, we were even more confused!"

"Wait till you see what else I've got. I brought some acorns harvested by the women in my family. They're taped up like a kilo of cocaine," I said, making Lucas laugh.

After about thirty minutes, we arrived in a bland industrial district, driving through a toll gate and parking among beat-up delivery trucks. From the outside, the hangar-size structure with open sides didn't look like much, but once we stepped inside, I stopped in amazement, snapping photos with my dad's Canon.

This was, without a doubt, the largest market I had ever seen—the size of three football fields lined up—and definitely the most colorful: rows and rows of fresh produce stacked on pallets, crates, wagons, and truck beds. From where I stood, I spotted long bundles of garlic chives; fat pieces of galangal, turmeric, and sunchoke; fancy, delicate greens like mâche, frisée, mizuna, and Lolla Rossa lettuce; and dozens of different types of tropical fruits extending out in every direction.

Lucas and I walked through the potato section of the market, which took my breath away. Before I'd started working at DC Ranch, I'd only ever cooked russets and red potatoes; I still remember how thrilled I was to discover Yukon Gold potatoes and fingerlings.

"So many colors," I muttered, taking in potatoes of every shape and size in various shades of purple, yellow, red, brown, and mahogany. Lucas nodded, explaining that many of the vendors specialized in rare varietals indigenous to their growing area.

We walked by a stand of shaggy greens that I immediately recognized as lamb's-quarters.

"These are my cousins," I told Lucas. "They taste like spinach, but sweeter. We use this all the time in Apache Land!"

Lucas translated what I had said to a leathery old man sitting on a stool, who broke into a big smile, revealing missing teeth. He picked up a bushel and extended it to me like a bouquet of flowers.

"He says they're his cousins, too," Lucas conveyed, grinning, "and that makes you his family."

I thanked the farmer and we continued wandering. Most of the market's salespeople were short and dark like me, and each time we stopped to talk to vendors, I was greeted with enthusiasm and kindness. They fed me chunks of melon, coconut, papaya, and mango out of the palms of their hands and inquired whether I recognized their yucca or rutabagas. They badgered Lucas with questions about what foods Apaches ate.

Right next to a woman selling plump, almost-black açaí berries out of big woven baskets, I spotted a wiry young man hawking a strange food I'd never seen before; they looked like miniature bell peppers, red, orange, and yellow, with strange, pale green protrusions that reminded me of witches' noses, hooked and stumpy, where their stems should be.

Sensing my interest, the vendor dropped a couple in my palm.

"What's this?" I asked Lucas.

"I think you call them cashew nuts. They're still attached to their fruit."

Up until that very moment, I had always associated cashews with white people—they were way too expensive for those of us on the Rez.

The salesman spoke in rapid Portuguese.

"He explains that cashew is a tree native to South America, even though the biggest producers in the world today are India and Africa." He listened some more. "Portuguese settlers transported the plant to their territory in Goa sometime in the fifteen hundreds and it spread to other countries from there."

I stared down at the fresh cashews in my hand. I had no idea about any of this. Even a chef like me sometimes failed to be curious about the foods he encountered. *What else didn't I know?*

"He wants you to taste," Lucas said.

"Do I peel it?"

Lucas shook his head. "You can bite into it like an apple."

I opened my eyes in surprise, making a show of bringing the little red not-pepper up to my mouth. I crunched it in half, chewing the flesh thoughtfully.

"It's delicious. Sweet and astringent." I asked Lucas to buy me a little bag. "What do people do with it?"

"It's for eating and making juice. People also make it into a liquor." Lucas eyed me mischievously. We'd shared some drinks at the welcome dinner, and he'd already clocked me as a party animal. "Maybe we can try some later, after a caipirinha."

It was time to hit the road—I was due to teach a class about my research into Native American cuisine in a couple hours. We walked back down a different aisle, taking in pyramids of chilies, familiar friends like jalapeños and serranos alongside varietals I'd never heard of, like these tiny yellow peppers that the sign told me were called Pimenta Cumari along with clusters of Brazilian "rainbow chilies," which were just as beautiful as they sounded: violet, orange, and red peppers clustered together on the same branch.

As we left the market, a cook's paradise, I felt a wave of melancholy.

"I wish we had this in America," I muttered as we ducked back into the car.

Lucas looked confused. "A food market?"

I shook my head. "A massive place for Native people to sell their foods and take pride in what they've grown."

Like many Americans, I'd grown up associating the word *farmer* with an image of a ruddy white guy in denim overalls and a straw hat driving a John Deere, but as I'd gotten deeper into studying Native foodways, my perception had changed. For the Indigenous farmers who'd grown food for their communities all across the Americas for thousands and thousands of years before the arrival of European colonizers, agriculture was a form of communication with all creation. They were scientists, inventors, revolutionaries, warriors, and caregivers, standing at the axis of time, land, the cosmos, and humanity, sustaining life against great odds. I thought of all the happy days I'd spent in my great-grandfather's garden all those years ago, listening to him sing to his plantings.

I turned to look out the passenger-side window. I didn't want Lucas to see me cry.

\+ + + +

The next day I met Yone, the chef-owner of a small restaurant located on a street of modest homes and businesses and hidden behind a tall, white-stone wall, with its name—Suri—spelled out in cursive steel letters. Lucas and I passed through a narrow arch into a courtyard filled with potted plants, ferns, and all kinds of tropical trees, and entered the restaurant through a glass door flanked by big arched windows. Inside, the space was similarly pretty and welcoming, with a dozen Brazilian redwood tables, some covered with tiles and others set with colorful woven placemats, and bright, folksy paintings of strong, brown workers and lush greenery hanging on the walls. Early in the afternoon, it was mostly empty, except for a few people sitting at the small bar.

"You'll love Yone," Lucas repeated. "The two of you are like flour from the same sack."

I'd known Lucas for only a few days, but he already felt like a good friend—his accent and funny sayings reminded me of talking to a Native elder. In addition to driving me around to my speaking engagements and serving as my translator, Lucas had sous-cheffed all my cooking demonstrations and tasting dinners. He was also, it turned out, an excellent drinking buddy.

After a wiry, curly-haired server in his twenties approached us, kissing Lucas on both cheeks, we pushed through swinging doors into the restaurant's clean, mom-and-pop-size kitchen.

Yone was a beautiful, fortysomething woman with a mop of dark wavy hair tapered short at her neck and twinkling, slanted eyes. She wore a white blouse with a black apron tied around her waist. As soon as she saw Lucas, she shrieked, clapping her hands like a kid unwrapping a present. Yone didn't speak a word of English, but when Lucas explained that I was a Native American chef in town for the festival, Yone pulled me in for a strong hug, then grabbed my hand and pulled me back out into the dining room.

The three of us sat down at a four-top in the corner, under a cascade of hanging plants, while Lucas translated Yone's backstory. She was mixed—her ancestors were Japanese, African, Portuguese, and Indigenous—and for more than a decade, she'd specialized in traditional Japanese cuisine. A couple of years ago, she'd decided to try something new, shifting her focus to dishes influenced by her Brazilian heritage. At Suri, she'd developed strong relationships with farmers and suppliers throughout the Amazon region.

Yone spoke rapidly and laughed easily. She talked about how her cooking style changed once she started incorporating traditional foods like tucupi, cassava, chayote, aguaje, and tambaqui fish, becoming simpler and more down-to-earth.

"The more the food changes, the more she is changing, too," Lucas relayed.

"What does she mean by that?" I asked, waiting for his translation.

"She used to care very much about ratings and professional opinions. She wished for her food to be reviewed in the right magazines, or maybe for some rich, handsome boss to help her open a fancy restaurant like in a Hollywood movie. But she says that the more successful she is, the less she enjoyed what she was doing. She says she forgot why she first gets into cooking. The new ingredients and dishes reminded her."

Yone said something more, which made Lucas chuckle.

"The foods reminded her she wanted to make people happy and connect them with good memories. She wanted to make people smile . . . in their bellies."

"That's great." I turned to Yone, grinning, and she spoke directly to me.

"She wants to know why you became a chef," Lucas reported.

I took my time, searching for the right words.

"I went to cooking school during a very tough time in my life. It was kind of my only option. Once I discovered I was really good at it, I decided I was going to work hard and get a job at some fancy place in New York or California, like Le Bernardin or the French Laundry." I wondered if Yone had heard of either of those places. "I wanted to show all those fancy French cooks that I was just as good as them."

Lucas translated for Yone, who threw back her head and cackled.

"She's picturing you wearing a big white chef's hat and fussing with a soufflé," Lucas explained. "She thinks it's hilarious."

"Yeah, it is a bit ridiculous." I looked around the cheerful space Yone had created. "It would be cool to have a place like this, somewhere where people in my community would feel welcome."

The server who had met us at the door returned with a bottle of cachaça and Yone poured us shots, the first of many we would share during the early dinner she served us: spiny lobster fritters we doctored with small limes; a comforting bowl of feijoada, the national dish of Brazil, a black bean stew accompanied by garlicky collard greens and farofa, crunchy toasted cassava flour; and a type of Amazonian river fish steamed in banana leaves, which Yone finished with big spoonfuls of sweet chili dressing.

Chili peppers were Yone's passion, it turned out. Along the back wall of her restaurant, she'd created a shrine to this seminal Indigenous cultivar—a six-foot-long table covered in a white tablecloth and every variety of chili imaginable: red, yellow, orange, and blackish-purple sliced fresh; chilies that had been roasted and pickled; chili pastes and salsas; a three-tiered pyramid of hot sauce bottles.

"I love chilies," Yone exclaimed as she got up to fetch little bowls of condiments for our table. "And I want you to love chilies, too."

I sampled every variation she brought over, washing them all down with cold bottles of Brazilian beer. At some point we were joined by one of Yone's cousins, who had traveled from the Amazon to attend the Indigenous festival. The dude was hardcore Native, walking in shirtless, with a sharp bone through his nose and a giant feather headdress that went down to his knees.

"He just finished performing a ceremonial dance," Lucas explained, and I tried not to stare like a creep. Yone spoke to her cousin in their Indigenous language, explaining who I was. He bowed his head, and Yone translated what he was saying to Lucas, who translated for me.

"He's honored to meet an Apache Indian from up north, and he hopes you are feeling welcome in Brazil. He calls you 'brother.'"

We clinked beer bottles, and Yone got up to visit her shrine once more, returning with a small glass bowl of tiny, bright red and orange chilies, each smaller than a dime and with a pointy tip, like a spinning top. They were pretty, and I immediately visualized using them as a garnish.

"These are really cool," I said, picking one up by its dainty green stem. "Are they hot?"

Lucas grinned. "Try it."

I bit in. At first, the chili tasted kind of fruity and sunny, but it quickly turned into flames in my mouth. I felt my face go red, fanning my mouth dramatically with both hands and grinning to show I was enjoying myself.

Yone and her cousin laughed. They were impressed that I could eat chilies like they did.

"Those are too hot for me," Lucas said, handing me the additional caipirinha I'd ordered. "They're called pimenta biquinho."

After that evening, I saw these little Brazilian chilies everywhere, in the stores where we shopped for ingredients and written up in the menus of several of the restaurants where Lucas and I ate. Before I flew back to the United States, I bought a few jars of pickled pimenta biquinhos to take back with me, along with a bag of seeds. Unfortunately, a customs officer ended up confiscating all of it.

Thankfully, I got to keep a different souvenir of my visit with Yone—a traditional Indigenous headdress crafted from a long string of black and white feathers that she presented to me at the end of our meal together. It hangs on the wall of my living room to this day, a reminder of a wonderfully fiery meal and an inspiring encounter with an Indigenous chef who'd decided, years before I did, that she didn't have to fit a set mold to consider herself a success. What did the French know about chilies? They were missing out on all the fun.

\+ + + +

Like Yone, I have always had a thing for chilies. Long before I learned that they were an ancient Indigenous cultivar, I used to compete with my friends to see who could spoon the most El Pato hot sauce onto their sloppy joe or macaroni. The Apache cafeteria ladies at Whiteriver Elementary would place three small bowls of the condiment on each folding table, along with a white plastic spoon. I would sometimes drink El Pato straight from the bowl—it showed I was a true Apache.

Open the kitchen cupboards of almost any home on our Rez and you're sure to find a few cans of so-called Duck Sauce, which gets its name from the picture on the yellow label. We use El Pato at breakfast, lunch, and dinner, on everything from eggs to roast beef to Doritos. It wasn't unusual to get a can of the hot sauce while trick-or-treating on Halloween. The person handing it out always put it in our candy bags with a big, goofy grin.

Once I started working in restaurants, I realized that almost every American chef has their chili of choice, although this can, of course, change over time. If someone was to force me to choose my favorite, it would probably be the chipotle, which I first tasted while working at the Country Club at DC Ranch, where we used them to make a dipping sauce that accompanied empanadas filled with duck confit, chopped dried cherries, and herbs. I was immediately smitten with the smoky flavor, so the next time I went to the grocery store, I searched for chipotles in the produce section. When I couldn't find them, I approached an employee at an empty checkout line and asked.

"Chipotles are on aisle four." The salesclerk I spoke to was a tall redhead who looked like she'd never been more bored in her life. "With the other canned chilies."

"No," I said, keeping my voice polite. "Do you carry fresh chipotle peppers?"

After confirming with her coworkers on either side of her, the redhead shook her head resolutely. "We only carry canned."

The next day, back at work I asked Chef Olson if he knew where I could find fresh chipotles.

"They don't exist," he said matter-of-factly.

I stared blankly.

"A chipotle is a smoked jalapeño," he explained. "You use ripe red jalapeños and smoke them anywhere from four to sixteen hours to give them that rich flavor. In Mexico, they usually use pecan wood, but you could also use mesquite, cherry, apple, or hickory."

I was intrigued. What an adventure—using traditional Indigenous cooking methods like dehydration and smoking, a crisp, tangy jalapeño can become the edible equivalent of inhaling a bonfire.

In the years that followed, I found other examples of chilies transforming like this. A bird's beak chili, when dried, turns into an árbol, taking on notes of molasses, brown sugar, roasted tomatoes, and a hint of smoke. When processed, poblanos become anchos, Anaheims become Colorados, and mirasol chilies become guajillos. What I love is that, even if the chili pepper's color or flavor profile changes dramatically, they somehow remain themselves. I take comfort in that whenever I reflect on my own journey.

Though we now associate chilies with various world cuisines—

from Thai and Szechuan to Jamaican and Sicilian—the plant actually originated in the low-lying rainforests of Brazil, in the region that Yone's Indigenous relatives call home.

Chili peppers are officially considered a fruit, and in some places, people refer to them as chili berries. Botanists have identified twenty-six wild species of chilies, along with five domesticated species, each of which has several varieties. The two most popular domesticated species are *Capsicum chinense*, which includes habaneros and Scotch bonnets, and *Capsicum annuum*, which includes bell peppers, jalapeños, and paprika, but there are hundreds of chili varietals of every shape, size, color, and spice level around the world. One of the very spiciest is bhut jolokia, which the Indian Army uses to produce chili grenades.

Archaeological evidence suggests that Native communities began growing chilies more than six thousand years ago, eons before the pyramids of Giza were constructed. These Indigenous farmers, who selected and planted different chili varietals over many, many generations, would have had an intimate knowledge of each pepper's distinct flavor and bite, as would the Indigenous chefs who cooked with them daily.

Indigenous people were also well aware of chilies' medicinal properties long before Western science began studying the healing properties of capsaicin and using the compound in the production of medications like Icy Hot and Capsagel. The Mayans had more than thirty different health-related uses for chilies, including treatment of stomachaches, arthritis, skin rashes, and dog and snake bites.

I remember one night, in the early NACA days, I was out with my skater friends in Phoenix, sitting on our boards at some random loading dock, smoking a joint and drinking tall bottles of Heineken. I'd been doing some research for a class I'd been hired to teach at Sur La Table, where we'd be making árbol chili salsa and frying our own tortilla chips.

"Yo, did you know that ALL FUCKIN' CHILIES are Native?" I was high as a kite, yelling like a crazy person. "All of the chilies in Asia and Italy and India, they all came from the Americas, from Native farmers?"

"Damn, does that mean that even, like, kung pao beef is Native?" asked my buddy Chris, who was sitting next to me.

I blew out and passed him the joint. "Yeah, man, without us they wouldn't be cooking with those little dried red chilies. You couldn't get those in China or wherever until Columbus's dumb ass got lost and rolled up on us!"

In the Southwest, chilies have *always* been an integral part of Indigenous culture and life. In 2023, I read about an amazing discovery by a team of evolutionary biologists from the University of Colorado who identified a fossil retrieved from a local dig as a chili pepper dating back fifty million years! Today, Hatch, New Mexico—which sits four hours southeast of my father's hometown—is often referred to as the Chile Capital of the World. Green chilies are so iconic in New Mexico that you can ask for them as a topping on your hamburger or hot dog at most fast-food chains.

One of the most far-fetched scenes in *Breaking Bad* was the one where Jesse tries to get Tuco Salamanca to try a batch of poisoned meth by telling him it contains a secret ingredient, chili powder, and Tuco says, "I hate chili powder," ensuring the assassination attempt fails.

There's no way dude hates chili powder, I remember thinking to myself. *He's a Native from Mexico.*

Where I come from, our relationship with chilies is an important element of our identity: a badge of pride—and a source of vitality and joy.

+ + + +

If my time in Brazil affirmed my belief in the beauty and richness of Indigenous culture, my next trip—to Germany in October of the same year—proved strange and disorienting. I was on edge the entire eight days I was there.

Just like in London, I'd been hired by a large food distributor to produce fancy dinners for large-scale buyers at the InterContinental Hotel in Cologne during a major food expo. My relationship with Kim was hanging on by a thread. Before, during, and after my trip to Brazil, I had been drinking and partying openly. I was getting interesting gigs, so why should I try to stop? Why should I hide it? *Work hard, play hard.*

I was very much enjoying the ride, although I was tired of arguing with Kim. I also felt some guilt about little Ari seeing me come home all messed up. Before I left for Germany, I promised Kim I'd try to stop again. I knew my words were hollow, but I refused to give up on our relationship. I still loved Kim and the family we'd created. This gig seemed like a perfect opportunity to show her that I was in a different place.

I'm just going to do the work this time, I remember telling myself. *I'm not gonna drink or get high.*

After landing at the Düsseldorf Airport, I caught a train and, as I exited the Cologne station to try to catch a taxi, I stumbled upon a monument to the bombing of Germany during World War II. It was an old hunk of a bridge that was all bent and full of shrapnel holes, like Swiss cheese; the English translation next to the German plaque read: *This is an actual piece of the bridge that was destroyed by the American Allied Forces.*

I stood there, frozen. *Dang*, I thought, *Grandpa Bob helped do this.*

My mind raced as I looked at the mangled monument. *What if someone found out I was the grandson of a Navajo Code Talker? Did people know the story of how our Native culture had helped defeat their city? Was it dangerous for me to be here? What if some skinhead came along looking for a brown dude to mess with?*

As it turned out, I had very few interactions with locals during the entire six days I spent in Cologne. The cooks in the hotel kitchen barely spoke English, so their bosses had printed out translations of my menus and mise en place sheets. I overcame the language barrier just as I had during my previous international gigs, by demonstrating what I wanted the other cooks to do and using the French terms that have become the universal language of professional kitchens everywhere.

"Cut this chiffonade," I'd tell the chefs, and they knew to slice the greens into thin strips. When I said *chinois* or *brunoise* or *julienne* or *mirepoix*, they understood just what I meant.

When I wasn't at work, I kept to myself, roaming the city, looking for ways to occupy my time. I remember seeing all these lively biergartens and thinking, *Man, this sucks. There's great beer all around me and here I am trying to be a sober dumbass.* I really, really wanted to throw back big, heavy steins of beer, but instead I took myself to a movie theater to see *Ratatouille*, a movie I love. Even though it was dubbed into German, I still got emotional during the scene when Remy's father and brother show up in Paris and razz him for cooking gourmet food. I knew the dialogue by heart.

"Take a good, long look," Remy's dad says as they walk into a shop where bottles of poison line the shelves. "Now, *this* is what happens when a rat gets a little too comfortable around humans. The world we live in belongs to the enemy. We must live carefully."

The following day, I visited the famous Cologne Cathedral, where the steps leading up to the observatory tower were so old, they were concave and slippery. When I got to the top, I admired the high, domed ceilings. Gilded in real gold with dark, elaborate paintings of saints and the Christian "heaven," the opulent Gothic interior was awe-inspiring—and very menacing. A procession of violent images flashed through my mind: conquistadors massacring Aztecs, Olmecs, and Incas; priests condemning Natives to have their limbs violently amputated for refusing to convert to Christianity; malnourished boarding school students getting their braids lopped off by nuns. I had to sit down for a moment. It was disorienting carrying this alternate version of history around with me everywhere I went, constantly questioning everything I'd been taught in school and at my parents' church.

When I left the cathedral to go change for that evening's shift, I turned down a new street, passing a shop with a huge display window—you could have fit a small car in there. I stopped in my tracks. There were a number of mannequins decked out in long, braided black wigs and headbands with cheap plastic beads. They wore corny headdresses and leather pants. Behind them, there was a small teepee in front of a painted backdrop of pine trees. Small signs with German words were scattered all around. I had no clue what they said.

I'd known about the Germans' obsession with Native Americans ever since high school, when we lived in the capital of the Navajo Nation, close to Canyon de Chelly and Chinle and other tourist attractions. The vast majority of visitors from overseas came from Germany. In my senior year, my English teacher was an annoying German man who told us rambling stories about living in postwar Berlin and was constantly telling us our culture was "fascinating." I had found his extreme interest in us a bit creepy, but I never gave it much energy, never wondered about the how and the why. But standing there that morning, staring at the kinds of artifacts you might see in a cheesy Hollywood movie about Plains Indians—fake ceremonial clothing and objects that were completely different from those of my own Ndee and Diné cultures—I was rattled.

What the hell is this place?

The store was closed, so I tried looking through the locked front door, but the glass was frosted. I couldn't tell if it was a costume shop or a novelty shop or a store for antiques. I never figured it out, but I was deeply upset to see Native Americans presented in such a stereotypical way.

A few days later, back at the Düsseldorf Airport, I sat at a round table taking bites off a dry ham sandwich, writing impressions from the week in my notebook, including what it had felt like looking through the glass at these caricature "Indians."

Maybe I'm not actually real, I scrawled. *Maybe people just see me as a cartoon.*

I snapped back to the present when I heard an American voice coming out of the TV hanging over the bar across from me.

"We're here at such-and-such stadium," some sportscaster said. I watched as the camera slowly panned across a half-empty college football stadium. "The venue seats around eighty thousand, but today, there are only around forty thousand fans in the stands."

Forty thousand. I took a sip of lukewarm coffee, the number curdling in my gut.

This was, more or less, the official number of Western Apache people in the United States today, around fifteen thousand of them members of my White Mountain Apache Tribe.

Holy shit, I thought. *There aren't even enough of us to fill up a stadium.*

An entire people—with an incredibly rich history and culture—and we couldn't fill a single college football stadium in a country littered with stadiums from coast to coast.

I looked down at my notebook and, for some reason, my mind flashed to the opening scene from the movie *The Terminator.* I was young the first time I saw the movie, maybe six years old. As the movie begins, a floodlight sweeps over a wasteland of devastation—a dark, empty playground; blasted buildings; busted-up bones all over the ground.

As a kid, the scene scared me plenty. But sitting in the airport in Germany, thinking about all those empty seats in the stadium, that scene hit me in an entirely different way.

Fuck, I thought, *that's what it's like to be Native.*

For Indigenous people in much of the Americas, the world had already ended once. I was sitting on the other side of the apocalypse in a place I didn't belong, eating a mediocre ham sandwich.

Suddenly, I was desperate to get on the plane and fly back to Phoenix. I wanted to see if I could patch things up with Kim, move back into a cozy apartment, and show that I could be a better partner and father. I wanted to prove to the world (and myself) that I wasn't just another drunk, messed-up Indian cliché.

+ + + +

A month after returning from Germany, I was back at the Phoenix airport, boarding a flight to Kansai International Airport. I had demonstrated that I could stay sober on a production trip, and Kim agreed that the Intertribal Agriculture Council's invitation to produce a special dinner on their behalf at the Imperial Hotel of Osaka was too good an opportunity to pass up. After so many broken promises, she was wary of me, but I gave my word that I'd stay put for a while once I got back. We'd give Ari a proper Christmas and make time to visit both our families.

Being in Japan was a dream come true. As the sleek, silent bus slid up the coast from Kansai to Osaka, I admired the big, regal moon reflected in the ocean. Suddenly, on the other side of the bus, the cityscape came into view—tall, sleek skyscrapers amid a sea of massive neon signs flickering Japanese characters—and I felt overwhelmed with emotion.

With my forehead pressed onto the cool glass, I thought about what Native America might have become had the Europeans not invaded and ripped our cultures apart. I imagined great, sophisticated cities inhabited by millions of Tlingit, Haida, Heiltsuk, Nuxalk, Tsimshian, Kwakwaka'wakw, and Nuu-chah-nulth in the Northwest and millions of Abenaki, Iroquois, Mohawk, Mohegan,

Seneca, and Wampanoag in the Northeast, epic desert towns with hundreds of thousands of Tohono O'odham, Hopi, Zuni, Apache, and Navajo peoples. I pictured large, modern buildings inspired by Indigenous architecture—dome-shaped wigwams and wickiups, teepees, longhouses, and boxy Anasazi cliff dwellings—and massive plasma screens with words in different Native languages scrolling across.

The banquet was scheduled for November 28, giving me four days to shop, prep, and get the hotel cooks up to speed. We were expecting one hundred and twenty guests, and I planned on serving them seven courses, including a new dish I was very proud of: squash blossoms stuffed with lump crab and fried in "Navajo tempura," a batter made from white corn flour mixed with a hint of chili powder. I would serve the fried delicacy with something I called Sauce Nana, a shockingly green blend of blanched and pureed lambsquarters and sunflower sprouts named after a badass Apache warrior who was in his eighties when he rode with Geronimo and whose story reminded me of the old master samurais.

The cooks at the Imperial Hotel were amazing. They moved quickly and deliberately, operating in a state of calm, respectful unison that was completely different from the craziness and posturing of the fine-dining kitchens I was used to. I had never experienced cleanliness like this either. It seemed like every scrap that hit the floor was immediately caught or swept up by a porter. All the chefs wore tall white toques, neckerchiefs, checkered pants, long aprons, and kitchen shoes polished to a gleaming black. I sensed their respect for the uniform, so after my first day in their kitchen, I switched from my black chef's coat and striped bib apron to my more formal white coat with the NACA embroidery. I attached my eagle feather to a delicate silver chain that I clipped on to my apron. The chefs banged out their prep assignments—they were even faster than me—and when they reported back for their next task, they'd stand at attention as if I were their drill instructor. I loved it.

Through my interpreter, Mike, I asked the other cooks about ingredients I'd never seen before: dried smoked squid, eel, sticky natto, little dried fermented fish that looked like tadpoles. Osaka was the first place I ever encountered shishito peppers, which have since become pretty trendy in the United States. When I asked about them, one of the chefs in the kitchen blistered a handful in a smoking pan, finishing them with a dash of sesame oil and yuzu salt. They were delicious.

Mike translated what the cook said, that shishitos were a local chili variety derived from Spanish padrón peppers.

"How'd they get here?" I asked him.

"The Portuguese brought them over," Mike conveyed, "most likely sometime in the sixteenth century."

From the Americas to Europe to Japan. Centuries before me, chilies had traced the same path around the globe.

+ + + +

In the days leading up to the event, the hotel staff and I worked like ants, efficient and determined, but there was still plenty of time for me to explore. When I wasn't working, I hit the streets on my skateboard, fascinated by everything I passed, the beautiful shrines and parks, the endless parade of intriguing, inviting restaurants. On a visit to Dotonbori Street one evening, I went from izakaya to izakaya, eating the best street food I'd ever tasted. One spot specialized in chicken sashimi.

"The chef says they killed the chicken this morning and it's really fresh," Mike told me. "I sure as hell wouldn't eat it, though, and neither should you."

It sounded like a challenge, so of course I ordered the dish. When the server placed the glazed-blue plate in front of me, everyone in the tiny restaurant turned to see how I'd react.

It was a pink, glistening breast of chicken, flash seared, thinly sliced, and dressed in sesame oil and house-made soy sauce. I put my nose to the plate—it smelled clean, fresh, and a little like a barnyard—and picked up one piece with my chopsticks, bringing it to my mouth. It tasted nothing like cooked chicken, nothing like raw fish, but an entirely new flavor. I got a small hit of adrenaline from that first bite. Eating raw poultry was thrilling and scary, but so delicious I finished the whole portion by myself.

"Give me your next-of-kin contact info," Mike joked. "Just in case you die on the plane in a few days."

I encountered so many new foods and flavors in Japan. From a culinary perspective, it was a completely different world, and yet there was something deeply familiar about the cuisine.

The Japanese were extremely proud of their foods and fiercely protective of the traditions and rituals around them, and many of their most popular ingredients were extremely funky, things that a lot of the American chefs I knew would find too pungent or bitter, too ugly and strange. Just like our beloved Apache foods—like acorns, sumac berries, wild carrots, and yucca blossoms—traditional Japanese ingredients seemed to be cherished for their distinct identities, allowed to just be themselves. The cuisine's simple, unadorned preparations stood in stark contrast to the classical French kitchen, where complicated, finicky sauces were put on a pedestal.

Observing all of the ancient artwork and temples in Osaka, I realized there was a direct relation between the nation's history and the characteristics of its cuisine. The old ways were woven into the current culture—the Japanese cooks I collaborated with were working with the same ingredients that their ancestors had been cooking with for thousands of years. In putting their own twist on traditional dishes, today's chefs were linking past, present, and future, strengthening a culinary culture that had evolved over millennia. This way of cooking was a beautiful thing, but it also made me a little sad.

The story of Native American foods and cuisines was so radically different, full of disruption, erasure, and confusion. I wanted to believe that the work I was doing to excavate the history of our cultivars and to champion our contributions and traditions could inspire Native Americans to feel proud about our food culture, but the task sometimes felt daunting.

Despite the heaviness of my thoughts, the city consistently inspired me. The Japanese elders I skated past all looked like they could be from Chinle, Tuba City, Tohatchi, Crownpoint, or one of the other towns on the Navajo Nation, where my father was from. Everywhere I went, I was treated with quiet respect.

One afternoon, I came across a set of marble steps outside a massive office building. The drop was six feet high, perfect for the kind of classic eighties-style big grabs I loved. I ollied the stairs on my first try, but right as I landed, I saw two Japanese cops walking toward me.

Shit, I thought, *I'm gonna go to Japanese jail.*

Instead, the policemen stopped and gave me a slow "golf clap," just like Wayne and Garth do on *Wayne's World*. They were wearing white gloves.

Japan is fucking dope, I thought as I skated away.

A couple days later, I passed a shop that caught my eye and jumped off my skateboard to get a closer look. Over the entrance hung a large blue banner with some Japanese characters and a picture of a katana sword, irresistible to a Wu-Tang fan like me. I slid open the glass, walking into a tiny shop with glass shelves displaying beautiful knives of every sort.

In the far corner, next to an antique cash register, an old man sat on a stool bent over an anvil. Behind him was a brightly lit cabinet holding a samurai's armor and weapons. Wisps of smoke rose from an incense holder.

I stood in awe, breathing in the aroma of steel.

The silence was broken when a tiny old woman emerged from a doorway and started speaking to me in rapid Japanese.

"Uhhhh, hmmm, I'm interested in your chef's knives," I stuttered. I had been saving as much as I could in the lead-up to the trip so I could get myself some of the country's famous hand-forged blades.

She and the old man both stared blankly, so I mimed chopping and stirring. "Kitchen knife? Cooking?"

I held up a finger, sliding my backpack off to pull out the Japanese cookbook I'd bought earlier in the day. I opened the book to the back flap, pointing at the photo of the author dressed in his formal chef's uniform, then at myself.

The old woman's eyes lit up and she immediately began pulling knives for me, placing them on a tray lined in burgundy felt. I examined each one she presented to me, putting aside two Japanese chef's knives, a paring knife, a beautiful santoku blade with a mahogany handle, and two Yanagiba slicers that looked like small katanas. All together, I spent the equivalent of $1,300, my entire budget.

Just as I was preparing to leave the store, a new customer came in, a sharply dressed man about my age. It was clear from the shopkeeper's greeting that he was a regular.

I smiled at him and he bowed his head. The old woman said something.

"They want to know where you are from." The young man's English was perfect.

I told him I was a Native American from the White Mountains of Arizona, and explained what I was doing in Osaka.

"I am going to cherish these knives forever." I gestured toward the ancient armor and sword in the display cabinet. "Where are those from?"

My new interpreter smiled. "His great-grandfather made that katana," he said, gesturing at the old man. "And he learned from him how to make swords in the traditional way. But, of course, now there is more of a market for knives."

"Wow." I couldn't believe I was in the presence of an expert sword-maker. "Would he be willing to sign one of my knives?"

When the young man asked him, the shopkeeper nodded his head once decisively.

I handed him back my new santoku knife and he placed it on his anvil. The two men went back and forth a few times and finally, the businessman took a pen and paper from the old lady and wrote something I couldn't make out.

I watched closely as the knife-maker etched a few Japanese characters on one side of the blade.

"His family seal," the young man explained.

Then he flipped the knife over and carefully carved English letters into the steel, consulting the slip of paper the young man had handed him. When he was done, they spelled out APACHE CHEF.

I was incredibly moved.

"Arigato. Arigato. Arigato." I thanked him over and over, bowing my head. The old man had given me my own katana.

I tried to pay him, but he wouldn't take any more money; it was one of the nicest things anyone had ever done for me. I had no way of knowing at the time that this personalized mahogany-handled knife he'd proudly presented to me would end up saving my life.

+ + + +

The banquet in the ballroom of Osaka's Imperial Hotel remains one of the high points of my career as a chef. The hotel printed out elegant menus with each of the seven courses written in both English and Japanese and flanked by sage-green borders adorned with a simple geometric design. They included the council's seal and the words *Made By American Indians*. I keep a copy in my desk drawer to this day.

Even though we couldn't properly communicate, the Japanese cooks who assisted me showed me their dedication and respect with their actions on the line. They worked cleanly, diligently, and quietly, mindful of every small detail, using laser thermometers to check the exact temperature of the bone china plates, chilling the silverware for the cold dishes and heating them for the hot dishes. I called out directions in English and my interpreter for the night, a petite young woman, repeated my instruction in Japanese.

"Two minutes, fire first course," I commanded. "Fire Acorn Stew and Racket Bread—make it beautiful, please!"

Each time my translator spoke, the chefs responded in unison: "Hai, Chef!"

I felt so proud watching them construct all these exquisite Western Apache dishes I had composed as an act of rebellion and resurgence. The chef in charge of the Acorn Stew stacked three Apache dumplings, the size of gnocchi, in a pyramid in the center of each four-ounce bowl next to three perfect cubes of acorn-braised beef. Each bowl was placed on a plate, along with two small Apache Racket Breads. Before each tray went out with a china teakettle full of piping-hot broth that would be poured ceremonially table-side, I scooped up acorn flour with a silver demitasse spoon I'd taken from Mary Elaine's, sprinkling some across each plate, a gold-colored dusting.

Each course went off without flaw—the service team was prompt and exacting. I had not seen such excellence in action since being on the line at Mary Elaine's. For those two and a half hours, I felt positive I was one of the best Native chefs in the world.

At the end of the dinner, I was asked to speak to the guests, walking out to a standing ovation. Everyone listened intently as I talked about my work with NACA, this special menu, and the importance of supporting Native American farmers and ranchers and purchasing their products.

The interpreter walked me around to several of the tables, where many of the diners singled out the Acorn Stew as their favorite dish of the night.

"They say the flavors reminded them of Japanese home cooking and that the presentation was very beautiful," she conveyed.

After we cleaned up for the evening, Mike invited a few of the other cooks to join us for my last night in the city and we went from bar to bar, eating and drinking until the early morning hours. The night was a blur. I barely got three hours of sleep before I had to get up and pack for the airport. I stumbled around my tiny hotel room, stuffing belongings into my duffel bag. I grabbed my passport from the safe and slid it into the front pocket of my backpack. My hand froze.

Fuck. Where was my eagle feather?

I had brought it to the kitchen the day before to watch over our preparations. It had definitely been in this pocket. I dumped everything out on the bed: receipts and menus and notebooks and a box of Japanese sweets I'd bought for Ari, but no plume.

I tried not to panic, retracing my steps, trying to remember when I might have opened my bag. I couldn't recall how I'd gotten back to the hotel or any of the names of the bars we'd gone to. And even if I could, there was no time for me to go back.

What a shitty way to end such an incredible trip. I had fifteen minutes before my taxi to the bus station arrived. I hopped in the shower, giving myself a pep talk.

That was such an amazing dinner, Nephi. You can go see the medicine man and ask him for another feather. You've got your lucky knife now.

The truth is that I was terrified. In the Apache way, my plume was there to guide me and watch over me. I'd had it since I was thirteen and I knew its power to be real.

The plume had taken hits for me, protecting against grave danger. Losing or breaking it was a sign, a warning that something bad was hovering nearby. Although I'd performed at the height of my powers the previous night, I worried that my plume had left me because I continued to disrespect the gift given to me by Creator. With all the drinking and drugging, I was constantly endangering my body and spirit. It was an ominous feeling. I couldn't shake it for the entire fifteen-hour flight back home.

SIX

HOT TUB TIME MACHINE

After riding high in Japan, my homecoming felt like a crash-landing. With a full-blown recession looming in early 2008, no one was hiring. I spent weeks pounding the pavement, dropping off my résumé at hotels and restaurants all over the greater Phoenix area, including a few of the small eateries in Mekong Supermarket, but I didn't get a single callback. I did land one exciting gig designing the curriculum for a Native American cuisine course at a small, private culinary school in North Scottsdale, but it was temporary and the pay was next to nothing. I kept taking on whatever contract work I could find, filling in for cooks who were out sick and running workshops through NACA, but I felt like I was treading water. What kind of delusional idiot was I, thinking I could support a family with random restaurant work?

The accumulating stress only made me want to party harder. Cocaine was accessible in the kitchens I passed through, and, although I couldn't afford to buy it on my own, I discovered that the drug gave me the same rush I got from producing big events like the ones in Cologne and Osaka. I was too wrapped up in my own struggles to sit with the destruction and pain I was causing the people I loved most. Each time Kim had enough and kicked me out, I couch-surfed with friends.

Finally, in the fall, I got a call from the Smithsonian's National Museum of the American Indian. The previous year, I had submitted a piece for their anthology *The Land Has Memory*, and now they wanted me to come out to DC for five days to do a cooking demonstration in the center court of the museum and to facilitate four ninety-minute trainings for their staff. Morning sessions would be dedicated to discussions of food in Native American history, while afternoon sessions would involve working with the staff of the Mitsitam Native Foods Café, the museum's highly regarded restaurant. It was organized into five different stations, each representing the Native cuisine of a different region: the Great Plains, Northern Woodlands, Pacific Northwest Coast, Mesoamerica, and South America.

This was a major milestone—I'd attracted the attention of one of the most prominent institutions involved with educating the public on Native American history and culture. Working with the museum's staff was a phenomenal opportunity, a chance to set the record straight about how foodways were too often an afterthought in official versions of history and get more people talking about the stories of Indigenous cultivars.

The week was a mixed bag. The staff were very engaged, particularly when I presented my boarding school food research, which they thought would make a great exhibit. Two hundred and fifty people showed up for my public cooking class and afterward some of the staff took me up to the roof of Mitsitam to show me the perfect view of the Capitol building. A few local Natives who attended the event invited me to a sports bar within walking distance from the museum, where we had a lively conversation about cooking and restaurants and then some of us hit another bar, where we did shots. I don't remember getting back to the hotel, although I think I remember staggering down the street and flipping off some famous monuments. I missed my morning session the next day, waking up at 11:47 a.m. The facilitator I'd been working with was upset, but I think she was more embarrassed for me. I offered to double up that afternoon's sessions, but she declined, wishing me well in my "future endeavors."

Even after that, I still decided to go out again on my last night in DC and get totally shit-faced. I stumbled back to my hotel again in the early morning, packing in a rush to get to Reagan National Airport in time for my flight back to Phoenix.

After a couple of breakfast beers at the airport sports bar, I decided it would be a good idea to call Kim and ask if I could move back in with her and Ari. I was too far gone to remember much about the conversation, but I do know it devolved into a loud, ugly argument. Apparently, I threatened to take my own life, which is when someone alerted the authorities. I have a vague recollection of a couple of airport cops slamming me to the ground and handcuffing me. They booked me for public intoxication and resisting arrest and I was transported to a jail in Virginia.

When I woke up the next morning, I was in solitary confinement. Dehydrated and nauseous, I came back to reality with that bitter mix of fear, anger, and regret that I'd come to know well roiling inside me. I asked the detention officer who came to check on me what I was doing there.

"You're on suicide watch, Mr. Craig," he explained, handing me a standard jail meal: a dry bologna sandwich, a mealy apple, and a carton of lukewarm milk. I wasn't sure I could keep it down.

I was miles away from anyone who cared about me, and my precious roll of chef's knives was back in Arizona, along with everything else inside my checked suitcase. Even if the police decided to release me, I had only a few dollar bills in my wallet and, without the tools of my trade, there was no way I could earn enough money to buy another plane ticket. I was fucked.

The next day, after cycling in and out of a restless sleep, a couple of corrections officers came by.

One of them rumbled, "Roll up and step out"—prison speak for "get ready to be released." I was relieved but also anxious. *Where would I go?*

"We're releasing you to doctors from Johns Hopkins for a psych evaluation," the other guard explained, answering my silent question.

"You're either very lucky or really unlucky," the first guy added.

I was processed out and given the clothes I'd been wearing when I came in: a black hoodie and camouflage cargo pants that reeked of tobacco and spilled beer. An officer directed me to take a seat and wait, and after several minutes, two somber, familiar faces appeared, peering in at me through the thick wired glass.

It was Dr. Allison Barlow and Dr. Mathuram Santosham, the instructors who'd led the epidemiology and biostatistics course I'd taken during the Winter Institute almost four years earlier. I learned later that, during that terrible airport phone call, I'd yelled, "The fucking pigs are here now," and Kim had called my parents to tell them I might be in serious trouble. They both knew Dr. Mathu, the founder and director emeritus of the Johns Hopkins Center for Indigenous Health, and had reached out to see if he could help them track me down. I was ashamed to think about how often the people in my life had to clean up my messes.

"How long will I be here? I gotta rebook my flight. I don't have any clothes. I need to go home." As we drove from suburban Virginia to downtown Baltimore, I badgered my former teachers with practical questions, my mind latching on to mundane details so I wouldn't have to process the magnitude of my reckless behavior.

"It will take as long as it needs to," said Dr. Barlow, a prominent researcher specializing in Native American health, before kindly shifting the conversation to my work at Mitsitam.

When we pulled up to the hospital, Dr. Mathu turned around and spoke to me in a calm, firm tone. "We want you safe, Nephi. You do important work and your family is worried about you. Plus, the court will drop a few charges if you comply with this evaluation."

I was touched by the doctors' concern, but it also stung. My last experience at Johns Hopkins was as a participant in a prestigious public health program. Now, here I was being locked up in the psych ward.

What a fool I was, imagining that I was someone who could help the people in my community. The only thing I was good at was blowing things up.

\+ + + +

"What are you so afraid of?"

Dr. Ericson, the head psychiatrist at the Hopkins facility, was a bald white man who projected his voice and enunciated each word carefully like one of those town square orators in a Western movie. On the way to the hospital, Dr. Barlow had assured me he was one of the best in the field, a claim that all of the nurses and counselors on the ward repeated, but I had my doubts. I'd left our first few sessions feeling even worse about myself than when I'd gone in. I was pretty sure therapy wasn't my thing—I'd been through a bunch of different treatment programs in four different states, and I hadn't experienced any transformative breakthroughs. I was a problem no one could solve.

"I'm afraid I might be insane," I blurted out, hoping to beat the doctor to the punch. Detoxing from my bender, my mind had cleared, making me acutely aware of the suffering all around me—the dozens of patients who were obviously mentally ill. Clearly, the experts thought I belonged here.

"I'm afraid I'm going to drink myself to death. I'm afraid there's something seriously defective about me . . . I mean, who in the hell thinks they can change history and revitalize an entire cuisine?"

Dr. Ericson scribbled away on his yellow pad.

"I'm afraid that nothing I do matters. The only thing I'm good at is cooking, but I can't support my family and no one around me understands what I'm trying to achieve or why. I'm afraid people don't respect me and talk about what a failure I am."

I hunched over, resting my head in my hands. I'd been in the psych ward about three months at this point. I just wanted to get through this session, which Dr. Ericson had told me would be our last.

"I'm afraid of feeling like this, like I'm not sure I want to live."

I closed my eyes. I'd never said these things out loud before. Finally, Dr. Ericson broke the silence.

"Do you want to know what I think?" he asked, clasping his veiny hands like a preacher about to deliver a sermon. "You're a smart young man, Mr. Craig. In my assessment, you are *not* clinically depressed. What's actually going on is that you are chemically inducing your depression and psychosis."

I scowled, daring him to continue.

"You're spiraling down because of the drinking and the drugs. You've made a choice to avoid hard emotions and you're harming yourself in the process. By not dealing with your grief and your anger, you're dragging yourself down."

Dr. Ericson's words pierced straight to the heart. For eighteen years, ever since the attack I still had never told anyone about, I'd been swinging back and forth between two familiar emotions—rage and numbness, rage and numbness—like a skater trapped on a ramp with no exit. Lately, ever since I'd lost my plume, my anxiety had felt all-consuming. This was a trick I didn't know how to land.

"That's your diagnosis? You're not gonna prescribe me some medicine or something?"

Dr. Ericson shook his head. "Son, I strongly recommend that you commit to this work, that you continue getting Cognitive Behavioral Therapy, probably for the rest of your life. There's nothing inherently wrong with you, but nothing will change until you get to the root of your self-destructive thinking and behavior."

In a sick way, I'd hoped this big-shot psychiatrist would provide me with an excuse for all of my awful behavior, making the people who'd written me off feel sorry. But for the first time, I began to see that if I had any hope of changing my downward trajectory, I would have to start paying better attention to what I was feeling, studying myself with the same focus and intensity I had brought to investigating the history of Indigenous foods.

+ + + +

Three days after my last conversation with Dr. Ericson, I was released to a long-term treatment program at a homeless shelter where I could stay until I stabilized and saved up enough money to make my way home. I was leaving the psych ward with no official diagnosis other than being an addict. I hadn't gotten a pass for my selfish, fucked-up behavior.

From the jump, Baltimore Station was totally different from any other rehab I'd been to. Located in a converted redbrick fire station in South Baltimore, the shelter had a casual, informal vibe and was designed to house residents for eighteen to twenty-four months. Owen, the guy in charge of my intake interview, was dressed in jeans and a ripped T-shirt. After asking me the usual series of biographical questions—name, date of birth, next of kin—he shifted gears dramatically.

"You ever kill anyone?"

I shook my head.

"You got AIDS? Ever been tested?"

Another head shake.

"You ever pay to fuck around with them hoes out there?"

"You got any tracks?"

"You stashin' anything right now?"

After answering no to all of his questions, Owen asked me to stand up so he could search my pockets, socks, and shoes. He looked around for my bag.

"You ain't got no clothes?"

"Nah, man, I just came from the psych ward at Hopkins and before that I was in jail."

Owen grinned. "No shit. Well, we're gonna help you get your shit together here." His expression darkened. "That is, if you do your part to save your own motherfuckin' life and stop doing all that dumb shit out on them streets."

Nobody at any of the treatment centers I'd been to had ever spoken to me like this.

"Dr. Barlow said a guy named Woody would be my counselor or something," I said. "Is he here?"

Owen's head snapped up from his paperwork. "Woody ain't nobody's fucking counselor. He's the clinical director."

After handing me a piece of paper with my bunk number on it—the Station had recently been renovated with a new, fifty-bed addition that was still pending a fire inspection—Owen brought me to the donation closet where I grabbed some pants and shirts, then led me upstairs.

It was almost lights-out. When Owen introduced me, the other men in my room grunted and nodded, telling me their names and that's about it. I placed my new clothes and shoes in the cubby next to my bunk and lay down with a book on depression I'd received from one of the counselors at Johns Hopkins. It was a relief to be out of the mental ward with all the strange nighttime noises. As I flipped through a chapter on adverse childhood experiences and the roots of mental illness, I thought about my first roommate at the psych ward, a young guy who smeared feces all over the walls and needed to be extracted by orderlies in orange biohazard suits. I thought about the pretty white-haired woman who never spoke or made eye contact the entire time I was committed. Every evening at five forty-five, like clockwork, an elegant older man in an expensive coat and polished shoes would come in, take off his wool hat, and sit down next to her, holding and rubbing her hand. He'd help her stand up and they'd walk together in circles around the common room while he talked to her about his day, although her expression never changed.

I shoved the book under my bed and closed my eyes, thinking about this couple. Their steadfast, dignified devotion reminded me of my parents. My mind skittered to my own failed relationships. *What did it take to create that kind of love and companionship?* I wondered. *Did I have that inside of me? Was I even capable of being that kind of man? And would someone ever show up for me in that way?*

+ + + +

My first morning at the Station, I was sitting outside with a few of the other guys, drinking coffee and smoking Newports, when a brown Buick pulled up to the curb. I watched as a tall Black man with a smooth, broad face unfolded himself from the car, talking into one of those old-school Bluetooth phones that went in one ear. He was wearing tan slacks, a black shirt, and a tan wool overcoat. He wore a golden do-rag under a tan-and-gold flat-brimmed baseball cap tilted to the side, and he sported a thick gold chain.

As he passed us, deep in conversation with someone on the other end of the line, he tipped his head in greeting. One of my roommates, Andre, caught me staring after him as he entered the building.

"Woody. Is. A. Bad. Motherfucker." He emphasized each word, like a poem.

"That's the clinical director?" I was surprised.

Another one of the residents, a guy from D.C. called Jake, chuckled. "Just wait 'til we go to group. Lots of people say they keep it real, but Woody actually does."

Born in 1942, Wynwood Curry was a Vietnam War veteran with the 82nd Airborne Division. He served two tours as a paratrooper, attending language school during his army service to become a Vietnamese translator, which ended up giving him profound insights and empathy for the "enemy." After returning from combat, Woody struggled with PTSD and active drug addiction, cycling through bouts of recovery and relapse. Eventually he turned it around, obtaining multiple graduate degrees from Johns Hopkins and training as a Certified Addiction Counselor.

People who knew him from the Baltimore Station or one of the other addiction recovery programs he designed often described Woody as a combination of the Buddha and Richard Pryor: part spiritual guru, part give-no-fucks comedian. During his five decades as a counselor and therapist, Woody changed thousands of people's lives, mine included. He turned the Baltimore Station into one of the most successful rehabilitation programs in the country. Over the two-plus months I spent at the Station, I listened attentively to every word Woody said. I trusted his swagger.

There were sixty men living at the Station when I arrived, and only two of them were white—all the rest were African American, apart from me, the lone Native. Many of the residents were military veterans and most, but not all, were struggling with addiction. The Baltimore Station is where I first realized that recovery was not just about drugs and alcohol—it could mean recovering from combat or violence, from police brutality, incarceration, or homelessness.

Every person in that converted firehouse was in recovery from a military-industrial complex that devalued human life. Addiction was just the tip of the iceberg.

Every weekday, Woody led a psycho-educational group in the cafeteria. As soon as breakfast was over, a few guys would fold up the tables and roll them into the corner, and a couple others would pass a large dust mop over the linoleum floors, which were always sparkling clean, probably because there were so many vets living there. There were large plaques of every branch of the United States military above the swinging kitchen doors—each time I walked by the Marine Corps plaque, I'd pay respects to my dad, my uncle Harrison, and Grandpa Bob, the Navajo Code Talker, saying "Semper Fi" under my breath.

My first day at the Station, I followed the other men's lead, helping arrange folding chairs in a semicircle facing the kitchen. James, a fellow hip-hop fan who would become one of my friends at the shelter, wheeled out a proper desk chair.

When Woody strutted into the room, everyone took their seat and stopped talking. He sat on his throne and scanned the room. I felt his eyes linger on me, the new guy.

"Y'all muthafuckas just don't get it!" He clasped his hands—I hadn't noticed his gold bracelets until then. Some of the guys around me chuckled nervously.

"Don't laugh, this shit ain't funny. I just came from a conversation about some muthafucka who says he's gonna leave another program after three weeks because he loves his woman." Woody rubbed his eyes, like a weary father. "This son of a bitch is just like all of you, talking some bullshit and calling it love."

How did he know I'd been thinking about my relationship? It wouldn't surprise me if this dude could read minds.

"You need to keep the focus on you, not some other motherfucker outside of you," he continued. "You been running 'round the world chasing a chemical to feel good, doing dumb-ass shit, getting locked up, put in a nuthouse, in and out of the ER. Then you get up in here, the drugs wear off, and you want to start chasing this love shit again."

Woody was glaring at us now.

"Where the fuck was your love when you were out there rippin' and runnin' and not giving a fuck about a goddamn thing? Where was all this love when you were thinking, 'I got me some money—fuck the landlord, fuck gas and electric, fuck the kids and the ol' lady, fuck everything, I'ma get high'?"

No one had ever pegged me so precisely. Somehow Woody knew exactly who I was. He understood the crazy life I'd been living.

"Love is a verb!" Woody punched a fist into his open palm. "You're feeling sorry for yourself, thinking how you need someone to care about you, to really love you, but guess what? That's something you need to learn to do for your muthafuckin' self!"

Woody shook his head.

"You being in here is an act of love, but you can't even see it. You sticking it out in rehab is the most powerful act of love."

I opened up the notebook I'd brought to the session, jotting down, *Rehab is an act of love.* It was the first of many Woodyisms I'd record, some profound, others hilarious. His favorite diss was, *You're like a one-eyed cat peepin' in a seafood store—you ain't seeing shit!*

The first few days, I brought the notebook to every session until Woody called me out while I was frantically scribbling.

"Hey, Phi." He'd given me the nickname as soon as I introduced myself to him, right after that first circle. "The fuck you doin'? Drawin' some shit?"

"I'm taking notes, sir!" My Camp Pendleton days and professional kitchens instilled in me the instinct to be deferential to my "superiors." A few of the guys snickered.

"Man, don't give me that 'sir' bullshit," said Woody. "Put the damn book away and just fucking listen."

Woody's groups were more lecture than talk circle, but they sent you on a journey within yourself. You laughed and grieved, sat with your deep shame and felt glimmers of hope. I rarely cried in any of the other rehabs I'd been to, but at the Station, I sobbed frequently. Seeing all of these self-described "street-life thugs," "hustlers," and hardened military veterans silently wipe tears from their faces melted away my brittle cynicism.

Over and over during my stay at the Baltimore Station, I was struck by how Woody tried to show the men under his care that beneath all the labels society was quick to slap on us—"deadbeat dad," "criminal," "convict," "combat vet," "drunk," "addict"—we were vulnerable people. He saw us as intelligent human beings with strong survival skills that had helped us get through the hell of combat, incarceration, and addiction. He used the language of the street because that was the culture of violence that had shaped us, but he harnessed it to teach us to tend to our emotions, to be kinder to ourselves.

Woody was the only one at the Station who knew about my background as a chef, and he advised me to make myself useful by working in the kitchen, which was overseen by two cooks: Rick and Gina. I told both of them that I had a lot of experience working in restaurants, but I didn't elaborate and so they put me on dishwashing duty. I found the work very satisfying. I'd quietly fill the three-compartment stainless sink with water—wash, rinse, sanitize—and methodically make my way through all the dirty dishes. I mopped my station dry and wiped the counters down regularly, using kitchen jargon like *behind* and *corner* as I moved around the tight kitchen. Gina teased me about it, calling me "Pro."

After all the drama of the last few years, it was a relief to leave the cooking to others. I was happy just to follow instructions and keep my shit clean.

+ + + +

Up until I arrived at the Baltimore Station, most of my own experiences with clinical environments had been sterile and whitewashed. Other than NARA in Portland, the rehab programs I'd gone through were either faith-based or grounded in the twelve-step philosophy—and I often felt like they had little to do with my lived experiences. A taciturn Apache, I would leave every spill-your-guts, pity-party session feeling confused and depleted.

Woody's background as a Black man, vet, and recovered addict meant he knew how to communicate and connect deeply with people struggling to keep their heads above water. He wasn't like any of the AA Big Book thumpers, pastors, white clinicians, or counselors who had "actively listened" to my tired, well-articulated excuses about my drug use and poor choices. People in the throes of addiction have the ability to detect "book smart" in people—and when we do, we automatically put up a barrier—but there was nothing textbook about Woody's methods, and I believe that's why they actually worked.

I remember how Woody reacted when I told him that the head psychologist at Johns Hopkins had recommended I stick with Cognitive Behavioral Therapy.

"Don't worry about that bullshit yet. Just sit still up in here and listen," he advised me.

Much later, I would come to realize that the various therapists who worked at the Baltimore Station were steeped in CBT concepts, even if they didn't talk about them that way. In every group and educational session, their goal was to help us see that, when we followed their advice about staying clean and staying out of trouble, our thoughts—about who we were, what we were capable of, and what we needed and wanted—also started to change.

"Honesty is not what comes out of your fuckin' mouth; honesty is what you do," Woody told us once. "You think you're being honest by talking about 'I didn't have a daddy.' 'I got beat up a lot.' 'That woman left me and broke my heart.'" Woody's normally deep voice went high, imitating someone making excuses. "But what's coming out of your mouth is just a story, some shit you put together to help you live with yourself. It's all lies. The truth is that the drugs didn't fuck you up; the drugs made you fuck *yourself* up!"

I thought about Dr. Ericson's observation that my addictions had triggered my depression and not the other way around.

"Stop *saying* you want to get better. The only honest thing to do is to stop doing that shit. Those of you that have been here for a while know that it's easier now, but here's the secret—it's not that this rehab shit got any easier; it's that you got better at doing it!"

Woody looked around the circle, his gold chain flashing in the fluorescent light.

"*That's* how recovery works—you get better with it the more you do it."

Sitting there in that narrow, brick-walled cafeteria, I was suddenly transported to the kitchen at Mary Elaine's, remembering how terrified I was when I started working there, how I doubted my abilities and questioned whether I was good enough. Working day after day in that high-end kitchen, where excellence was expected every step of the way, *made* me good. Really, really good.

I appreciated Woody's framing of recovery as something that you got better at the more you committed and practiced. It was exactly like cooking. You could talk a big game about how great you were, but there was no way to fake it once you stepped into the kitchen. The proof was in the pudding, as that corny-ass saying goes.

Thanks to my professional experiences—culinary school, DC Ranch, Mary Elaine's, establishing NACA—I knew what I was capable of. Whenever I picked up a knife and sliced and diced with precision, whenever I perfectly seared a piece of meat or adjusted a sauce on the fly, I'd get a hit of confidence and clarity: *This was what I was meant to do.* Cooking made sense to me, and because of that, it pushed me to keep going and get even stronger.

It was Woody and the other counselors at the Station who guided me toward this realization—cooking was more than a vocation for me. Working in the kitchen was a way to keep my mind in order and practice staying grounded. Sitting there in that hard folding chair that day, I dared to hope. Maybe cooking could help me get a handle on my darkest impulses and thoughts.

Maybe my thing is culinary therapy, I thought, smiling to myself. *Culinary Cognitive Behavioral Therapy.*

+ + + +

By April 2009, my mind had cleared and I felt hopeful again, letting myself daydream about starting a new life on the East Coast. One evening, after finishing kitchen clean-up duty, I went outside to call Kim from my old silver Samsung flip phone.

We hadn't spoken for months, since the night of our airport blowup, but she sounded relieved, even happy, to hear from me. My heart ached as she filled me in on Ari, about how much he was talking, and how well he was doing in his kindergarten class.

"He's obsessed with SpongeBob and your dad. It's so cute. He calls him 'Gampa.'" Kim laughed, a sparkling sound. "He asks to come and see you in Whiteriver, Nephi, but I think he also somehow understands that you are far away. I tell him that you were sick and you're in the hospital getting better."

The line went silent. I lit a Newport.

"How are you doing?" Kim's voice was softer now, more guarded.

"I'm doing real good. I like it here." I took a deep drag. "I've got a lead on a couple of chef jobs, but I'm taking my time. Baltimore's a tough city, but it's pretty cool—the houses are redbrick and all different colors and there's a really nice waterfront. I think you would like it."

"We tried that in Washington . . ." I could sense I was making Kim upset. I took a deep breath and kept going, before I could lose my nerve.

"Listen, I know things were really bad this winter, but I'm in a much better place. I haven't had a drink since that day I called you, and I haven't used. A big change could be good for us. I think we could have a good life here."

I heard voices in the background and wondered who was there with Kim. I felt the acid of the orange I'd just eaten rise up to my throat.

"I can't do this anymore, Nephi. It's not good for any of us." Kim sniffled. "It's over."

I felt my own tears welling up, but what came out instead was anger.

"Fuck you."

I yelled some more, but Kim had already hung up. I was shaking. I glanced down the grimy street, where right around the corner you could score just about any drug you wanted.

I was on autopilot now, driven by rage. I stamped out my cigarette and ran upstairs to grab my backpack from under my bed, stuffing it with my clothes and books. James, who was up in his bunk relaxing and listening to Raekwon the Chef on his boom box, looked up.

"What's up, Nephi? Where you goin'?"

I couldn't meet his eyes. "I gotta get out of here. I need to get back home and see what's up with my family. I hear some stupid shit is going down."

"Why don't you cool it? You know nothing good comes from acting on a big emotion."

Usually James's deep, jazzy voice put me at ease. Not today.

"I'm done sitting still," I said, stomping out the door. I never said goodbye, and I'm still sad that this was our last exchange—James was a real one, and the impact of the Baltimore Station program was truly profound, even if I couldn't fully grasp it at the time. I don't know how my life would have gone differently if I'd stuck it out and stayed at the shelter for a year or more, which many of the residents did, but I do know that this unique community would have continued to help me stabilize and heal.

I took a quick detour through the cafeteria, snatching a handful of saltine packets and some fruit from the snack basket. I walked out of the firehouse, turning left onto Light Street and to the shady money-transfer store where the Station residents knew you could cash out your Maryland food stamp card in an emergency. I used the money at the liquor store next door, grabbing two fifths of Bacardi and a six-pack of beer.

Next, I headed for the Greyhound station, a twenty-minute walk away, where I used the last of my cash to buy a one-way bus ticket to Phoenix. I snuck shots of Bacardi along the way.

I kept drinking at the bus station and was faded by the time we stopped in Pittsburgh. Next thing I remember, I woke up handcuffed to a gurney in the hallway of a hospital. I had no idea how I'd gotten there. When a doctor finally came by to check on me, he told me that someone had called the police because I was stumbling around and yelling. When the cops showed up, I cussed them out and struggled, so they restrained me and brought me to UPMC Mercy hospital.

"You're lucky nobody pressed charges," he said.

Another white guy in a uniform telling me I was lucky—that pissed me off.

"I'm free to go, then," I said, letting him know I was aware he couldn't legally keep me there. "So get these fucking cuffs off. I have to catch a bus."

The doctor called over the security guard to unlock the handcuffs, making a last-ditch effort to convince me to go straight to rehab. I tuned him out.

As soon as a nurse removed my IVs, I riffled through my pockets for my bus ticket and sat down to lace my shoestrings back into my shoes. I returned to the Greyhound station through thick fog, passing by an empty sports arena, and managed to convince the teller on duty to honor my one-way ticket and let me on the next bus.

I had a few hours to kill. I suddenly remembered that, after the station attendant had threatened to call the police on me, I'd hidden my almost-full bottle of Bacardi in the last stall of the men's bathroom. My heart raced as I entered the foul-smelling space. I was relieved to find the bottle still there, behind the base of the toilet.

+ + + +

It was an awful trip home. I drank steadily, and when we stopped in St. Louis just before dawn, I polished off the last banana I'd stashed in my bag. By the time the bus got to Amarillo, I was dehydrated, sick, and shaky. When we got to Albuquerque, I bummed some change and called a friend who agreed to let me crash with him. I couch-surfed in Phoenix for a few months, obliterating myself with drugs and alcohol.

One morning, in early fall of 2009, I woke up vomiting blood. I worried that I might actually die—it was clear to me that I needed to get out of the city. Broke, strung out, and exhausted, I returned home to Whiteriver. It seemed like my only remaining option.

My mom and dad knew that I'd probably be in less danger with them than if I were out on the streets, and they were relieved to have me home. I told them I'd do my best to not drink or get high, but I also said I couldn't promise—given how many times I'd tried and failed to stay sober, there were no guarantees. I think they were just grateful that I was still alive at this point, which broke my heart.

My first week back, my buddy Roland called and invited me out to drink some beers with him and a few other friends from the Rez.

"Yo, Nephi, you coming to the job fair tomorrow?" he asked me when he dropped me back at home. "Ski season is starting."

All throughout our teens, Roland had held various jobs at Sunrise Park Resort—the largest ski resort in Arizona, which was owned and operated by our White Mountain Apache Tribe—doing lift maintenance, washing dishes, working as a parking attendant and gift shop clerk. I remember him joking that they should make him general manager.

I played it cool. "I'm going back to Phoenix in the new year, or I might look for a job in New York . . . but, sure, I'll come check it out."

By the time I showed up at the lodge the next day, the lobby was packed. I weaved my way through the crowd looking for the Sunrise booth, which seemed like my best bet for finding a food and beverage position. A few people sat behind a folding table covered with job applications, stickers, pens, and other job fair swag.

"Do you have any culinary positions open?" I couldn't believe it had come to this, from Mary Elaine's to a nothing hotel restaurant in the middle of nowhere.

A tall Apache guy stood up and stared me down.

"I'm Kyle, the kitchen manager at the Summit Restaurant." His voice was raspy, like a smoker's. "Do you have a résumé?"

I reached into my coat pocket and pulled out a letter-size envelope.

"I'm Nephi Craig. I grew up here in Whiteriver." He unfolded my CV and started reading, his face blank.

"I've been a chef for ten years," I continued.

Finally, Kyle looked up. He grabbed an application form from the table behind him.

"Fill this out. You want a job as a line cook?"

It was a huge step down, but I was too desperate to look offended. I said yes, and he hired me on the spot.

+ + + +

Two weeks later, on a bright, cold Thursday in the first week of October, I showed up for my first shift. The resort ran a shuttle for employees, but I didn't want to risk being late, so I asked my uncle Brian to give me a ride. When we pulled up to the two-story wooden hotel, Brian clucked his tongue.

"Fuhh, everybody says this place is haunted." The hotel, he explained, had burned to the ground in 1971 before being rebuilt. The story was that some people died in the fire, although I have never found evidence of that.

I thanked Brian, grabbing my backpack out of the back seat. The last time I'd set foot in the building was in the mid-eighties, probably for a special family occasion. Back then, the place seemed impossibly large and elegant—I was surprised we had something so grand on the Rez. I don't remember much about the dinner we had, but I do remember the chef stationed in the middle of the fancy dining room, a big white guy in a tall paper hat standing next to some red heat lamps. He held a long fork and knife with which he carved up a big, bloody roast, placing slabs of meat on silver platters that were carried around by servers in bow ties. It was far-out—I thought his job looked pretty cool.

Twenty years later, the carpet in the lobby had changed, but not much else. Everything still had that eighties log cabin vibe: dark wood beams, rough stonework, and a funky color scheme of orange, mahogany, and teal.

Dang, I thought, *it's just like that movie,* Hot Tub Time Machine.

A friendly front-desk clerk instructed me to head upstairs and wait in the dining room. "The staff meeting'll start once the van gets here."

When the rest of the crew arrived fifteen minutes later, I was even more convinced I had passed through a portal into an alternate reality. As I looked around, I realized that every single kitchen worker appeared to be Native—brown cooks, brown servers, brown dishwashers, brown porters—and several of them were bantering in our language. Other than in Japan, I'd never worked in a restaurant where there weren't a bunch of white dudes at the top of the pyramid. Kyle, the kitchen manager who'd hired me, barged out of the swinging doors. He was the Apache in charge here, doing double duty as the head chef.

"Hey, good afternoon. Welcome back to those of you returning, and welcome to the new people this season!" Kyle talked like a manager on a TV show. "I think we have a pretty good team this year, but as those of you who've worked here for a while know, most people only stick around a few weeks before they quit or get fired." He snickered, but I already knew I wasn't going to stay at this job for more than a couple of months.

Kyle had the team go around, all fifteen of us, and introduce ourselves, even though it was obvious that most everyone already knew each other. When it was my turn, I kept it short and sweet, omitting any information about my professional experience. I didn't want to stand out.

"Today, we're going to set up the kitchen and do some prep work," Kyle continued. "Most of you remember our menu, so we're not gonna spend much time going over it."

He looked over at the tall tattooed guy leaning on one of the tables to my right. "Marv, I want you to show Nephi around, walk him through the kitchen and show him how we do things."

Marv nodded and tipped his head at me.

"We open tomorrow night and I expect it to be real busy, so let's all get to work."

I followed Marv into the kitchen, making sure to keep my face neutral as I took in all the old, second-rate equipment and the big mess.

How the fuck are we going to open tomorrow? I thought, keeping my mouth shut.

Crappy conditions aside, the thing that struck me right away was the warmth of the team. Everyone (besides Kyle) seemed to have real affection for each other. There was laughter, joking, teasing, and cussing, and music blasting from an old CD boom box: Too Short, Eazy-E, Bone Thugs-N-Harmony, Master P, Cash Money Millionaires, Bob and Ziggy Marley. It felt like a house party on the Rez.

For years, I'd been searching for a powerful sense of connection in the kitchens that I'd worked in, but I'd never quite fit in—not at school, not at DC Ranch, not at Mary Elaine's. I'd done guest stages at great restaurants around the country, traveled around the world questioning my path and my purpose.

Was it possible that this banged-up kitchen was what I'd been looking for all along?

My excitement flagged when Marv showed me the walk-ins. Whenever I enter a new kitchen, my cook instincts kick in and I scan the space, seeking out the freshest produce and proteins to work with. But here, pretty much everything was canned, frozen, or shrink-wrapped.

There were giant #10 cans of beans and corn stacked precariously on the shelves, and gallon jugs of pico de gallo. The chest freezers were stuffed with frozen, precooked "rotisserie chicken," individually Cryovaced steaks and fish fillets, sacks of huge frozen shrimp, and bags of frozen vegetable medley, that wacky mix of broccoli, squash, cauliflower, and rubbery green beans familiar to anyone who's eaten in an institutional cafeteria. In the fridge there were bags and bags of prechopped salad mix, a sad combo of tired romaine, purple cabbage, and slivered carrots; supermarket packages of presliced tomatoes and onions; bags of blue cheese crumbles; and many trays of freezer-burned Stouffer's frozen lasagna. I had never seen so many different varieties of frozen potatoes—cubes, tater tots, french fries, waffle fries, and hash browns.

This is how we're opening, I realized. *It's all heat-and-serve shit.*

I thought about getting out while I still could, but it had been a long time since I'd had steady work. Plus, it would be a relief to work a dinner rush again.

Unlike any other restaurant kitchen I'd worked, there was no obvious hierarchy at Sunrise. The place was a free-for-all. Kyle didn't assign anyone specific stations or tasks—we were expected to just claim them, depending on what we felt like doing that day.

"I'll go help the girls at concessions with the Pepsi machine," said Freddie, who I would discover was always looking for an excuse to get out of the kitchen and talk to pretty young women.

"I bet you can't wait to make the pasta sauce with that feet-cheese," said Vinny, a kitchen supervisor who had already been at Sunrise for four or five years when I got there, poking fun at Marv's hatred for blue cheese. Vinny had been a friend of my older brother's, way back in the eighties, before we moved to Navajo Land. He immediately stood out to me because he was the only other cook in the Sunrise kitchen who kept and sharpened his own knife.

"Yo, Nephi, it's been a loooong-ass time since I seen ya." The dishwasher, OJ, also knew me—he used to hang out at the old-school skate park my brother and I helped build in Whiteriver back in the nineties. He wore a camouflage bandanna on his head. "I heard you went to culinary school. You gonna bust out or what?"

I smiled. It was nice to see familiar faces.

"I'll get started on the mashed potatoes." I remembered the crate of nice-looking russets I'd spotted in the walk-in. I went to fetch them, placing the box on an empty stretch of counter space and rummaging around in an overstuffed drawer for a peeler.

"What are you doing with those?" Ivan motioned to the potatoes. He reached up to the shelf above us, pulling down a box. "We use the powdered ones. The fresh ones are only for the baked sides."

"Okay." I made an effort to keep my face neutral, but I was horrified. There was nothing more basic than preparing mashed potatoes from scratch.

It was so comforting for me to look around the kitchen and see all these familiar Apache faces. At the same time, I couldn't help but wonder what our ancestors would think if they were to walk in and see the confused, wacky food we were preparing—the steak gorgonzola with a way-too-sweet balsamic reduction or the trout almondine smothered in an electric-blue blueberry-brandy beurre blanc. Every ingredient here would be a baffling stranger, even the trusted potato.

+ + + +

Growing up in a White Mountain Apache and Navajo household, I pretty much took potatoes for granted. On a basic level, I knew that potatoes were an Indigenous food, although I had no idea about their rich, fascinating history. They were just there, an everyday ingredient, diced up in venison stew, boiled or baked on an open fire, crisped in a skillet and served with scrambled eggs or Spam. I had once heard a cool story about how our people started eating potatoes by observing Bear, watching as she dug up these funny, lumpy roots that she devoured and fed to her cubs.

In Apache Land, fried potatoes are a staple at community gatherings—at every wake, ceremony, and camp, you'll find bags and bags of russet potatoes ready to be cooked and served. My Navajo grandmother would light up when she talked about potatoes. They were a crucial ingredient in one of her favorite dishes, mutton stew, made with mutton necks that had been cut on a band saw and simmered for hours. About halfway through the cooking process, she'd add green chili and peeled, diced potatoes that fell apart in the golden, fatty broth, becoming fluffy, almost like mashed potatoes.

Like every young chef, I spent a good deal of time learning how to prepare all kinds of potatoes and make them perfectly. In addition to roasted grandma-style potatoes and everyday mashers, which I could make in my sleep, I'd perfected my creamy potato chowder, shepherd's pie, scalloped potatoes, potato gnocchi, and countless rich, French variations like pommes Anna, pommes fondantes, and dauphinoise potatoes. Just like my grandma Nancy, I appreciated potatoes, although I also saw how they were used as menu fillers for bored, burnt-out chefs, an easy way to please a crowd with minimal effort.

Once I started digging around for information about Indigenous cultivars, however, I discovered there's nothing fluffy, beige, or boring about the story of the potato, which began its journey in the Andes region of central Peru, where wild varieties of the so-called *Solanum tuberosum* plant became a treasured Indigenous food.

In Apache culture, there are many age-old oral stories that convey important information about our foods and their cultural importance. The same, I learned, is true of the ancient Andean peoples, who considered potatoes to be gifts from Pachamama, the Earth Mother; the story goes that, in exchange for giving them this hardy, edible root, Pachamama charged humans with taking care of the land. It filled me with pride to learn that it was Indigenous farmers who started domesticating potatoes some ten thousand years ago and that—long before the Spanish conquistadors set foot on the continent—they had cultivated well over three thousand different varietals. I'm sure that this knowledge would have only intensified Grandma Nancy's passion for potatoes.

The fact that you can find plentiful varieties of potatoes in most grocery stores and farmers' markets today is a direct result of Indigenous people's scientific experimentation. Season after season,

Andean farmers planted spuds in different soils, at varying altitudes, seeking the perfect potato for every climate. And they dropped different combinations of seeds and tubers into the ground together to create new sizes, shapes, colors, and flavors, much like the white, yellow, black, red, and blue corn varieties I encountered growing up on the Rez. Potatoes provided communities with a reliable source of nutrition that could be stored for months, significantly improving Indigenous people's food security.

By the rise of the vast Inca empire in the early thirteenth century, potatoes had become a cornerstone of Indigenous culture in South America. Historians believe that Incan measurements of time corresponded to how long it took to cook potatoes to different consistencies—and that potatoes were used both to predict the weather and aid with childbirth.

Thanks to the potato, the Indigenous peoples of the Andes also came up with a significant culinary innovation: freeze-drying food. *Chuño* is the name for a type of preserved potato that was first produced before the rise of the Incas and remains popular in South American Indigenous communities to this day. Chuño is made by leaving spuds out in icy overnight temperatures and then letting them shrivel up in the sunlight. Once this process is repeated several times, the potatoes are covered with a cloth and stomped on to remove any remaining moisture. By the end of the cycle, the spuds are transformed into compact white or black pellets that can last for more than a decade, making chuño an important household staple that's used in soups and stews. When I found out about this Indigenous innovation, I immediately thought of our own labor-intensive Apache process for drying corn—we call it *nadá'łeeshbizh* or *łeshbéézhihíí*—which also preserves a revered ingredient for years and years.

I loved learning about another amazing aspect of the potato's history, one that unfolded closer to home, in the American Southwest. In recent years, the small but mighty Four Corners potato varietal has gotten a lot of attention for being a nutritional and agricultural powerhouse. Known in botanical circles as *Solanum jamesii*, this type of potato has twice the protein, iron, calcium, and magnesium of an organic red potato, and it's also incredibly prolific, with one tuber yielding hundreds of new spuds in just four months. One article I read branded the Four Corners potato "the ancient potato of the future"—because of its resistance to high temperatures, drought, and disease, it could be a potentially life-saving crop for our changing climate.

In 2017, anthropologists from the University of Utah discovered traces of Four Corner potato starch on stone tools that had been excavated from an archaeological dig in the southern part of the state and dated to around 10000 BC. The potato's roots in North America, it turns out, are just as ancient as in South America, leading some experts to suggest that it should be considered the fourth, lost sibling of the so-called Three Sister crops: corn, beans, and squash.

The Four Corners potato, in fact, grows wild deep beneath the pinyon pines and juniper of the Mogollon Rim—it was one of the foods my Western Apache ancestors would have traditionally foraged, along with the Hopi, Kawaik, Navajo, Southern Paiute, Zuni, Tewa, and Zia peoples of the area. It makes me sad to think that I had no deep connection to this wild, mighty tuber growing up.

Our cultural ties to this ancient Indigenous food were yet another casualty of colonization and the terrible violence and land loss we've endured.

Like all things Indigenous, the potato doesn't get the respect it deserves. But its history has prompted me to reevaluate the spud. It is not just a humble staple—it's a miracle, a potent symbol of resilience and abundance.

+ + + +

By my second week at Sunrise, I was feeling comfortable. Some of the other cooks in the kitchen had been working together for four or five seasons, and the vibe was friendly and relaxed. People talked openly about what was going on in their lives, bragging about their children's accomplishments in school but also sharing news about relatives who were struggling.

Tabatha talked about her cousin who had recently gone to prison for selling drugs and violating his probation.

Another line cook asked if anyone knew what had happened to their coworker Mike, who hadn't come back for the season.

"It was a car accident," said Marv. "Wrapped their ride around a tree running from Highway Patrol."

In every other restaurant I'd worked, people acted like they had no life outside the kitchen. The only acceptable topics of conversation were food related—gossip about other kitchens and discussions of restaurant culture—or sports. Talking about your relationship or your family was often laughed at or met with sharp, sarcastic remarks.

Given how much I struggled in my personal life, I had been

happy to compartmentalize with the best of them, but it was a relief to let my guard down. Over the course of the last few shifts, I'd chatted with the cooks next to me about my father—whom everybody on the Rez knew and loved—and about how my son, Ari, was scheduled to come visit in a couple of weeks and I hoped to take him snowboarding.

It wasn't my choice to move back to Whiteriver, but after being rootless for so long, it felt good to be back in our sacred mountains, cooking with an all–White Mountain Apache culinary team. I knew from my travels all over the States and around the world that this experience was something rare and special.

Even so, my professional standards were not up for negotiation. When I got to Sunrise, I was the only cook who came in each shift with their own knife roll and toolbox. By habit, I would set up my station meticulously, paying attention to detail. The other cooks would walk over and admire how organized it looked.

"Mise en place, man. It's how you live your life in a kitchen," I told them.

My coworkers would sometimes huddle around to watch me work.

"Damn, Nephi, where'd you learn to do that?" OJ asked as I speedily medium-diced a bunch of zucchinis.

"It looks so pretty," said Vina, the morning kitchen supervisor, who had been at the hotel for more than two decades when I met her. She looked tough, but her voice was sweet as she admired my cutting board. I wasn't a sous chef or even a lead line cook, but it was clear to all of the other cooks that I had the most training of anyone in that kitchen. After observing my chef's knives and knife skills, several of the cooks asked me to help them learn.

"We call them classic cuts," I explained to Vina, demonstrating how to bâtonnet carrots. "They're like speaking a language. Once you learn classic cuts and kitchen terminology, you can do this work anywhere in the world."

"Terma-what?! Keee-ya, show guy," OJ said, using the Apache slang for someone who's acting all fancy.

All the cooks asked to check out my black Wüsthof knife roll filled with my treasured knives from Japan, along with a few more I'd picked up in New York City and some I'd had since culinary school.

"Yo, Nephi, where can we pick up some good knives?" Vinny asked me one day. Most of what was in the kitchen was made of cheap stamped steel with white plastic handles; everyone was always fighting over the sharpest ones in the box.

Kyle didn't mind me showing the other cooks new tricks, although he did razz me one day when he caught me demonstrating how to chiffonade greens as he walked through to his office. "Don't do too good of a job," he said, pointing at me and glaring.

His bad attitude didn't detract from my excitement about the team's enthusiasm for sharpening their cooking skills. I watched them become more confident and capable. It felt like a positive sign. I exerted my influence in little ways, making tweaks to how we were working. I recommended the other cooks stop using the "salt and pepper mix" they kept in a big tub so they could have more control over the flavor profile of each dish. I taught them how to get nice caramelization on fish or chicken by adding a small dollop of unsalted butter in the last minute of sautéing.

It appalled me that our Indigenous kitchen was so far removed from our ancestral heritage, that the ingredients we worked with were mechanized, processed, extracted, powdered, doused with chemicals, and shrink-wrapped. I hated that our salad dressing came out of a bottle, that we used store-bought stock and powdered bases, that all our sauces were overly sweet.

But, despite all that, I loved being back in the contained chaos of a busy kitchen. I left each shift tired and happy. I finally felt like part of a tight-knit community.

SEVEN

DEATH OF A SUPERHERO

I still planned to move on to some bigger, better job once the ski season was over, but even I could admit that being home was good for me. Living at ten thousand feet, in a wild environment, has a way of putting things in perspective. I wanted to live up to my own high expectations and make my ancestors proud, although that didn't mean I had stopped partying. Even without a lot of money, staying high is easy if you know the right people. I just got better at hiding what I was doing.

I made a point of spending time with my parents and cooking for them on my days off. Throughout his life, my dad had taken pride in being a meat-and-potato Navajo, but by the time I came back to Whiteriver, he had pretty much cut animal protein from his diet—he complained that it bothered his stomach. When I was a kid and my mom went out of town, my dad would sometimes prepare a big pot of pintos to last us the week, so now we cooked a lot of beans together. This seminal Indigenous cultivar was a great source of protein, I told him, and would help him stay strong.

One afternoon, the two of us were driving in my dad's truck

down to Kayenta, on the Navajo Nation. I was my dad's roadie for many of his performances, helping load and unload his equipment and the boxes of CDs and cassette tapes we would sell. Our road trips were special—my dad asked me questions about life and work and family, or, sometimes, we'd ride for miles and miles in comfortable silence. On this trip, Hank Williams was playing on the radio and my dad turned it up loud. It made me smile to hear him singing along.

"I was wondering something, son." My dad turned off the music, his tone dead serious. I looked over at him, worried he was going to ride me for coming home after my shift the previous night all buzzed out.

He stalled, formulating the question.

"Is there a way . . . there's gotta be a way . . . I think you can . . . So, is it possible to make vegetables taste like mutton?"

I chuckled, feeling relieved. My dad was extremely competent in so many areas—he could speak Navajo and Apache, tie cowboy knots, use a chain saw, fix cars, play guitar; but *I* was the food expert. My father loved watching me in the kitchen, complimenting my knife skills and the way I got the skin on a roast chicken perfectly crisp and golden each time. He was always extremely grateful for everything my mother and I put on the table, even the simplest omelet. I think it came from growing up in a big Navajo family with seven siblings and very little money and food.

"I was thinking about it 'cuz of that squash you grilled last week," he explained. "It was so good! It almost tasted like steak."

"Can you make vegetables taste like mutton?" I repeated the question, showing him I was taking it seriously. "Yeah, man, you probably could."

I loved seeing my dad's big grin peeking out from under his

bushy mustache. I realized he hadn't been smiling as much as usual since I'd been home.

"I'd start by roasting ten pounds of mutton bones and then simmering them in water for twelve hours to make a lamb demi-glace. After that, I'd strain the liquid, discard the bones, and slowly simmer it down again until it gets real thick and gelatinous. You're basically making glue out of all these bones."

Whether he was building shelves or changing an alternator, my father was unfailingly meticulous—once a marine, always a marine. I could tell he was impressed by my confidence and know-how.

"I'd roast a bunch of your favorite vegetables like zucchini, onions, and potatoes, then coat them in the mutton glue for a few minutes to let them get all glossy and sticky."

My dad told me I was making him hungry.

"We should definitely try it someday soon," I said. It still haunts me that we never did.

+ + + +

Halloween has always been a big deal in our family. Every year, we'd decorate our house inside and out and my dad would set up his sound system, blasting spooky monster noises and kooky music. My parents would invite everyone over for a costume party, and our yard would be crowded with people eating, dancing, and shrieking with laughter. The gathering was also an excuse to celebrate a bunch of October birthdays, including my younger brother Shiloh's and Ari's. In Whiteriver, birthday parties tend to be blowouts, with tons of people and even more food. When so many are struggling or in dire straits, another year of being alive warrants a big celebration.

I made arrangements to get Ari for the weekend, and we spent the day of his birthday preparing for the party, making papier-mâché skulls to hang from the huge apple tree in my parents' front lawn. We strung them up the next morning, and people started arriving in the early afternoon, carrying their potluck dishes. Soon, the long folding table we'd set up outside was covered in pots of beans, bowls of potato salad, charred hot dogs, steamed broccoli and carrots, and baked ham tented with foil. We placed stacks of fry bread and Apache tortillas next to bowls of fresh yellow chilies and bags of potato chips. Someone brought orange Halloween cupcakes, and we placed them next to the large sheet cake my parents had bought for the birthday boys.

All my favorite people were there: both my brothers and their families, tons of cousins, friends, and relatives from Whiskey Flats and beyond. Ari ran around, dressed as Bumblebee from the Transformers. I'd recently started dating a pretty woman from Whiteriver named Nalin, the daughter of my parents' church friends—and she was there, too.

Nalin and I had a lot in common, and from the beginning, I'd been open about my past. She knew all about my world travels, my struggles, my addiction, and my stints in jail and rehab. Like me, she had a kid and was navigating the bumps of co-parenting. I was feeling optimistic about our relationship.

Usually, my father was the life of the party, welcoming everyone with hugs and jokes. But that day I noticed him sitting off to the side in a rusty lawn chair drinking a cup of Postum, which he called Mormon coffee. I could tell something was on his mind. Around five o'clock, my mom told us she was going to drive my dad up the road to the Indian Health Service hospital. We were worried, but

Dad smiled and said he didn't think it was a big deal, he just wanted to be checked out. He promised he'd be back for cake and presents.

He never got to see Ari blow out his candles surrounded by a gaggle of cute little Apache pumpkins, witches, ninjas, skeletons, princesses, and grim reapers. After the party wrapped, around eight, my older brother, Dustinn, left with his family to drive back to Mesa. I was carrying the sound system over to the shed when my mom's car pulled into the driveway. She was alone.

"Dad's getting flown out to Phoenix in a helicopter." Her face was pale in the moonlight. "Get Shiloh. We need to drive down tonight. They say he needs emergency surgery."

Whatever was going on was beyond the scope of the basic care offered by our Rez's medical center.

+ + + +

We drove down to Banner Health as fast as we could without breaking the law. When we were finally allowed in to see my dad in the ER, he was propped up in a hospital bed wearing a blue paper gown. He looked weak and sad—the only other time I'd seen him like this was when I was six years old and we rushed from Whiteriver to Albuquerque after we got a call that he'd been in a car wreck. Though I'd later learn that he'd been drinking and driving when he crashed our truck, it was extremely upsetting to see him sitting in a wheelchair with a neck brace on. I recalled bursting into tears. Now, I contorted my face into a reassuring smile, willing myself not to cry when my dad told us that the doctors had found a mass in his gut.

"Everything should be okay when they remove it," he said, reaching for my mom's hand. "But they need to do it tonight."

As soon as our family friend Carol arrived, she and my mom left the room to take care of some paperwork. Before we had time to ask my father for more details, a nurse came in to say they were all ready for him in the operating room.

"Can we have a minute to say a prayer?" My dad's voice was calm.

The nurse nodded and stepped out to give us our privacy.

"Come here, you boys." Dad reached out both hands, and Shiloh and I each took one as he began his prayer in the Navajo language before switching back to English. "Diyiin Shitaá'. Give me and my family strength. Watch over our family far and near, so that they be blessed with what they stand in need of. Bless the doctors in this hospital." His voice shook as he repeated the Navajo phrase "Hózhó Náhásdlíí'" four times. It means *Walk in beauty.*

I remember the last thing he said to us before being wheeled out: "You boys need to be strong now. Please tell Mom I said I love her and that everything is going to be okay."

I was in complete shock. Out of the corner of my eye, I saw tears streaming down Shiloh's face. The nurse came back in to wheel my father out on the gurney. Where the hospital bed had been a moment ago I spotted my dad's brown cowboy boots, his thick gray wool socks tucked inside them. That's when I finally let myself break down.

\+ + + +

Two hours later, a white guy in blue scrubs came out to the waiting room and introduced himself as Dr. Scott, my dad's surgeon. He towered over my mom, who stood up to shake his hand.

"I'm just going to be really straight with you, Mrs. Craig," he said. "Vincent has a rare form of cancer. It's called a gastrointestinal stromal tumor, or GIST."

My mother let out a wail, and Carol and my brother helped her sit back down. I stayed standing, concentrating on catching every word.

"We hoped to remove it, but it's metastasized. It's attached to a major artery near his spine, and if we remove it, he will die on the operating table."

He said everything so matter-of-factly. I wanted to shake him.

"So, what's the next step here?" My tone was sharp.

"We did the only thing we could, which is close him back up," he replied, smoothing his hands on his coat. "We need to stabilize him and then we can talk about the treatment options. But I need you to understand, we're talking about a stage-four diagnosis."

My mother was slumped over now, weeping on her friend's shoulder.

"I'm so sorry," Dr. Scott said, telling us to head home and get some rest.

We got back to Dustinn's house after three in the morning. I tried to sleep, but my mind kept running through everything I'd read on my phone about GIST. The prognosis wasn't great, especially when the cancer had spread to other parts of the body, but more than half of those patients survived. My dad was a fighter. Our job was to be strong like him and make sure he was getting the right care.

The days passed, and my dad slowly recovered from surgery, staying awake for longer and longer stretches of time, during which he chatted with a steady stream of visitors: relatives, friends, and work colleagues, people from every part of his life.

My mother encouraged me to return home and get back to work, reassuring me that he was receiving excellent care. "He's in God's hands," she added.

I was hesitant—I didn't share my mom's faith in the medical establishment or organized religion. Ever since the operation, my dad had looked ashy and worn, like someone sick with the flu. But he also urged me not to jeopardize my position at Sunrise.

"They really need you, son," he said, winking mischievously.

Back in that worn-out kitchen, my dad was on my mind constantly, and I spent entire shifts feeling edgy. I was less forgiving of all the crappy tools and bullshit ingredients we were working with, and I started to openly talk shit about the menu, and about Kyle and his sloppy management. I stopped helping my coworkers or teaching them new stuff. I was a miserable asshole.

One night in late January, toward the end of a particularly slow dinner service, I decided I needed to leave and go get fucked up. Without saying a word to anyone, I slipped out of the kitchen, hitching a ride back down to the neighborhood we called Dark Shadows, to the house of a bootlegger I knew.

When I got there, one of my cousins was hanging out front, smoking and stomping his feet to stay warm.

"Fuck this N.I. bullshit," he said, referring to the crappy Natural Ice the bootlegger sold for a dollar a can. "We're gonna make a beer run up the hill. Wanna roll with us?"

I was happy to put even more distance between myself and work. We piled into his friend's black Altima, four of us crammed in the back seat.

"You still at Sunrise?" Up in the passenger seat, my cousin was rolling a joint.

"Yeah, I'm supposed to be there right now, but I felt like boozin' it." My cousin's rowdy crowd brought out my swagger.

The six of us drove to the Circle K on the edge of Pinetop, and, feeling flush, I bought myself two fifths of Bacardi and a twelve-pack of Heineken, and pitched in for two thirty-packs of Budweiser. We drove around drinking and smoking blunts until a cop pulled out behind us, tailing us. We knew better than to mess with these border-town cops, so we decided to turn around and head back to the Rez. Right when we passed the casino, my cousin's friend lost control of the car on the icy road, sliding into a small ditch.

Everyone got thrown around, cigarette sparks flying, beer sloshing all over us. We climbed out of the car, laughing and cursing, trying unsuccessfully to teeter it back onto the road. Within minutes, the red-blue lights of a cop car cut through the swirling snow. My cousin and his friend, along with one of the young women who was riding with us, took off running. It made me laugh out loud to see their footprints in the snow.

I just stood there. I had nothing to hide—I hadn't been driving and I'd bought my liquor legally. There was no law against partying. The tribal cops weren't interested in my rambling, drunken story. When one of them tried to cuff me, I yanked my arms away. The fucker tried tasing me, but the charge didn't go through my thick winter jacket.

"Fuckin' missed, suckers!" I cackled, parroting the line from the movie *Lost Boys*.

That pissed them off. A second cop grabbed me and tased me in the neck, bringing me down to the ground. They hog-tied me, threw me in the back of a unit, and locked me up in the Whiteriver jail for the night.

As soon as I was released the next day, I called my cousin to see if he was okay, but I didn't call into work—I had already made up my mind I wasn't going back. Why would I? I could get a better job anywhere in the world. Right now, my number one priority was being close to my dad.

+ + + +

In March, we got good news. The doctors decided my dad was stable enough to return to Whiteriver and receive his care from Indian Health Service. A crowd gathered at the hospital to send him off. The nurses and doctors all came to say goodbye. They loved my dad, who was always peppering them with silly questions and telling jokes, doing what he'd done our whole lives—using humor to lighten the mood and protect us from grim realities.

My extended family piled into four cars and caravaned behind the ambulance for the entire 175-mile trip. The mood was both solemn and happy. When we drove onto the Rez, I saw a yellow balloon tied to a lamppost with a handwritten sign that read *HOORAY! VINCENT CRAIG!*, and once we pulled off the highway on the north side of town, there was a large group of people gathered by the entrance to the hospital. I felt tears well up as I spotted family members and elders, little kids with puppies, friends, and police officers standing under a large WELCOME banner with hearts, happy faces, and handprints in cheerful colors.

It wasn't until we got to the medical center in Whiteriver that we learned that every single bump in the road, every curve, had caused my dad excruciating pain. Still, the fact that he was strong enough to return to Whiteriver gave me hope. For the first time in months, I didn't feel rage bubble up every time I opened my mouth. My dad would spend a couple of days in the medical center for observation before moving back home, so we got busy, clearing space for a hospital bed in our small living room, stocking up on the protein drinks the doctors prescribed, and arranging my dad's Neil Diamond, Johnny Horton, and Michael Martin Murphey CDs on a side table within arm's reach, next to a small boom box.

But after two weeks, it became clear that Dad was in too much pain and that the nurses' daily visits were not sufficient. He needed a much higher level of care than could be provided at any of the hospitals in the White Mountains. He was transferred to Kindred Hospital, a small oncology facility down in Scottsdale.

I still wasn't working, so I stayed with my dad overnight, relieving my mom, who watched him during the day. It was dark by the time I walked into his room each evening, and often I had a few drinks in me, which I knew made my parents sad. I wasn't happy about it, either, but I couldn't stop.

One Friday night, I sat in the chair my mother had pulled up next to my father's bed. We had been channel-surfing and when we came across the movie *Amadeus*, my dad told me to leave it on. It was such a relief to hear him laughing.

During one of the commercial breaks, I clicked the mute button.

I cleared my throat. "You're going to beat it, Dad. You're gonna beat the monster man."

In my dad's comic strip, Muttonman—who was faster than the Bureau of Indian Affairs and could leap over Shiprock in a single bound—was the only one who could stand up to the Frybread Monster, a radioactive blob of dough that grew out of control, just like my dad's cancer.

My father grabbed my hand, his grip much stronger than I expected. "You got to do it, too, son. I know you can beat it. The alcohol and drugs, they're not for our people. Don't let the moth sickness get you."

I squeezed his hand. This wasn't the conversation I wanted to be having—my dad called alcoholism "the moth sickness" because addicts are drawn to drinking and drugging despite the fact that it'll burn and kill them. I could count on one hand the number of times my father and I had talked directly about our struggles with alcoholism. He entered recovery when I was twelve, right around the time I started using regularly, but before that, he'd done his best to hide his drinking from us kids. He was good at compartmentalizing, a skill I'd definitely inherited.

My father looked at me tenderly and kindly changed the topic, joking about the first meal we'd eat together after he got out of the hospital. I played along, but my insides felt curdled. I didn't want to talk about food.

I sometimes wonder how things would have turned out if my dad had taken a tougher stance with me. I never said this to his face, but I resented him for being so good at sobriety, just like he was good at everything else.

I resented his faith in me, his belief that I was capable of kicking my addictions, even when they were the only way I knew to numb the fury and self-pity consuming me from inside. I resented the supposedly loving god who would make this good man suffer.

+ + + +

The nights were long and brutal. After the doctors put a feeding tube into my father, I'd sit for hours watching the nutrients and morphine slowly dripping out of their ghostly sacks. I was angry at everyone—the nurses who woke my dad any time he finally slipped into a deep sleep to check his vitals and the oncologists who stuck to their story that no environmental factors had contributed to my dad's cancer despite the fact that he'd grown up next to uranium mines. In his shows, my dad liked to joke that his hometown, Crownpoint, was the only place in the world that Natives glowed in the dark.

One night, I fell into a deep sleep, startling awake before sunrise to hear my dad making these horrible gurgling noises. I clicked on the bedside lamp. The front of my dad's gown was drenched in blood and something that looked like coffee grinds. He was confused and afraid, so I grabbed his hand, holding on to him and yelling for the staff to come help us. When the nurses arrived, they asked me to step out into the hallway. I slid down the wall, swiping away tears. My dad's blood was all over my shirt and my shoes. I looked at my hands, taking deep, furious breaths to try to calm my heartbeat.

Another night, my dad's hand slid off the side of his bed while he slept and his gold wedding band, the one that was so snug we marveled it didn't cut off his circulation, slipped off and pinged when it hit the floor. I jumped up, using the light of my phone screen to find it. It was smooth and cool, heavier than I expected—it had lived on his ring finger since before I was born. I tried to slip the ring back on, but it was evident that it was not going to stay. I folded it up in a scrap of paper, putting it into my pocket to give to my mom.

The days passed and my dad spoke less and less because of the pain. His impeccably groomed mustache grew, as did his beard whiskers. When I came in that evening, I made a joke about it.

"Wow, Dad, I didn't know your eyebrows could grow that long!"

His eyes twinkled.

"Do you want me to give you a shave and trim?"

He nodded yes.

I had a pack of triple-blade razors in the backpack I carried back and forth from my brother's house to the hospital, so I asked the nurses for shaving cream and some scissors. I filled a plastic pan with hot water from the sink and laid out my equipment, mise en place–style. I started by carefully snipping his mustache and then rubbing shaving cream onto his strong jaw in gentle circles. I drew the razor down both cheeks, and he automatically tipped his chin up so I could shave under it.

I wiped his face with a clean towel. "There. A new man!"

For the first time in days, my father spoke, his voice raspy. "Th-thank you, son."

I hugged him and he wrapped his arms around me. My dad inhaled loudly, letting out a single shuddering wail. He wailed like this six times in succession, the saddest sound I'd ever heard. I didn't know how to console him. After he quieted down and fell asleep, I walked out to the alley beside the hospital to smoke a cigarette and cried for almost an hour straight.

+ + + +

On one of our last road trips together, to a performance out in Tuba City in early 2009, my father and I drove through Holbrook, Winslow, and Flagstaff, stopping to look at the Moenkopi dinosaur tracks for the first time since I was a little boy. Seeing those massive footprints got us talking about ancient Navajo history, and as we headed to the venue and set up the stage, I told my father the story of the Anasazi bean, an ancient heirloom that had come back from the dead.

Like the potato, beans originated as a wild plant that ranged from the Andes up into modern-day Mexico before becoming an important agricultural crop throughout the Americas. Among the tens of thousands of types of cultivated and hybridized beans, there was a reddish-brown-and-white varietal popular with Indigenous farmers in the Southwest, I told my dad, a cool-looking bean that had many different names.

"Cave beans. Aztec beans. And New Mexico Appaloosa, because it kind of resembles those speckled horses. In the 1980s, a Colorado company called Adobe Milling trademarked the name Anasazi bean."

"That's a Navajo word," my father remarked. "It's our name for the Pueblo people." (Years later, I would learn that modern-day Puebloans don't appreciate the Anasazi label because its Navajo language meaning can be interpreted as *ancient enemy*.)

I nodded. "It was an important part of their diet."

I explained how Anasazi beans are unusually high in fiber, making them especially filling. They'd also been shown to significantly reduce inflammation and lower cholesterol. I gave my dad a pointed look—this was before he'd cut back on junk food and added more veggies to his diet.

"People say they make you toot less than other beans, too," I added.

My dad laughed—he appreciated a good fart joke.

"What were you saying about them being resurrected?" he asked.

"In the late twelve hundreds, there was a drought that lasted more than a quarter century, forcing the Pueblo people to abandon their homes in southern Colorado and Utah, along with their gardens," I explained. "By the time other Indigenous groups, including the Navajo, moved into the region centuries later, the Anasazi bean was thought to have disappeared."

There are different stories of how it came roaring back to life in the twentieth century. I read one account about a group of archaeologists in the 1950s who'd discovered some speckled, old beans in a clay pot and managed to sprout them, but other sources attributed this discovery to some local farmers. Eventually, the founder of Adobe Milling started selling Anasazi beans to gardeners and farmers interested in heirloom crops.

"I believe there's even a farm in Whiteriver that's growing them," I told my dad.

I clarified that I didn't think the return of the Anasazi bean was *actually* a miracle.

"From a scientific perspective, there's no way a centuries-old bean could be viable. Some of the Puebloan farmers must have held on to some dried beans, planting them in their new homes and trading them with their neighbors," I said.

Still, I thought it was cool that an ancient crop had become popular again.

"That's what I'm talking about when I say that food can help us time-travel and experience a bit of our history," I said. "And I guess you could say there's something miraculous about that."

\+ + + +

My dad's health continued to deteriorate. He looked withered in his hospital bed, all these wires snaking around him. I could tell by his expression that he was in pain all the time.

In late April, the oncologist met with my mother and me and told us my father had three weeks to live. They were transitioning him to hospice care. I'd never experienced such a feeling of helplessness. None of the things I held sacred—my eagle feather; the pollen; the Apache and Navajo prayers, medicine, and ceremony—were going to save my father.

My dad was my hero: an artist, storyteller, and cowboy, the funniest Navajo I knew. He was a natural leader, looked up to by so many different types of people, and a kind, prayerful family man who always did his best to shield the people he loved from suffering. Throughout my life, at my worst and my best, he had loved, supported, and tolerated me. He had admired my mom, calling her his "muse" and doing his best to make her happy.

Vincent Craig was a true Renaissance man on the Rez.

And when he died—on May 15, 2010, at 9:10 p.m., the spring after I turned thirty—my father was eighteen years sober.

+ + + +

Once Dad was gone, everything got quiet. Eventually, everyone but me and my brother Shiloh left the room. We sat holding his hands, and I felt a kind of peace I'd never felt before wash over me. I think there was something about the magnitude of the pain and loss that made me feel the expansive, cosmic nature of love—how it could kick your ass and remind you how small you were. I whispered, "It's over now, Dad. I love you."

By the next day, news of Vincent Craig's passing had spread throughout Native America—the *Navajo Times* published a lengthy obituary. We were fortunate to have had time to have the difficult conversations about my father's last wishes while he was still lucid, and now we threw ourselves into funeral arrangements. I phoned every single police agency my father worked for to request an escort for a fallen officer. I called the United States Marine Corps Honor Guard to get a sixteen-gun salute. I spoke to my dad's boss at Overseas Aircraft, his last place of employment, and they agreed to arrange a flyover. My brothers made arrangements for the burial itself, including a procession of Apache cowboys.

Four days after his death, hundreds of people packed into the big Mormon church in Lakeside to say goodbye. My brothers and I all spoke, sharing our favorite memories of our father, and my dad's close friend, Ronnie Peaches, talked about how the Apache people had adopted this famous Navajo as one of their own.

At the end of the service, a posse of Apache and Navajo pallbearers walked my father's casket out while a Vietnam-era Huey chopper hovered overhead, beating the air. We all looked up, silent, feeling a deep sense of pride in our fallen hero. More than a hundred vehicles followed the black hearse back to the Rez, escorted by police cars from each of the tribal departments my father had worked for. As we drove through the border towns of Show Low and Pinetop, dozens of white families stood on the roadside holding signs with messages like *Goodbye Vincent, until we meet again.*

We transported my dad's body to the smaller Latter-Day Saints church in Fort Apache, where we had hung up some framed *Muttonman* strips and arranged my father's saddle, ropes, and guitars around a big photograph of his face. People came from far and wide to pay respects, crying and laughing at his comics until it was time for the final procession to the grave, where a marine kneeled in front of my mother and presented her with a United States flag. Before we lowered my father into the earth, we swapped the flag out, shrouding the casket in a bright red Navajo blanket. In the Apache way, we also sent him off with food and drink, including a canteen of water and a big bag of corn chips we'd placed alongside his body. Before we left the cemetery, we sprinkled ashes gathered from cooking fires all around the edges of his grave.

+ + + +

I had been busy in the lead-up to the funeral, but now the hours stretched ahead, empty and foreboding. There was no one I wanted to talk to. There was nothing I wanted to do. I hadn't answered any NACA emails in months, and I had no interest in making new connections or drumming up speaking engagements. The fear of living without my dad was so huge it quickly morphed into something much more horrible, a demon of rage, mistrust, and despondency. I went days without seeing anyone, avoiding Nalin's calls, not thinking about Ari. The only thing I wanted was to be left alone, to drink, smoke, and snort myself into oblivion.

I spent that summer unemployed and homeless, mobbing out on the streets of Whiteriver each night. Once, in the backyard of a notoriously dangerous party house, I was standing by a roaring fire when a heavyset, mean-looking Apache with long, scruffy hair and a pistol in his waistband staggered up to me and put both hands on my shoulders, staring at me with his drunk, dead eyes.

Do I owe him money? Have I pissed off his buddy? I braced myself for violence, startled to see tears well up in his bloodshot eyes.

"Fuuhh, Nephi," he slurred, his breath boozy. "I'm so fuckin' sorry. We loved your dad, man. Vincent Craig was the shit! Fuckin' A, why the good ones always gotta die?"

He told me how he and his family had cried when they heard the news and that a bunch of them had attended the funeral. I stood there scowling, trying to look tough, but when he told me how he was a Boy Scout back when my dad was a Scoutmaster, my eyes welled up.

"He always called me and the other little Apache guys 'son,'" he recalled. "We'd sit up in our tent at night and whisper about how we wished he really was our dad."

I met so many people like that scary-looking Apache that summer, people who wanted to tell me how much my dad meant to them and how sorry they were for me, my brothers, and my mom. Even in my drunken stupor, those encounters imprinted on my brain, but I just kept spiraling. I barely ate anything that didn't come from a bag in the convenience store. I was totally malnourished.

My mind and body were rarely in sync, but sometime in late August, I woke from a drunken stupor keenly aware that I was hurting, not just emotionally and spiritually but also physically. My hands wouldn't stop shaking and my entire body ached, down to the bones. In a rare moment of clarity, I sensed that I was being consumed by grief and the emptiness that enveloped me after I lost my dad. I needed to go back to the Native American Rehabilitation Association center up in Portland, I decided. I'd gone through rehab there nine years earlier and I remembered the place fondly. It seemed like the perfect place to go lick my wounds, surrounded by natural beauty and other Natives struggling to keep their heads above water. When I called, a woman named Lela picked up the phone and told me she remembered me. "You were the young skater chef from Apache Land!"

I was relieved when she informed me that they had a bed open. NARA was the first rehab center I'd ever gone to. Maybe it could also be the last.

When I arrived at the treatment center, I discovered very little had changed since I'd been there in 2001. But as comforting as I still found the place, I was unable to truly let my guard down. I couldn't speak about losing my dad without getting angry, and I felt frustrated that I hadn't dreamed about him once since he'd been gone. Then, two weeks into my treatment, it finally happened—I dreamed I was at one of my father's shows, but the whole time, my dad never acknowledged me or heard a word I was saying. It was like he didn't even know who I was.

I woke up in tears. *After all these months, I dream about you and you don't have shit to say?*

It felt like my dad had finally given up on me.

+ + + +

A few days after the sad dream, I placed my weekly call to my mother. We had a hard time talking about everything that had happened—as a young girl, my mom had witnessed addiction destroy her family and she still found the topic painful. We stuck to news of what was happening in Whiteriver.

"Everyone's talking about the big changes at Sunrise," she reported. Mom knew some of the older employees at the front desk in the hotel, and they'd told her that the head chef position had opened up—somehow, Kyle had failed up and been promoted to hotel manager. "They think you should apply."

I snorted. "Do they know I'm in friggin' rehab again?"

My mother wasn't fazed. She had plenty of practice dodging my dark moods.

"Think about it, sonny. We mailed you a package, and I included an envelope with a tribal application. It's stamped and everything."

The box from home arrived the next day, and after the staff went through it, they handed me the contents: a tube of toothpaste, a new toothbrush, a pack of white socks, two plain black T-shirts, a bag of Doritos, and the job application, which I unfolded as soon as I got back to my room. I stared at it for a long time, feeling worn out—it was hard to imagine managing a kitchen. Still, for a few days, it was all I could think about.

I filled out the application and placed it in the outgoing mail the next day.

Early in October, after I had left NARA and returned to Phoenix to look for work, I got a call—somehow, the executive chef job at Sunrise was mine if I wanted it. Part of me worried that it was too early in my recovery, but a bigger part of me wanted to be home. It was almost Halloween, a year since my father was rushed to the hospital, and I wanted to see Ari, who would be turning seven soon. I had an irrational hope that this time everything would be different. How many times had I said that to myself? How many times had I really believed it?

Either way, I started working the next week, barely a month out of rehab. As grateful as I was for the opportunity, I was also overwhelmed. In my new role, I was responsible for budgeting and straightening out the food and beverage program's financials. I also needed to start meeting with all the vendors and sales reps, figure out how to operate the point-of-sale systems, and build a new menu, one that lived up to my high standards. At the same time, I didn't want to overwhelm the team.

It wasn't easy switching roles—I went from being in the trenches with my coworkers to being their supervisor. I knew that now that I was executive chef, the staff would naturally talk shit about me. I did my best to accept that, but it stung. I had never stopped wanting to belong, and I could tell that some of the more seasoned cooks were wary of me, especially Vina, who had been at Sunrise since I was still in Pampers. She had seen dozens of chefs come and go, including ambitious white boys from across the country who'd been pummeled with culture shock, and Native cooks that lasted only one or two seasons. She acted standoffish with me, making it clear she thought I was another unreliable drunk and that I wouldn't be there for long.

Instead of getting bogged down in kitchen dynamics, I resolved to make the food my focus. Under my watch, there'd be no more boxed broth, no more powdered potatoes. We'd make stock from scratch each day and peel, chop, boil, and mash the potatoes every shift, adding just the right amount of cream.

Before the start of the ski season, I organized an all-day intensive training in culinary culture, providing my staff with a booklet of kitchen terms, techniques, and ingredients that were on our menu. I showed them videos from chefs like Anthony Bourdain, Thomas Keller, and Daniel Boulud and talked about the rigor and discipline of professional cooking.

I wanted my team to work at a higher standard than they thought possible for themselves, but I also wanted them to understand that their indigeneity was a strength, not a liability—they belonged in a professional kitchen just as much as our ancestral foods did. Early on, I gave a pep talk about Indigenous cultivars and how foundational they were to almost every world cuisine.

I started tweaking our menu, keeping it simple so I didn't crush everyone with all the changes. That confused trout almondine was the first thing to go—I replaced it with roast salmon in a corn sauce with a Three Sisters side, a simple mixture of sautéed corn, squash, and beans. It sold like crazy from day one. Next, I added pozole and that was a big hit, too.

I immediately began sourcing as many ingredients as possible from Indigenous growers. I reached out to Tohono O'odham Community Action, the grassroots agriculture-revitalization organization I'd done a dinner for, to see if I could buy cholla buds and tepary beans from them. Historically, the Tohono O'odham people had been desert farmers and tepary beans were one of their important crops.

During our pre-shift meeting, I set a five-pound bag of white teparies down on the table we were standing around, telling my staff the story of the Tohono O'odham Tribe and their efforts to use these heirloom beans to make their community more healthy.

"They've been studying how tepary beans regulate blood sugars in diabetics," I told the cooks. "What's also cool about these beans is that they're drought-resistant—they're being used to bolster food security in Africa."

"But aren't beans Mexican food?" A young man named Leon, who was new to the team, spoke up. "They're our enemies, man!"

I let the chuckles die down.

"That's a misconception," I explained. "You ever hear the phrase 'We didn't cross the borders, the borders crossed us'? That's what's up. An imaginary line was drawn between Native people up here and down there. It's just one of those racist ideas we were taught."

I scooped up a handful of the beans, instructing the staff to pass them around.

"Go ahead, show guy!" Marv held the handsome pale beans in his palm, grinning.

I explained to the team that, from now on, we'd be preparing our bean sides very simply, simmering them in water. Ever since culinary school, I had defaulted to the classical method of preparing Native cultivars like quinoa and beans—cooking them in chicken stock with carrots, celery, onion, and other Eurasian aromatics like thyme—but when I started catering to my father's sensitivities, I had experimented with something new and pared down. Cooking the beans in water is most likely how our ancestors would have done it, and I was pleased with how clean they tasted.

"You can really taste the unique profile of each type of bean this way," I continued, observing that Anasazi beans were lighter, creamier, and slightly sweeter than pinto beans, and they cooked more quickly, too.

Large scarlet runner beans—dense, rich, almost meaty—were a favorite with carnivores. Tepary beans were one of my favorite heirlooms. Brown teparies in particular have a unique flavor—if you close your eyes, you can taste the desert soil.

"I call white tepary beans 'desert pearls' on some of my menus," I continued. "They get creamy and smooth, delicate enough to pair with almost anything."

The staff listened intently.

"You're like one of those wine guys," said Freddie, the girl-crazy cook.

"A sommelier," said Tabatha.

"A bean sommelier." I looked around the circle, encouraging my cooks to give it a try. "How would you describe a pinto bean?"

"Tastes chaaaamp," said OJ, our resident class clown, making everyone laugh.

The cooks in my kitchen quickly embraced our new menu—the flavors were fresh and delicious and they took pride in how pretty our dishes looked when they went out.

Occasionally, when we served my simplified beans, I worried that I was being too basic. What would my culinary school instructors say if they tasted a forkful?

"There's no depth," I imagined Chef Dominic complaining. "It's so . . . plain."

In my mind, the Native ingredients talked back, telling my snooty instructor that they were very happy with the changes I was making.

This is who we really are, I imagined the Anasazis proclaiming. *And if you don't like it, well, too fuckin' bad!*

Once we opened for the season in November 2010, it quickly became apparent that our customers were pleased with the new menu. Although Yelp reviews for the hotel remained harsh as ever—people complained about the dated décor and uncomfortable beds—there were *many* positive mentions of our restaurant. People were surprised that this *Hot Tub Time Machine* dump was putting out such fresh, clean, and delicious food.

What other classical cooking rules have I been following blindly? I wondered. *What else am I embellishing unnecessarily?*

Leaning into simplicity was a relief. Outside of our kitchen, my staff and I were all dealing with the hardship and mayhem of everyday Rez life. There was something wonderful about letting the foods speak for themselves.

+ + + +

A year after I first sabotaged my job at Sunrise, walking out in the middle of a shift to get wasted, I did it again. This time, I missed three shifts in a row during an ugly bender, and after a string of increasingly frantic messages, the resort manager informed me they were terminating my position. Listening to my boss's voicemail, I was much too high to feel ashamed.

At this point in my journey, there was nothing surprising about another relapse. When you're in deep with your addictions, you simply make the decision to get high and drunk, holding on to some false hope that you won't go as far as blacking out and wrecking your life. It's like rolling the dice.

Within weeks, I was out on the streets again, in bad shape, running with a down-and-out crew. I hated crashing at my mom's place, knowing that I was adding to her pain and grief, but I had run out of options. Nalin and I had broken up—she said she didn't want to see me again until I cleaned up my act. I tried to spend as little time as possible in the Whiskey Flats house, which wasn't all that difficult considering how I was spending my nights.

One morning in late February, I woke up in my childhood bedroom enveloped in the dank smell of cigarettes and liquor.

How the fuck did I get home?

I sat up and surveyed the room. My wallet was there on the floor, along with my shoes, but there was no trace of my weed or vodka. It was six fifteen a.m. and my buzz was fading fast.

As reality crept back in, I remembered sitting around a campfire the night before with a dozen rowdy Apaches, talking shit and laughing it up late into the night. I recalled telling a rambling story about skateboarding around Osaka.

"Boo-shiiit!" one of my wasted buddies had ribbed me. "You ain't never been to fuckin' Japan!"

"For real, man." I dropped my empty beer can and crushed it with my foot. "I was out there in 2007 cooking at the Imperial Hotel. It was fucking life-changing."

"No shit, what did you cook?" another guy asked. He sounded genuinely impressed.

I closed my eyes for a moment, imagining that immaculate kitchen, the beautiful, synchronized dance of those Japanese chefs.

"Bundi'tunneh and Acorn Stew."

The circle went quiet for a moment, and then everyone busted out laughing. Most Apache men can't fry an egg, never mind prepare a traditional stew.

"I did a nine-course menu of Native foods. It's called a tasting dinner. I smuggled acorn, nadá'łeeshbízh corn, piñons, wild tea, and a small Racket in my suitcase, past Japanese Customs." I had their attention now. "While I was there, I bought some chef's knives from the great-great-grandson of a real-life fucking samurai. They're like small katanas."

"Keee-yeah! Go on and bring one over tomorrow," said the tall metalhead sitting to my right. "I wanna check it out. Maybe I'll buy it off of you."

He looked around the circle, sneering like, *Can you believe this bullshit?*

The rest of the night was a blur, but somehow I didn't forget about my potential buyer. I'd already sold several of the knives I'd collected over the course of my twelve years of cooking professionally to get money for booze and drugs, but I'd held on to my favorites—the hand-forged blades I'd bought in Japan. Now, I walked over to the dresser where I'd stashed them and slipped them into my backpack, sneaking out into the cold February day.

+ + + +

Death showed up regularly in my dreams that spring. I'd pass out and see myself laid out in a cavernous room full of hospice beds with other dying addicts. There were always beeping machines and long bags of black bile hanging down to the floor. Everything was bathed in a sick green light.

I'd catch my reflection in a window or mirror and know that I was going to die of cirrhosis or get shanked out in the streets, that I was probably going to meet a violent end like so many of my friends and family on the Rez. I started hallucinating more and more frequently.

During one particularly intense episode of delirium tremens in my childhood bedroom, I heard the boom of Apache drums and people cussing me out in Apache, watching as the wall cracked open, revealing the whole universe. I saw loved ones who had already passed away gesturing for me to come join them and Apache Crown Dancers dancing in the Milky Way. These visions dissolved, and I watched horrified as Ari ran away from me and all of Whiteriver went up in flames. I heard the mechanical *clack* of loading handguns and rifles all around me, and menacing voices.

"Yo, Nephi. You ain't shit," they taunted. "We're gonna come and kill you!"

It felt so real, I was terrified—I almost wished that they would.

In early June, I woke up on the floor of my mom's living room with tears streaming down my cheeks. I'd been thrashing around, yelling in my sleep, and my terrified mother had called for help. I remember looking up and seeing two police officers and two mental health professionals from the reservation standing over me.

I sat up, startled. I hadn't shaved in days. I was embarrassed of how raggedy I looked with my patchy goatee and whiskers.

"What did I do?" I was more worried about the cops than anything else. I thought they were there to arrest me for something I did during my blackout.

Dr. Brown, one of the mental health professionals from Indian Health Service, told me to sit down on the couch.

"Nephi, you're in very bad shape. I know you're hurting inside. We all knew your dad, all of us were at the funeral." He spoke softly, which I appreciated. "He would be so sad to see you like this. You're going to drink yourself to death if you don't stop."

My mom was weeping. The two Apache police officers stood next to her, solemn. They didn't have any of that normal combative cop energy.

They weren't telling me anything I didn't know. Through angry tears, I snapped at them. "I know death is near. I feel it all the time—it's out there fucking following me."

My mom hated hearing me swear. Her tone changed.

"Son, you have two choices," she said, looking me straight in the eyes. "You can either go to jail or you can go with Dr. Brown to detox. You can't stay here any longer."

I felt the anger drain out of my body. I was so tired. I looked down at my hands. My knuckles were bruised and scratched up from fighting, breaking doors, and falling down, and my fingernails were black with dirt.

"Fuck it. Take me away then."

I think I'd made the police nervous, because they spoke sternly. "To where?" I was no stranger to acting tough and getting myself thrown in jail.

I shook my head, smiling pathetically. "Detox, man."

They drove me to Holbrook, Arizona, the small, depressing interstate town where, over a century earlier, my great-grandpa was put on a train and sent to Carlisle. Holbrook borders the Navajo Nation, and the streets are full of unhoused Native people doing just about anything to feed their addictions and stay numb to the awful reality that's built up around them. The stabilization unit in Holbrook was not a treatment center—you could only stay and detox for seventy-two hours. When I finally dried out after three days, the people who ran the joint told me they had to release me. I did the only thing I could think of, leaving and getting wasted so I could check myself in again.

That first night back, after a crappy yet comforting dinner—a lumpy, mystery-meat Salisbury steak with powdered mashed potatoes and mushy canned green beans, alongside a Styrofoam bowl of pinto beans and bacon—I rolled myself a cigarette and went outside to sit on a big, gray rock. It was unusually windy and cold. I sat, feeling the food digesting in my stomach. The yellow grass rustled loudly. I wondered if I could brew it into a tea.

"I can't do this no more, Dad." I inhaled and exhaled smoke. I was talking to my father and I was talking to Creator, sending up a prayer. "I don't give a shit where I go, but I really just need a bed. I'm not going to die of alcoholism."

I had traveled all over the world, worked in extremely challenging conditions, navigated tough kitchens and multiple stints in jail. I had created my own opportunities, launching a national organization and moving up the ranks to become the boss of my own kitchen, forging a path that didn't exist for brown, Indigenous chefs like me, but I had no clue how to be sober. All I knew was that I was done living this way.

"I don't know how to do this," I told the moon, "but I'm going to do whatever it takes."

I was done fighting with the world, done being angry. Death was no longer this big romantic notion—a way to quiet my clamoring, damaged ego for good—and there was no mystery to being an addict. My life had become a living hell.

In this moment of clarity and surrender, I thought about Woody and one of his favorite sayings: "A drowning man will grab a sword." I thought about my dad on his deathbed looking at me with sad eyes, telling me that alcohol was not for our people, and about the visions I'd seen during my episode of delirium tremens, watching little Ari holding his teddy bear and walking away from me.

I want to find heaven, I told Creator. *I want to create it here on Earth.*

I wiped away my tears. I could feel my dad all around me. He was telling me that he knew I, too, would be a good father someday.

The next day, I called the Rainbow Treatment Center back in Whiteriver, along with every rehab center I'd ever been to, but no one had a spot available. I even called the Salvation Army—I was willing to go to a faith-based program if that's what was needed.

I made one last call, to a program in Tucson the people at Holbrook had recommended, one that I'd never heard about—the Amity Foundation Circle Tree Ranch. I said who I was and that I was finally ready. The guy on the other end of the line listened quietly and told me they had a bed open for me.

EIGHT

COOKING FROM SCRATCH

By the time I rolled through Amity Circle Tree Ranch's arched red gate in the summer of 2011, I had completed nine rehabs and run away from another five. This place seemed different, or maybe it was me. I was finally done with the chaos.

Located on sixty acres just outside of Tucson, in the Tanque Verde Valley, Amity was once a working ranch and then a boarding school. To get there, we drove through the Sonoran Desert—jagged rocks, cactuses, and mesquite trees on repeat—arriving at a fenced-in compound with big, old trees and eight adobe-and-brick buildings arranged in a circle. These, I'd soon find out, were the "lodges" where we patients slept. One of two big buildings farther in was Bear Hall, where most of the group sessions were held. There was a long stained-glass window above the front double doors and the two seven-foot statues of Chinese dragons standing inside the entrance.

The entire place gave off the vibe of a small, quaint town in an old Western movie or one of those Scottsdale spas. It was the first rehab facility I'd ever been to that had a serious salad bar.

In the promotional materials I'd seen, Amity billed itself a "therapeutic community." Some of its founders had been members of Synanon, a San Francisco cult originally founded by hardcore heroin addicts who banded together to help each other get clean. Breaking from faith-based programs like AA, Amity integrated spiritual practices such as meditation, mindfulness, and a sweat lodge that, at the time I was there, was overseen by an elder named Ron, a Pascua Yaqui who ran it in the Lakota style. The focus of the program was creating a supportive environment where people could feel safe processing the traumas that fed their addictive tendencies.

I was brought into an office, where I sat down across from Rachel, the intake coordinator. She went over the rules; I smiled at "If you're high, you fly"—it reminded me of something Owen or Woody might say.

"For the next thirty days, you have one job and one job only," said Rachel, handing me a stack of workbooks with titles like *Thresholds of Change* and *Resentment, Rationalization, Resistance, Reaction & Perseverance.* "You'll be stabilizing."

I would not be participating in any formal therapeutic activities for the first month, she explained. There'd be no contact with anyone outside of the Ranch, no phone calls, no nothing. I'd be staying at Threshold House, together with all the other guys who were in the early days of detox, fresh off the street or out of jail. It was the first building you saw as you entered the grounds, the one with a nice porch where residents could sit and look out into the courtyard. There was a different Threshold residence for women, near the family housing.

Rachel called in one of the clients who was assigned to work in the administrative offices. It turned out to be Larson, a guy I knew from Window Rock High. We greeted each other warmly and he led me on a quick tour. At Threshold House, he introduced me to a few guys who were hanging around outside, before leading me inside to a large bedroom with two bunks on each wall.

"Get ready to do a whole lot of nothing," he said, leaving me to unpack.

Larson wasn't kidding. Each morning after breakfast, the Amity community gathered for a morning check-in where they recited the Amity Philosophy, introduced newcomers, and went over announcements about groups, job assignments, and activities. The only expectation for those of us in Threshold was that we occupy ourselves and stay out of trouble. The days stretched out, long and hot.

I kept to myself, only speaking when I was spoken to. I'd learned that the first few days in rehab can be really aggravating—you're trying to figure out all the different personalities, who's cool, who's serious, who to stay away from. As soon as morning meeting was over, I'd go sit under the big mesquite tree in front of Threshold House, then I'd spend the hundred-degree afternoons in my room, where I'd bust open my workbook, reflecting on straightforward prompts like "How did you participate in getting where you are today?" I sat thinking about that question for what felt like hours, but all I wrote, in all caps, was *CONSISTENTLY BEING ON A SELF-DESTRUCTIVE PATH.*

It was as simple as that. I was tired of making excuses, and I was ready to tread new ground.

Once I completed Threshold, I was assigned to a lodge overseen by David Nunez, a big, buff Mexican who'd done a couple of long stints in prison. David was all tatted up, with a shaved head, mustache, and goatee—he gave off a major do-not-fuck-with-me vibe. Our supervisors at Amity weren't called therapists or counselors, they were called demonstrators. They were real-world examples of how to live your recovery in public.

What I love about people in recovery is that, while they often appear hard as nails on the surface, they possess a level of humility and optimism that only comes from surviving the horrors of active addiction, with all the violence and devastation.

David was like that.

Despite his tough exterior, you could tell he cared deeply for the men and women under his watch and believed in their ability to pull through. In one of the first formal groups I participated in, David talked about how terrifying recovery was, but that we had no choice. He stood up, throwing a fist in the air.

"We are the fucking marines of this shit!" Of course, it was the perfect analogy for me. "We take the work seriously and we go in ready to fight!"

Some of the Amity techniques definitely had a confrontational vibe. Once I got out of Threshold, I learned about "groupings," peer-led meetings where people held others in the program accountable for their actions and behaviors. If someone expressed concern about an individual, that person would be "grouped," which essentially meant they had to get in the middle of a circle of eight or so people who took turns calling them out on what they were or were not doing, how they were avoiding the work or displaying addict behavior. Grouping was a process borrowed directly from Synanon; apparently, in the old-school days, things would get physical, often turning into a borderline group beatdown.

There was no physical violence at Amity, but that didn't mean being grouped wasn't painful. About three weeks into my time in David's lodge, he came to find me at breakfast, telling me to show up at one of the small group rooms behind the main dining hall at four thirty that afternoon.

"What's going on?" I asked, looking up from my half-eaten omelet.

David grunted. "Just be there, man."

I arrived a few minutes early. I'd never been in this particular room before—the swamp cooler was putting up a fight against the three-digit heat, and losing. A bunch of people were already there, sitting in a big circle; I recognized Raymond, Dale, Rachel, Monique, Amy, Carlos, and Jonathan. Both Larson and David were there.

Aw, shit, I realized. *They're gonna group me.*

David motioned for me to get in the middle. I'd already participated in a handful of groupings, but being on this side was disorienting. I had to keep swiveling around to face the person who was talking—it was hard not to feel like a cornered animal.

Before we got started, David reviewed the guidelines.

"Everything's on the table. I expect everyone to be honest here. And, as usual, no acts or threats of violence. You'll be kicked out faster than you can say *bullshit*."

He stood up, tugging on his goatee, his huge silver ring pointed straight at me. "Nephi, I want you to listen good. I want you to see yourself in the shit your friends are describing."

I took a deep breath and nodded, but my stomach felt queasy. I'd been keeping my head down. I hadn't been running my mouth or misbehaving. *Why was I in the hot seat?*

David left the room, and Larson kicked things off.

"Right. So, basically, Nephi, we've been doing all this work about resentment, but it feels like you're holding back."

"You're withholding." Rachel, who'd been at Amity a year, often jumped in when she thought someone wasn't being direct enough.

Larson cleared his throat. "You brought up your parents judging you, or how your ex didn't trust you, but it didn't feel like you shared anything real, anything specific. Like, I have no clue what exactly you're resentful about. You're like a lone wolf."

"More like a mangy Rez mutt," said Carlos, a sarcastic Navajo who'd been at Amity for almost two years and was always looking to get a rise out of me. "You never play ball with us. At night, you never play games or shoot the shit."

I smirked. Before I could think better of it, I snapped back. "That's stupid. Who gives a shit about sports or Monopoly? I'm here to work on myself."

"Sounds like B.S. to me." Raymond was an older Navajo dude who I liked very much. "It's not stupid to participate. It's not stupid to talk to people who are in the same boat as you. They're the ones who will tell it like it is and hold you accountable. They're the ones who can help you out when shit gets hard."

Carlos jumped in. "Exactly. That's your problem right there, Nephi! You think you're too fucking smart for the rest of us. You don't share because you don't think we'll get you."

I felt my face burn.

"But you know what? You're not special. You think you're so deep, but it looks like you're just skimming the surface. You've gotten real good at sugarcoating your entire life."

Everyone took a turn, adding their own variation on the theme.

Finally, it got quiet and Rachel asked what I was taking away from the session.

"I'll hang out more. I'll even go to those stupid-ass ice-cream socials." From my dad, I'd learned to use humor to defuse tense situations. "I'm gonna think hard about my tendency to isolate."

+ + + +

My fellow residents were on to something—I *had* been retreating—but none of them realized what was occupying my time. Nobody knew I had unexpectedly become an old-school Apache farmer.

I discovered Amity's vegetable garden by accident. After completing the Threshold program, I'd created a morning routine for myself, waking up at six and going for a three-mile run before hitting the gym, which was a lot nicer than any other rehab gym I'd ever been to, with brand-new mats and a variety of free weights.

One day, on the edge of the property, I jogged past a narrow plot of earth, about half the size of my great-grandpa Joseph's garden. It was in rough shape, overgrown and dusty, but I could make out the floppy leaves of a squash vine sneaking through a tangle of weeds. I stopped in my tracks and took a deep breath, savoring the tang of tomato flowers and the musk of desert soil. Here and there, I spotted lines of black irrigation hoses, although it didn't look like they were really watering anything.

That morning, as I placed my breakfast plates in the dishwasher's bin, I asked my buddy Steven, one of the kitchen workers who I'd become friendly with, about the sad-looking garden. He'd been at Amity for five years, and I figured he might know what was up.

"That's Naya's garden. She was one of the founders, but she's retired now. Haven't been back there in a minute. She used to grow real sweet corn," he said, shaking his head. Like most Navajos, Steven got all misty-eyed when he talked about the most sacred food of the Indigenous Southwest. "Yo, Nephi, when you gonna come work with us, show us what's what with Apache cooking?"

I chuckled and told him I was off to group. My buddies knew I was a chef; some had even followed me on MySpace and read about my work with Native foods. A few times, they'd encouraged me to volunteer in the Amity kitchen, but—just like at the Baltimore Station—I felt like I needed a break. I wanted to focus on getting, and staying, clean.

But that neglected vegetable garden kept calling to me. The next day, I brought it up with David, asking if he knew who was taking care of it since it looked like it was dying. I wondered whether it would be okay for me to tend to it in my free time.

"Everyone was all excited to plant that garden, but then, you know how addicts are. Once their brains are used to the excitement, they get bored and forget about it." David shook his head, grimacing. "I'll ask around and get you an answer."

Later that week, David gave me the okay. I started early the next morning, heading over to the forgotten patch pre-breakfast, before the heat became unbearable.

I'd only ever lived in apartments and trailers and I had never had my own yard, but it turned out I'd retained a lot from my early years of helping my great-grandfather in his subsistence garden. I spent the first three days working on the irrigation, testing the lines and replacing busted pipes with an abandoned coil I found tossed in the back corner. After that, I waged a battle against the weeds, spending hours on my knees each day for a week.

As I cleared the overgrowth, I uncovered clumps of sad-looking crops: several varieties of squash, melon, and cucumbers, their vines crispy and yellowing; some dying beans; a few limp tomato plants and sunflowers. My most exciting discovery was a long row of corn stalks that spanned the length of the vegetable patch. Barely knee-high, they'd been dwarfed by the desert weeds. They tugged at my heartstrings.

Once the garden was all cleaned up, the corn became my first stop each morning. I'd walk down the row, gently patting each stalk on the head, talking to it like I'd spoken to Ari when he was little.

"What's up, buddy?"

"You gotta drink up that water so you can grow and get all tall."

"Déba'gosiní'mé." It was one of the Apache phrases I knew—*what a cute baby.*

I could tell that working in the garden was good for me, good for my recovery. I felt light inhaling the earth smells, happy even. Growing up, I'd heard about Navajo corn-gathering songs, although I didn't know a single one myself. I made myself chuckle singing made-up tunes to the corn stalks or humming "I Like Dirt" by the Red Hot Chili Peppers.

A week after my grouping, during evening circle, I finally opened up about the garden. I shared how weeding had become a sort of meditation for me, a way to let go of frustration and resentment.

"I talk to the plants about things that make me sad, like how I haven't really been there for my son since he was born, or how I'm still sick about my dad being gone." I took a deep breath. "Talking to the plants, it's like a funny farm for real."

David scowled. He'd encouraged me not to make a joke out of things that made me feel uncomfortable or vulnerable.

"Each time I pull a weed, I think about something I want to let go of, some grievance that's been playing over and over in my mind. 'My ex never really believed in me.' 'My mom has always thought I was bad.' 'My dad was better than me in every single way.'"

The room was still. Everyone was listening intently.

"I see now that if I don't figure out how to clear my anger and frustration with the people in my life, it might choke me, just like those weeds. If I don't root out my tendency to blame others, I might suffocate and rot."

"Fuck, yeah, Nephi, you've figured out a way to do the work."

David finally smiled—and then he said something that has since become a mantra for me.

"You're participating in your own evolution!"

+ + + +

Seven weeks into my time at Amity, I was authorized to have my first visit. As part of the self-study we'd been doing, I'd written apology letters to various people in my life, including Kim and Ari. Now, I wrote to say I wanted Ari to come visit with my mom.

On the Saturday after July Fourth, my mom, my seven-year-old boy, and my teenage cousin-sister Kyra, my uncle Edwin's daughter, showed up in the early afternoon. I'd gone through so many treatment programs since Ari was born and had been locked up all over the United States, but this was the first time Ari would see me in a place like this. In the days leading up to Family Day, I felt nervous, worried that it was a mistake to expose my son to this place and all these tough characters, but as soon as he stepped out of my mom's car, I was overcome with gratitude.

Rachel welcomed visitors at the front gate and brought them through the arches. After a brief official welcome, we were instructed to show our families around the compound and let them see where we lived, which was nice because at just about every other rehab, you had to stay in designated areas.

After I pointed out the various buildings where I spent my time, I led my visitors to the garden.

"I talk to Grandpa Ivins and Dad here, and I even talk to the plants," I said as we passed through the wire gate. My mom teared up.

I explained how much the plants had grown since I started taking care of them, especially the corn, which now stood taller than Ari. It made me smile to watch my son play in the dirt and splash around in the small water puddles while Kyra egged him on. It reminded me of my childhood in Whiteriver.

I pulled my mom over to the corner where the tomatoes were popping off.

"I feel so different here," I said, as we admired the ripe red and orange fruit. "I feel a little crazy, actually."

My mom looked over at me, her face lined with concern.

"I feel crazy for being at peace, for not acting all resistant. I think I've finally been brainwashed," I said, getting her to laugh. "I'm just glad I didn't need shock therapy."

It was blazing hot by now, so the four of us headed back to the main building, climbing the creaky stairs to find an empty meeting room. At the end of the hallway was a space with a small desk, earth-tone wool rugs, and a couple of worn leather chairs. Ari immediately curled up in one of them, looking around at the built-in shelves full of books and trinkets: painted Ganesh elephants, golden Buddhas, and a miniature Virgin Mary.

"You look good, sonny. It looks like you're eating well." My mom sat down in the chair next to Ari.

"Yeah, you look healthy. I can really tell you stopped drinking." The last time Kyra had seen me, I'd been passed out by the woodpile in my parents' backyard, where I often slept when I came home drunk late at night. She plopped down on the two-seater sofa next to me, grinning like she still thought of me as her cool older brother. It made me choke up.

"I like it here, but I'm looking forward to coming home. I miss Whiskey Flats." I laughed, but I really meant it.

"We miss your cooking," my mom said. "There's no one to build our morning fire."

Ari had been quiet all day, but now he spoke. "Yeah, Dad, remember how we would watch *SpongeBob*, and you always cooked us omelets? I can't wait for you to come home so we can do that again."

I missed those cozy mornings, too; ever since I was a kid, I'd enjoyed chopping wood and starting a fire to warm the house. But I kept my mouth shut—I had already told myself I was never going to be dependent on my mom again or move back into my childhood home. I was determined to find a place of my own, even if that meant living in a halfway house or a shelter.

Ari must have sensed my mood change, because his expression darkened. He folded up his skinny legs, leaning his chin on his knees.

I hadn't seen my son in more than four months, and he'd grown so much. His pants were too short and he needed a haircut. I was the one who always gave him a good, clean fade. It was a Craig tradition—in our family, fathers cut their sons' hair.

"You need a haircut, son." I felt sad, leaning forward to pass my hand through his thick black hair, making it all bushy. I looked him straight in the eyes. "I promise that I'm gonna do better."

"You really hurt me when I was small, Dad. I didn't like you." Ari spoke matter-of-factly, his voice neither warm nor angry. "You smelled like smoke when you came home. I'd hide under the bed, but you'd come pull me out and tell me to hang out with you, but I didn't want to."

Every word felt like a bee sting, making me flinch. Emotionally intelligent beyond his years, Ari softened the blow by acknowledging the offering I'd tucked into a letter for Kim.

"Mom gave me the drawing you sent, and I hung it in my room."

I'd filled an entire sheet of white paper with drawings, writing Ari's name in simple, 1990s-graffiti-style letters along with cool phrases like *Stand Strong Son*, *Diné Bizaad/Western Apache*, *Sons of Sacred Mountains*, *Enter the 36 Chambers*, and *Sobriety Endurance Life 2011*. In the top-right corner, I drew a broken heart with a Band-Aid across it and dragon wings coming out of it, shading it carefully. *Dad's gonna be ok,* I wrote next to it.

"I liked your picture." Ari smiled now. "I hope your heart gets better, Dad, so I can come stay with you more. Mom says she wants me to see you, but not when you are drinking."

I was a thirty-one-year-old man in early recovery, amazed by my son's composure. Tears streamed down my cheeks, but I didn't move to wipe them away.

"Thank you for telling me how you feel, son. You've always been so brave." My voice was shaky. "I feel so sad to know how I hurt you, and that I made you afraid."

Ari got up from his chair and wrapped his arms around my neck. I closed my eyes.

"I still love you, Dad." Kyra and my mother were crying. "I want you to get better."

"I'm gonna be all right." I held my son at arm's length so we could look at each other. "We're going to grow up together, okay? I'm gonna show you that it's safe to be with me."

Now, all four of us were crying.

It's a moment that, years later, plays in my mind like a movie, suspended in time. Woody had often told us, "You will never 'fix' your problems, you'll only learn to carry them." I finally understood exactly what he meant. That day, I felt—in every cell of my body—that I was ready. I could be accountable for the damage I had done. I had missed so many amazing moments with my son, but now I would slow down and really listen. I'd try my hardest to learn to be an emotionally present dad.

I pulled my boy close, feeling his heartbeat in my chest.

+ + + +

By the end of that summer, my rehabbed garden was going crazy, and I was bringing a daily offering to the cooks in the Amity kitchen: chubby cucumbers, skinny zucchini, broad beans, cherry tomatoes, and big, yellow sunflowers. I got a kick out of seeing my vegetables laid out on the salad bar.

Now and then, one of my buddies would show up to lend me a hand, although nobody came consistently. Like gardening, recovery can be tedious. You're baking in the sun, getting pricked, you're thirsty as fuck, your back aching. For a long time, I, too, had said I wanted to get clean, but I wasn't willing to get my hands dirty and do the grunt work, staying sober day after day after day.

At Amity, my relationship with the truth evolved. For as long as I could remember, the painful parts of my existence had filled me with terror; so many of my bad decisions were driven by the desire to push them away. After one particularly heart-breaking group session—where one of the men in my lodge spoke with astonishing courage about the sexual abuse he'd endured over the course of many years from his own family—I finally talked about what had happened to me when I was ten, hot tears of rage and shame pouring out of me.

I began to see how for two decades now, I'd put up a front, acting like a mean badass when I was really a scared little boy. I thought about how I'd felt when Nalin and I started going out—our chemistry and easy affection terrified me. Just as I'd done with countless other relationships, both personal and professional, I had put up a wall when I felt us growing closer, withdrawing into my drinking and pushing her away. I wanted someone good in my life, someone who really saw me and cared about me, but I had never truly believed that I deserved that. But now, as I opened up in group, sharing more of my story, I realized I was done moving through life feeling so alone.

Once puny, the corn in my garden was also rapidly transforming. The stalks now hovered above me and as I walked among them, I'd whisper, "I'm going to take care of you until you're tall and strong enough to bless me with some pollen to pray with."

In late August, before I harvested and brought a whole bucket of silky cobs to the ecstatic kitchen staff, I carefully collected some pollen from a few tassels, drying it in the sun on a piece of paper before stashing it in an empty Carmex tin.

Ever since I was a little boy, younger than Ari's age, I had heard that corn was "sacred." I distinctly recall riding around in my father's truck with my brother Dustinn one day listening to some old lady on KTNN 660 AM, "The Voice of the Navajo Nation," talking for several minutes about corn pollen. Her voice was croaky, with a thick Navajo accent. She sounded serious, like a grandma who's telling you something important.

"Everything we do is about the corn—we plant corn, we grow corn, we sing to the corn, and we eat the corn," she explained. "Corn is our mother, she takes care of us. Always. Corn is ceremony. It's our way of life, and will be forever."

"This lady means business," Dustinn observed, making my dad grin. I wasn't quite sure what it meant for a food to be a parent or a way of life, but the woman's words struck me as powerful and interesting.

Years later I learned that corn pollen grows on corn tassels, which are the male flowers of the corn plant. A single corn plant produces several million grains of pollen—infinite potential. All across Mesoamerica, where it originated as a wild grass before being cultivated by the region's farmers, corn became a pillar of Indigenous identity and culture. The Mayans considered themselves Corn People, just as many of today's Native communities—including the Zuni, Hopi, and Navajo—still do.

I remember sitting with my dad and my grandfather Bob Craig as they chatted in Navajo, trying to decipher their conversations. One of the only words I could make out was "tádídíín," the Navajo word for corn pollen. My grandpa once told us that, the night before the United States Marines stormed the shores of Iwo Jima, a group of Navajo Code Talkers had gathered on the bow of a huge battleship in the South Pacific, praying for the soldiers' protection with the corn pollen they'd carried with them in their medicine bags from the other side of the world. Now, seven decades later, I was in the process of receiving my own blessing from the corn. I had nurtured a humble crop back to health, and in turn, I felt, this ancient Mother Food would watch over me as I prepared to start a new way of life.

I was proud that I'd succeeded in transforming the Amity garden with my care and devotion. Despite the misconception—shaped by white anthropologists who labeled our people "nomads"—that Apaches were not farmers, our culture is actually rooted in an intimate and strategic relationship to land, water, and food. Generation after generation, Western Apaches cultivated a body of knowledge that would challenge any trained botanist. They learned about the timing of the seasons and the protocols of when the wild foods were ready; many of these lessons were passed down through song. Individuals were chosen as leaders because of their understanding of the region's landscape, because our lives literally depended on it. Once we were moved onto reservations, we were forced to augment our diet of wild foods with a variety of agricultural crops, including pumpkins, melons, beans, potatoes, barley, and sunflowers.

Long before contact with white settlers changed everything, corn was an important cultivar for our people. White Mountain Apaches planted corn fields each spring before heading down to lower elevations to set up clan camps, where they could hunt and gather. These Apache farmers were experts in a technique that people nowadays call "dry farming"—they'd plant the dried corn kernels two or three times deeper than you'd usually place seeds, where the soil retained more moisture. This meant that the corn would grow even with no one there to water and tend to it. Apaches,

Navajos, Hopis, Zunis, Pueblos, and other Southwestern tribes all practiced this technique for thousands of years.

The community would come back together for harvest in late summer. Corn was such a bountiful crop for our people that when the settlers arrived in the White Mountains, we traded it for cattle, establishing a new tradition of Apache cowboys that endures until this day.

Nadá łeeshbízh, or barbecued corn, is one of the few Western Apache food practices and techniques that has survived colonization. Nadá łeeshbízh refers to an involved, hands-on process of transformation that stretches back millennia, and, to this day, it's one of the most powerful flavors of home. The same way some people feel about blue cheese, white truffles, natto, jackfruit, fish sauce, bitter melon, caviar, or any food that is distinct, potent, and culturally revered, I feel about Apache barbecued corn.

To make Nadá łeeshbízh, you work with fresh corn that's just been harvested, still in its husks. It takes several people working together to dig a huge pit in the earth, which is then lined with stones. Next comes the task of building a roaring fire and keeping it going for many hours. Once the whole pit is full of fiery coals, you line it with loose, green husks collected from the field, piling the harvested corn in huge mounds, which are covered with more fresh husks and branches. Now, large sticks and branches are laid across the pit and a large piece of canvas is stretched across it (our ancestors probably used animal hides). Finally, the pit must be covered with more dirt to seal in the heat—and then the corn's left to cook for twelve to twenty-four hours.

Buried deep in our Mother Earth, the corn undergoes a slow process of caramelization, while the wood, smoke, and green husks add subtle umami accents. Initially, the red-hot stones roast and char the corn husks, but as the heat mellows, the corn bakes and then steams. The entire process happens in the dark.

After the cooking time is over, the dirt is scraped off and the canvas pulled back, releasing steam into the air. The smell that rushes out of the pit is unforgettable: fresh, sweet corn mixed with earth, stone, and fire, a tantalizing, ancient aroma. Before the work of processing the corn continues, every kid, adult, and elder pauses, helping themselves to a warm, smoky-sweet cob. Then, all the corn husks are removed and the cobs are hung to dry.

Over the course of a week or more, the flavors continue to condense and intensify. Once packed tightly together, the kernels slowly shrivel and pull away from each other—now they're ready to be removed from the cob. This can be achieved by firmly rubbing two cobs together, catching the loosened kernels in a basket or on a cloth, although I've seen some grandmothers fondly remove each individual kernel by hand, working meticulously, row by row.

Once each kernel has been transformed into a translucent, golden jewel, the corn becomes more valuable than any luxury ingredient. Dried Nadá łeeshbízh lasts for up to a year—my favorite way to use it is simmering it in a pot with beans and meat to produce a delicious corn stew called Dijíízhi that's pure Indigenous comfort food.

Tucked away in the Sonoran Desert, I was leaning into my cultural affinity for this amazing wild grass–turned–Indigenous cultivar. Me and the corn, we were in each other's corner. I was helping it grow, and it was teaching me what happens when you nurture the parts of yourself that are rooted in the soil, nurtured by the earth we all come from.

With the right mindset and behaviors, the right practices and nourishment, we are all capable of healing from devastation and transforming our lives. I already knew in my heart how to make it through recovery. I didn't have to become someone else—I just had to listen deeply to myself and trust the guidance of those who had come before me.

It took me more than a dozen tries, but this time, rehab stuck—in large part, because I really believed that I could change, that it was in my power to be the person I wanted to be. I was grounded and ready. It was time for me to mise en place my life.

+ + + +

I yearned to be back in our mountains. I kept thinking about that spot just down the road from Sunrise Park Resort where, on a clear night, you could see all the way down to the lights of Phoenix. I wanted to be back among the trees, under a tarp of massive sky.

In September, I wrote a letter to Ronnie Peaches, my dad's old friend who, at the time, was the resort's general manager, asking if the head chef position was still open. I was determined to try something new, laying all my cards on the table, so I started by saying how much I had enjoyed being at Sunrise, supervising an all-Native team and increasing sales with a popular new menu. I spent the rest of the letter explaining that I had relapsed after my father's death, and that I'd spent the whole summer in treatment.

My mentor here, David Nunez, has been encouraging me to formulate a plan for after I leave here, to set myself up with a solid routine, I wrote. *Please consider giving me another chance to show you what me and the team are capable of.*

A week after I mailed my letter, I got a short, typed response, inviting me to apply.

Underneath his name, Ronnie Peaches had added a friendly, handwritten note: *It's good to hear from you.*

I tried not to get my hopes up too much, but a month later, right around the time I was awarded my 120-day sobriety certificate, I received a phone call from Ronnie saying I'd gotten the job. I could stay in the hotel, he told me, in a room set aside for management. I cried tears of joy.

I arrived two days early. The hotel manager showed me to my kitchenette room on the second floor, which faced hills covered with pine trees and aspen as far as the eye could see—I had asked for a room with two beds so that my son could come stay with me.

It took me fewer than five minutes to unpack everything I'd brought in my duffel bag. I spent a lot of time in the empty kitchen that weekend, organizing the shelves and deep-cleaning all the surfaces, channeling my nervous energy. I had abandoned my team at the worst time, during the busiest part of the ski season. Ronnie had told me that Vina and Vinny, the two strongest cooks in the kitchen besides me, had done an excellent job overseeing the morning and evening shifts, respectively, and I worried they would be conflicted about having to report to me again. I knew I would be.

The hotel wouldn't officially open for business for over a month, but in a few days, we'd host the first of three groups of hunters who had paid top dollar to participate in Elk Camp. This was an annual event that drew wealthy men and women—businesspeople, entrepreneurs, bankers, and winery owners—from all over the United States who came to hunt in our mountains for ten days, accompanied by Apache guides. The kitchen crew was responsible for breakfast, lunch, and dinner, staying on-property and rotating between shifts that started at four a.m. and ended after ten o'clock at night. The pay was good and the hunters always tipped very well. I drew from my experience cooking in high-end kitchens to plan a varied, upscale menu I would present to my staff when they reported for work.

Monday morning, I went for a run around Sunrise Lake, admiring the reflection of the soft dawn sky and the bold colors of the autumn leaves. As soon as I got to the kitchen, I brewed a strong pot of coffee and calmed my nerves by passing through the walk-ins with a clipboard in hand, checking on the deliveries I'd ordered. I brewed a second pot of coffee for the staff.

A little before noon, the shuttle bus that had picked up hotel workers at stops all over the reservation—including Hon-Dah, Whiteriver, and Diamond Creek—pulled into the narrow parking lot, depositing a noisy crowd bundled up in winter coats and hats. Vina and the other old-timers from her morning crew were the first ones off, followed by Vinny, who wore a black Sunrise Park Resort hoodie. It was time to face them head-on.

I walked out into the dining room, perching casually on one of the cheap wooden tables and fixing my eyes on a big, brown stain in the middle of the gray carpet. We'd have to attack it with some of the heavy-duty cleaning liquid I'd found locked in the closet downstairs, next to the old heat lamps and silver, continental-style platters I remembered seeing as a boy.

As the staff filed up the carpeted stairs, I kept my expression neutral, ignoring the whispers and shocked looks.

"Everyone, circle up."

Most of the fifteen people in the room had been with me the previous season and were used to my pre-shift meetings. Not one of them had any idea I was about to run my own grouping.

I looked around the room, trying to make eye contact with everyone, although several people were pointedly staring out the windows.

"Before we talk about the new season, I want to share some information, talk openly with you about what's been going on with me and where I hope we're going as a team."

Marv, the intimidating Apache who'd first showed me around the Sunrise kitchen, stood right across from me, his large, tattooed arms folded across his chest, his face unreadable.

"As some of you probably heard, I just got out of rehab down in Tucson. I was there for three months, the longest I've ever stayed in a program, although I did spend the same amount of time in a mental hospital a few years ago."

A couple of the sous chefs opened their eyes in surprise.

"This was my ninth time in rehab, or the fourteenth, if you count all the times I bounced."

A few people chuckled.

I cleared my throat. "Here's the thing. I've worked in professional kitchens for about twelve years now, but I've never been honest with the cooks I've worked with about my struggles, about the drinking and drugging."

"Pretty sure they knew what was up," muttered a young guy I'd never met before, blowing air through his teeth. One of the old-timers shushed him.

"Every time I decided to try and stay sober, I never told anybody.

Even when I got my dream job and spent an entire year not drinking." I turned to look at the newbie. "I can see now that I was setting myself up for failure, and I'm determined to do things different this time around.

"After my dad died . . ." My voice cracked, but I willed myself to keep going. "After my dad died, I almost drank myself to death. I was lost, my heart was completely broken. Some of you saw me out there."

I sensed the group's silent intensity as they listened to me. Below us, I heard people passing through the lobby, snatches of conversation and laughter.

"I fought to come back to this kitchen because I think what we have here is special. I'm here to learn, teach, follow, support, and grow as part of this team—and to do that I need you to know where I'm at with my recovery, so I don't fuck it up again."

I took a deep breath.

"I'm not saying it's up to you to help me stay clean. But I am saying that I'll never get better if I don't learn to be accountable to the people around me. For most of my life, I was so ashamed of being an addict that I went around lying about everything, but I don't give a fuck about that anymore. I want to learn to live again, to feel things fully without turning to alcohol or drugs to help me cope. I want to apologize for how I acted before, and for not being straight with you."

Vinny smoothed his hands down his pants. "For real, man, that was shitty, the way you just dropped everything," he said.

OJ, my dishwasher friend, nodded. "Shit was crazy, but we made it through the season without you."

"Customers kept asking about you," said Carla, one of the servers. "I wanted to tell them that you were just another drunk chef, but I didn't because my brother was also lost in his addictions."

Vina nodded. "I thought for sure we'd never see you again."

"Yo, Nephi." Marv's voice was deeper than the others. "That shit took a lot of heart," he said, looking me square in the eyes. "I respect that."

"Yeah, thanks for being upfront with us, man," said Freddie. "But, sheeit, can we get to our stations now? I gotta work on my mise en place 'n shit!" His voice got all nasally pronouncing the French term. The team chuckled.

I was grateful to Freddie for shifting the conversation back to the present. I'd shared enough for one afternoon. I knew my staff was skeptical—where we're from, we've heard it all before; we know that most attempts at sobriety initially fail. I took them through the menu for that evening's Elk Camp dinner: corn chowder, cedar-planked roast salmon, roasted potatoes, and a Three Sisters salad. We'd have to wait and see if I had the guts to follow through, to stay diligent and humble, rooted in my recovery. We'd have to rewrite the rules of our kitchen. We were in this together, truly cooking from scratch.

\+ + + +

By classical French culinary standards, Mary Elaine's was the pinnacle of my career, but from my perspective, what the Sunrise team and I accomplished during my first year of recovery was truly unprecedented: the first restaurant in the country completely run by Natives doing high-end, technique-driven food in their ancestral homeland. And all of it in a banged-up old kitchen in a tired ski resort that looked like it was stuck in 1986.

Like many people in recovery, I felt compelled to stay busy. Even after Elk Camp was finished, I continued working from seven in the morning to midnight most days.

My routine was like clockwork. I'd wake up by six to work out, then shower and walk down the hall by seven to the kitchen, where the morning crew was already deep in breakfast service, serving the skiers who were ready to hit the slopes. I'd sit in my cramped office, handling paperwork and menu planning. I always left the door open—I loved listening to Vina run the show, expediting dishes in Apache. All of the daytime cooks and even some of the young servers spoke Apache, too. It fired me up.

The night crew would roll in at one to prep for when we opened at five. Their vibe was completely different. Most of the cooks, dishwashers, and servers were in their late teens and early twenties—Vinny, who was my brother Dustinn's age, five years older than me, was the oldest guy in the kitchen. The evening crew was full of energy, hyped to be employed for the winter ski season. They moved quickly, talked loudly, and told raunchy jokes. During prep, we'd listen to country music or KNNB 88.1 Apache Radio, but once the shift was over, we'd blast West Coast gangster rap, classic punk, and death metal. I was the last one to leave each night, shuffling down the hall to collapse in my bed.

One slow Wednesday in early December, I asked the front-desk manager on duty if I could use the fancy printer and laminator in the back office.

"Knock yourself out," he replied. "I gotta go check on the pool. The jets are busted again." People were always dropping shit from the walkway above the bean-shaped swimming pool that took up one whole side of the carpeted lobby.

I printed out three big signs that day, taping together multiple sheets of paper to make long, skinny banners.

I hung MENTAL MISE EN PLACE just above the stainless steel double sink. At this point, every single person in that kitchen had heard me talk about how working in the kitchen was an opportunity to clear our heads and be fully present, practicing putting aside any negative thoughts and problems that made our lives outside this place feel out of control.

The PARTICIPATE IN YOUR OWN EVOLUTION sign went above the door to my office. I hoped that by living my recovery publicly, I might encourage others to make positive changes in their lives.

Lastly, I hung SENSE OF URGENCY above the wall clock mounted just inside our swinging doors. It was a popular kitchen phrase coined by Chef Thomas Keller of the French Laundry, an appropriate motto for a bustling restaurant kitchen. For me, the phrase held a deeper, much more personal significance—it felt imperative that I share the story of Indigenous foods with other people who needed to hear or relearn it. Over the years, the knowledge I'd gathered had propelled me forward when everything else seemed hopeless. Thinking about how centuries of brutal history had disconnected our people from healthy, sustainable food traditions—and all that could be gained from reviving them—had given me a sense of purpose. I wanted to bring others in my community along.

Even though the days were long, every minute felt precious. My dad was gone, there was no time to waste. I had no idea how long this thing at Sunrise was going to last, but I wanted it to be great while it did.

Throughout November and December, the restaurant was extremely busy. Word had gotten out that the menu had changed for the better, and along with the winter tourists, we were getting a lot of customers from Whiteriver, Canyon Day, and McNary, and even from farther out on the reservation, from Cibecue and Carrizo. Our staff was firing on all cylinders. I felt so happy seeing cooks who I knew came from rough neighborhoods and families arrive in the kitchen excited to throw down and get cooking, and it made me proud to see young Apache women get rewarded with good tips at the end of a long, busy shift. I loved that our workplace was full of laughter and real talk about anything and everything, all aspects of life on the Rez.

One evening just before New Year's, I turned to Vinny as we scrubbed down the counters.

"I think we should do a Chef's Table." I'd been kicking the idea around for weeks. I told him about the Chef's Table at Mary Elaine's, how people would book a year in advance for a chance to sit in a tricked-out corner of our kitchen, watching all the action while our head chef personally served them, talking about each dish that was put in front of them.

"That sounds crazy," he responded. We were both grinning.

\+ + + +

If I placed a four-top table just right, like a diamond, it could fit in the corner just outside my office, with a clear view down the line. I used my own money to buy some small plates and bowls from IKEA, hung a pretty Pendleton blanket on the wall, and set up a digital monitor to project a slideshow of close-ups of different Native ingredients and action shots of our team. It was nowhere near as opulent as Mary Elaine's setup, with its framed French paintings, padded chairs, and expensive rug, but it was exactly right.

I started experimenting with dishes for the menu. My idea was to take diners on a culinary tour of Indigenous America from south to north, starting with a quinoa salad, a Three Sisters appetizer, and a starter-size serving of pozole, and ending with a homemade sorbet of wild berries.

I planned to kick off each dinner with a little bowl of Western Apache Seed Mix. I'd learned about seed mixes—and how they were most likely a snack our ancestors ate during scouting missions and probably left along the trail as little bundled offerings for hungry travelers—from Twila Cassadore, a forager and food educator who was helping run an organization called the Western Apache Diet Project down on the San Carlos Reservation. She and her co-director, Seth Pilsk, had come into the restaurant in the fall and we'd hit it off talking about Apache foodways. What made the seed mix I prepared for our Chef's Table distinctly White Mountain Apache was salted acorns and parched white corn; when they were available, I'd add roasted piñon nuts.

Since the line cooks were still getting used to their stations and our new menu, I prepped the first Chef's Table menu almost entirely by myself. The staff was baffled that I wanted to put a dining room table inside the kitchen, but I could tell they were curious about the food I was preparing.

"I'll train you to do this kind of thing before the end of the season," I told Vinny and a few other cooks as they observed me break down a whole Quinault River salmon.

"Hey, OJ, did you know that out in Northern Cali, Oregon, and

Washington, and all the way up in Canada and Alaska, the Natives love to eat the salmon's head? They save it for the elders, kinda like we do with beef tongue."

I picked up a heavy knife and split the head through the middle, making that awesome bone-cracking noise cooks love.

"Let's cook this one," I said, taking the two pieces of salmon head and placing them in a hot sauté pan with a little olive oil and salt. I threw it in a 400-degree oven for about fifteen minutes and once it came out, crispy and golden brown, I threw in a few knobs of butter and some fresh thyme, chopped parsley, and chili flakes. I plated both halves on a large plate lined with some ponderosa pine needles I was planning to use for the first Chef's Table dinner.

I had the whole team gather round, the salmon looking up at us, wide-eyed and surprised.

A few of the staff chuckled nervously, but I encouraged everyone to have a taste, telling them the best parts were the jowls, collar, cheeks, eyeballs, and brain.

I was happy to see everyone take a piece, laughing and daring their coworkers. A Native food had pushed the team out of their comfort zone and bonded them together.

The first Chef's Table was designed to get management's approval and, in addition to Ronnie Peaches, we'd be hosting Ronnie Lupe, our beloved tribal leader. As soon as our dishwasher, OJ, spotted Lupe's white tribal headquarters truck pull into the parking lot, he yelled, "Shoooow, Chairman is here! Chill out, yo. Let's do this."

"Guests in the kitchen," I yelled, channeling Chef Thompson. I trained the whole team to shout back in unison, "Yes, Chef! Guests in the kitchen," just like we did at Mary Elaine's.

In his button-up shirt, slacks, shiny black dress shoes, and neatly cut, short gray hair, Chairman Ronnie Lupe was the kind of man who commanded any room he walked into. He walked through the kitchen like a G, scanning the scene and greeting the staff. He had a baritone voice and glasses that made his eyes seem even more piercing and observant. When one of the cooks stepped forward to shake his hand, he said, "Tsik'neh?"

I thought it was cool of him to use the casual "What's up?"

One of the most prominent, influential Apache leaders of the modern era, Ronnie Lupe had been our tribal chairman since 1968. During his first administration, he'd spearheaded the construction of the Sunrise Park Resort and the hotel we were all standing in. Eventually, he was elected vice president of the National Congress of American Indians, becoming an inspirational icon all across Native America.

I knew that neither Ronnie had ever seen a team of Apaches like us. It felt like an important achievement, but I was also very intimidated. I was determined to show my bosses that they had made the right choice by bringing me back.

As soon as the two other guests arrived—the marketing manager and an Apache guy named James who worked on the ski mountain and doubled as a photographer in his free time—we sat our guests down and served them each a shooter of wild tea and an individual glass bowl of seed mix.

It was fun to watch Ronnie Lupe, this revered leader, scoop up a handful of seeds with his hand and pop them into his mouth.

"Kaaaaay yeeeaaah," Chairman said fondly, his serious demeanor melting away. "This reminds me of my grandma."

I smiled. I, too, remembered snacking on a mixture like this at my mom's aunt's house—Grandma Charlene kept it in an abalone shell on her kitchen table.

"I've made parched corn everywhere from New York to Osaka," I told my guests. "The trick is to get the pan very, very hot and constantly stir the dry corn until it cracks, then throw in some salt and a couple of ice cubes and keep toasting the corn until the pan dries up and the kernels are coated with salt, crunchy, smoky, and delicious."

The dinner went smoothly. While my team held down the dinner service, putting out burgers, bowls of pasta, roasted salmon, and a new addition of mine, Apache fries—small red potatoes that have been steamed, smashed, and fried, and seasoned with smoked paprika, chives, and lime, served with a chipotle aioli—I presented the foursome in the corner with one beautiful dish after another. Each time my servers and I dropped plates in unison, I described the inspiration behind the dish and gave a quick summary of the Indigenous ingredients showcased.

"I want to honor our Apache culture by developing menus that simply couldn't exist anywhere else in the world," I told my VIP guests.

Almost two hours after we started, I served the final main course, an elevated twist on Acorn Stew, inspired by the dish we'd served at the Osaka banquet all those years ago. In each delicate white bowl, I had arranged a few golden acorns, a couple of little football-shaped Apache dumplings made of acorn flour, and a pile of sliced New York strip steak. I ceremonially poured a china pitcher of piping-hot acorn bone broth over the solid ingredients. We served each bowl with a side of miniature Racket Bread that we'd cooked on an open fire built on one corner of the griddle.

Ronnie Peaches's eyes got really big. "You have to photograph this," he directed James. "And get pictures of the staff in action."

I watched as my boss composed a perfect spoonful of stew and brought it to his mouth, following it up with a bite of bread, which he dunked in the broth.

"Don't tell my wife, but this is the best Acorn Stew I've ever had."

Ronnie Lupe chuckled. "I was a little worried when I saw how small each dish you brought out was, but I'm so full." The chairman rubbed his belly.

"What you're doing here is really impressive," he continued, motioning for me to sit down in James's empty seat. "I never imagined our traditional foods could be served like this. You've made something special even more special—I can't wait for people to find out there are Apaches out here cooking like this."

I felt like jumping up and down, but I held it together, saying I'd go pack up some homemade chocolate truffles for our guests to take home and offering them coffee.

As I passed behind Vinny to grab a French press from the coffee bar, he turned and gave me a thumbs-up.

"That food was badass," he said, lowering his voice.

Topping each mug with a big dollop of piñon-infused whipped cream, I couldn't stop grinning. For years, I had prayed for clarity, and, finally, I felt like I had it. Serving our guests this coffee concoction I'd come up with myself brought me lots of joy. There was so much bitterness in our lives. Tonight felt like a celebration of all the sweetness.

+ + + +

One of the most significant gifts of early recovery was getting to spend more time with my son. Now that I had my own place, Ari came regularly to stay with me on the weekends. While I worked, he hung out in our room, watching cartoons and drawing, or wandered around the hotel, inevitably ending up in the arcade room, where he'd play *Q*bert*, *Asteroids*, and *Bubble Bobble* like a kid from the eighties. Whenever he got hungry, Ari would run over to the kitchen. Sometimes, I'd whip him up an omelet or a bowl of pasta, but usually the Apache ladies took matters into their own hands. Each morning, they fixed him a plate of eggs, sausage, hash browns, and Apache tortillas and sent him to sit in my office. Ari was always such a good kid—he knew he couldn't play around in the kitchen, but he loved to watch the line cooks working when I'd let him.

Once school ended, Ari started coming to stay with me for longer stretches. The hotel was a lot quieter during the offseason—overnight, it was often just me and the front-desk clerk. After the frenzy of the winter and spring, it was a treat to spend time outdoors together with my son. The two of us went on long walks and spent hours down by the lake, fishing. If Ari caught a big trout, I'd take it up to the kitchen to cook it, sautéing it in a pan with lemon and thyme or simply grilling it. I was happy that Ari was such a good eater. He liked vegetables and didn't shy away from trying new foods like calamari and shrimp; I remember him beaming with pride that summer when he tried his first oyster.

During my busier days, Ari would run around by himself in the woods, building huts, listening to the rustling of the leaves, and playing out grand adventures in his imagination, just like I'd done at his age. Being back in the sacred mountains as a person in recovery was strange and awesome. It felt like so much time had passed, and that no time had passed at all. I was hurtling through space, both a son and a father, launched on a wild trip of spiritual acceleration.

Other times, recovery felt like the most boring thing ever, although even then I didn't feel the urge to drink or light up a joint. In addition to my duties as executive chef, I oversaw and managed the hotel's full-service bar, the Black Diamond, selecting the wines, ordering all the alcohol, and collaborating with the bartenders on special drinks. I had full access to the liquor storage, but it was never a problem. Once I was transparent about my sobriety, my cravings fully subsided. I had distanced myself from people who thought it was cool or transgressive when I drank.

Like corn that's been cooked underground, I was transforming into a more vibrant, formidable version of myself. Initially, I hadn't told any of my professional connections about my new position; my brain had cycled through all kinds of tired, familiar tracks—*this place sucks*; *you're so much better than this*; *you should be making your name in New York or California*. But after Chef Olson, who was now the executive chef at Thunderbird Country Club outside Palm Springs, reached out to congratulate me on my new job, I sent him a thank-you email and even set up a phone call. I had some questions about ordering and bookkeeping that I was pretty sure he could answer.

More and more, I felt like I was on the right path. If I was going to make my mark as a Native chef, this was exactly where I needed to be, immersed in community and learning how Indigenous foods could lift us up and help us. If people wanted to experience our food, they needed to come to our remote mountains, just like the millions of tourists who drive for hours through the French countryside just to go to these little one-star and two-star eateries. I was an executive chef on the motherfucking Rez—this wasn't some performative bullshit. Me and my team were living the struggle, doing something both impossible and amazing.

There was nothing to compare us to. What we were doing at Sunrise was so outside the realm of conventional restaurants. I printed up one last sign, placing it right above the pass-through where the servers and cooks interacted so that, once I convinced management to cut a window into the wall that separated our kitchen from the dining room, everyone could see it: APACHES DO IT BETTER.

I wished with all my heart that my dad were alive to see this. I knew it would have made him chuckle.

NINE

DZIŁ ŁIGAI ŁAÍÍ BICH'AGÁSHÉHÍ

(THE WHITE MOUNTAINS AND HER BABIES)

Being an executive chef is a bit of a paradox. On the one hand, it's an individualistic endeavor. Through the dishes you create, you're attempting to impart your unique point of view, your culinary traditions and the people, places, and things that inspire you. On the other hand, you need a team to make your vision a reality. Balancing these two things can be tricky.

In my new role, I was discovering how much I enjoyed being a teacher. That electric charge I'd experienced when I first started as a professional cook—the realization that this was something I was good at, something that gave my life shape and purpose—was the same way I felt about mentoring the people in my kitchen. I felt both challenged and fulfilled.

Like the two executive chefs I'd learned from early on, Chef Olson at DC Ranch and Chef Bradford at Mary Elaine's, I was determined to hold my staff to the highest standards of excellence. At the same time, both my culinary mentors had shown me the importance of being fair—of seeing the humanity of the flawed, complicated people in your kitchen and treating them with respect, offering them opportunities to bounce back from mistakes.

At Sunrise, all of the challenges of working in and managing a restaurant—the low pay, the high pressure, the long hours, the resulting turnover and attrition—were magnified. For the people in my kitchen, the topics I'd highlighted while traveling the country and world to tell the story of Native foods—the injustice, poverty, and health disparities—were just *life*. Members of my team regularly called out because someone close to them had been killed or was dying, or they missed work because of their own struggles with addiction. Several of them, men and women, were directly impacted by domestic violence or incarceration.

Less dire, but just as detrimental to our daily routine, was the fact that most of my staff didn't have their own transportation, which meant they relied on the notoriously unreliable Sunrise-sponsored vans. My morning crew left Whiteriver and the other pickup locations before dawn in freezing weather, riding up the mountains in fifteen-seaters that had bald tires, faulty steering, squeaky brakes, and busted heaters. Vans broke down, people got sick from the cold, workers came in late or not at all.

For all of these reasons and more, we were chronically understaffed, and I regularly worked eighteen-plus hours a day. How to be a good boss was a question that was constantly on my mind. Given the extreme hardship my staff faced on a daily basis, what was the right way to be exacting and tough? What did it mean, in relation to the Natives in my kitchen, to be fair?

One afternoon, Nancy, one of the tough-as-nails line cooks who worked the morning shift with Vina, came by to give me a list of ingredients that needed to be ordered. My office at the back of the kitchen was more of a cubby—there was barely enough room in there for a small desk and a bookshelf—but Nancy lingered, gazing out the window, which had a spectacular view of the ski mountain. I turned away from my computer. There was something she wanted to tell me.

"A lot of us didn't trust you at first, Chef Nephi."

I flinched, then quickly nodded, eager to convey I was ready to listen.

"But you always come in early and you stay all day. You keep the walk-in organized and clean. You've taught everyone ways to do things better and faster. The food all looks and tastes amazing."

Nancy's compliments meant a lot, coming from someone who had worked at Sunrise for decades.

It was just as encouraging to see some of the younger cooks in my kitchen stepping up. While I'd been gone from Sunrise, the hotel managers had put Chef Vinny in charge of the bar and grill downstairs, but it was clear to me that he had more to offer than flipping burgers. As soon as I got the head chef position back, I asked Vinny if he'd be willing to come upstairs and work the line with us—his knife skills were on point, I told him, and I believed he had a lot of potential. Initially, Vinny had been hesitant to make the change, but he'd quickly taken off, holding down the busy sauté station and mastering classical sauces like demi-glace, velouté, beurre blancs, gastriques, and reductions. Now, Chef Vinny was the one guiding the younger line cooks on the grill and garde manger stations while I kept things running smoothly at the pass, making sure every dish we put out looked perfect and training the servers.

Even with all the progress we were making, there was still some skepticism in the air. I sensed it in the furtive looks the staff sometimes exchanged, the occasional eye roll, a mumbled aside. Like many of the people who worked with me, I'd once found comfort in the informal, messy, familiar dysfunction of the old Sunrise kitchen. I understood that working alongside this new, focused version of me was a big change, and that not everyone was adjusting. By the end of my first season back, a few of the guys who'd been around when I first got to the resort, including Freddie and Marv, ended up quitting.

I told myself not to take it personally. Most of the people I worked with had never met another Native who called himself a chef. From their perspective, that was a white thing, something they associated with the big-city guys who had rolled through this kitchen and lasted a year or two, tops. There was also this widespread misconception, one that I frequently encounter to this day, that the kind of food we were preparing at Sunrise was White People Food. It was too aesthetic, too carefully plated, too colorful and healthy.

I could argue how the "farm-to-table" and "hyper-local" ethos of New American and California cuisine reflected Indigenous food practices that predated the United States by hundreds of years, but at the end of the day, the Apaches in my kitchen didn't really care about food trends or follow industry news. They were concerned with supporting their families.

While it's undoubtedly true that, pre-colonization, our White Mountain Apache diet was entirely based on working with whatever was seasonal and bountiful, the fact that we believed that this kind of clean, local eating was foreign to us was a sad reflection of how our foodways had been ravaged. Generations of Native Americans were growing up with no sense that ours was the OG plant-based diet, heavy on fruits, vegetables, nuts, seeds, and grains.

Was it any wonder that my staff thought I was operating on a different wavelength? I was an Apache who liked to wax poetic about corn and chilies, tossing together facts about history, philosophy, and nutrition with a whole bunch of metaphors. At different points, I myself had felt like a crazy person for believing in an invisible legacy—a sophisticated Native American cuisine that had laid the foundation for so many others. The loneliness and isolation I'd experienced as a young chef was the reason I'd created the Native American Culinary Association in the first place; I was desperate to meet others who understood what had been lost and, like me, were passionate about claiming it back. The connections and inspiration I'd gained through the organization had kept me going through tough times. I wanted to share the power of this community.

For several years now, I'd put NACA on the back burner while I pieced my life back together, but it was time to make it a priority again. I wanted my staff to see for themselves that they were part of something much bigger: an underground movement dedicated to revitalizing and restoring Native American food traditions. I wanted them to believe, as I did, that this work could actually change our lives.

+ + + +

It was a brilliant fall. The tall aspens around the Sunrise Park Resort were painted red, orange, and yellow, and clumps of wild grasses stood knee-high.

Nalin and I had recently gotten back together, and I was determined to do things differently this time. At Circle Tree Ranch, I'd finally taken a hard look at my codependent tendencies—since my teens, I'd rarely been without a girlfriend, but those connections had come from a deeply insecure, selfish place. I sought out women to feel better about myself and impress my brothers and my friends. A few of the counselors I'd worked with over the years had suggested that part of me yearned to be "mothered," which I found disturbing and embarrassing. Once I thought about it, though, I realized that I was desperate to learn how to take care of myself emotionally.

Shortly after returning to Sunrise, I'd called Nalin on the phone. I wanted to be the one who told her I was back at the hotel. I thanked her for pushing me to get help for my addictions and explained that, for the first time in my life, sobriety was my number one priority. We talked on the phone frequently, and after a few months, I invited her over for dinner at the house in Whiskey Flats on one of my nights off. I made butternut squash ravioli from scratch and twirled it dramatically in a pan of simple brown butter–sage sauce, hoping to impress her.

It worked, but we agreed to take things slowly. Right from the beginning, I committed to one of Woody's universal principles of recovery: honesty. I practiced naming my insecurities, telling Nalin I didn't really know how to be a good partner, but that I was eager to learn. I confessed I needed help figuring out how to be a solid parent for Ari.

My recovery allowed me to open my heart fully. I listened carefully—and I learned. Nalin told me stories about her life before she met me, and about her decision to move back to the Rez to raise her daughter. Her love for our landscape and people was part of what attracted me to her—it made her even more beautiful. She knew so much about Apache culture, from our creation stories to different urban legends that circulated throughout the Rez, and her sharp use of Apache slang was unrivaled. I soaked it all up, asking her to slow down and explain things that seemed like second nature to her.

Nalin seemed to intuitively get what I was trying to achieve, without me ever having to explain it. She understood the recovery piece of my work as a chef and the cultural importance of the food. She appreciated the significance of creating a high-caliber kitchen up in our White Mountains. As I hammered out the details of the NACA conference, which had been scheduled for the first week of November, she acted as my sounding board.

Despite the objections of Sunrise's assistant manager, Roy, I had received permission to host the NACA event at the hotel in the quiet stretch between Elk Camp and the beginning of the ski season, which took care of our venue costs. A miserable old white guy who'd been at the resort for more than twenty-five years, Roy showed little interest in the community he worked in and treated us like unskilled labor. He'd come up with all kinds of ignorant, lame reasons as to why the conference wouldn't work, including "it's too far for people to travel to learn about fry bread." Thankfully, the Natives on the management team saw the value of the project, overriding him.

With the help of some NACA friends, I'd secured additional funding from a variety of groups, including the White Mountain Apache Tribe Office of Tourism, FoodCorps Arizona, and the Johns Hopkins Center for Indigenous Health. The money we raised would pay for group meals, hotel rooms, transportation, flyers, and posters. I earmarked a modest amount to order special chef's coats for every member of the Sunrise culinary team, including the servers. The coats were badass—black with the NACA logo on the left breast and the Sunrise logo and our colorful White Mountain Apache Tribal seal on the right shoulder—and I had them personalized with each person's name in both Apache and English.

+ + + +

Hosting that NACA conference in our White Mountains remains a highlight of my time at the Sunrise Park Resort. Over the course of three days, a hundred-plus participants gathered for inspiring workshops and boisterous community dinners.

At first, some of our guests seemed shocked by the location. The amenities at Sunrise Park Resort were a far cry from your typical conference center or big-chain hotel—there was no internet or phones in the rooms, only a small tube TV that barely worked. Everyone quickly caught on, though, as to why gathering in this place was so meaningful. Here we were, a diverse group of community members, elders, scholars, advocates, professional chefs, and culinary students—all of us Indigenous—sharing our collective wisdom in this sacred landscape. I imagined this is what our ancestors must have felt like during a war council, gathering together with other tribes to figure out ways to protect their people and landscapes.

"Us Natives will get it done no matter what," observed Arlie Doxtator, a Wisconsin-based chef who spoke at the conference about the Oneida people's foodways, as we stacked cracked pleather chairs in the old conference room. "We don't need all them bells and whistles!"

Everywhere you looked, the hotel buzzed with activity. People stood in front of the Indigenous foods timeline I'd tacked up on the large wall next to the fireplace, reading key facts about different cultivars from pre-contact times up to the present, and a constant flow of Native chefs came in and out of our kitchen to prep their cooking demos and pitch in for the group meals. Many of the academics jumped in to help as well, slipping borrowed white kitchen bib aprons over their casual business attire. People walked by in chef's stripes and bright-hued camp dresses, talking about food sovereignty or medicinal plants used by their tribe. The halls reverberated with lively conversations, loud music, and roaring laughter.

Many of my friends and colleagues attended the conference, including Chef Mark Mason and his sister Bleu, who I'd first met back in Window Rock, when we were part of the same skate crew. Now, the two of them owned and operated Black Sheep Cafe in Provo, Utah, which I considered one of the most important Native restaurants in the country. I loved catching up with Chris Rodriguez, a Seattle-based chef I'd first connected with in 2011. In addition to his culinary training, Chris held a master's degree in Latin American studies and he was well versed in Indigenous foods, resistance culture, and the Zapatista movement in Chiapas, Mexico. He was one of the first people I'd talked to about the term *decolonization*—when I asked him to send me an extract for his conference presentation, I expected a bold, strident statement about anti-colonial foodways, but instead he submitted a summary for a talk titled "Fathers in the Kitchen," during which he spoke about the importance of shifting Indigenous attitudes around gender roles, prepared baby food, and made the aunties in the room swoon.

On the last day of the conference, Andrea Beatty, a White Mountain Apache who was helping the Johns Hopkins Center for Indigenous Health develop a Traditional Apache Plants curriculum, gave a workshop called "Traditional White Mountain Apache Foods and Cooking."

Andrea showed up at the resort with several nieces and grandkids in tow—and one of them was carrying a large woven basket of fresh corn she and her neighbors had grown themselves.

"Chef Nephi! I finally made it. It's cooooold out here. Still warm in Cibecue." Andrea's light green Apache camp dress was almost the same color as the corn husks. She caught me eyeing them eagerly.

"I'm gonna teach everyone how to do Tamale'cho," she said, referring to Apache tamales, which are different from Mexican tamales in that they're made with fresh ground corn, not masa, and there's no filling, a kind of steamed corn cake. "I bet you fancy chefs don't even know how to make this, huh?"

For her presentation, Andrea wore the personalized chef's coat I'd had made for her, standing behind a table holding two large Apache grinding stones made of dark volcanic rock—the traditional tools for making Tamale'cho—and an array of colorful ingredients, including her homegrown corn, wild sumac berries, a basket of deer jerky, bunches of dried wild onions, and two glass jars, one filled with grass seeds and the other with tied bundles of wild tea.

A relative of the sunflower, this tall, spindly plant we call wild tea is known by a variety of names, including Cota, Greenthread, and Indian Tea, or, depending on who you're talking to, Navajo

Tea, Hopi Tea, or Apache Tea. While greenthread can easily be mistaken for other wild grasses, you can distinguish it by its thin, flimsy leaves and the small, butter-yellow flowers with their pretty red centers.

Wild tea grows all over the Southwest year-round, but it's typically harvested just as its flower buds start to open. You never pluck it out of the ground; instead, you snip it a few inches up the stem with a penknife, a pair of kitchen scissors, or the pinch of two fingers. Harvested in the right way, greenthread will continue to grow toward the sun.

For me, processing wild tea is a perfect example of Indigenous mindfulness. After I bring home the plants, I wash them in cold water and pat them dry with a clean dishcloth. Then, picking up three or four stalks at a time, I start folding them in two-inch intervals starting at the bottom, thickest parts: I let any flowers peek out from the top. Some people tie up their bundles with a piece of cotton string, but I've learned to wrap the folded bundle into itself in a figure-eight formation. As I set each completed bundle out to dry on a tray, I contemplate the power of simplicity.

Wild tea has many healing properties, including aiding digestion and reducing all sorts of inflammation. When you brew it, the water turns a cheerful shade of orange-red. I love the flavor of the tea—grassy, refreshing, a little piney. At Sunrise, we found different ways to incorporate it into our menu, making wild tea sorbets, popsicles, granitas, and gelées. I served a shot glass of the warm beverage at the start of every Chef's Table meal.

Andrea had requested we brew wild tea to accompany the Tamale'chos we had helped prepare in advance.

"This is the real way to do Apache corn," she said now, grinding a pile of the fresh corn kernels Chefs Vinny and Randall had set aside for her cooking demonstration between the heavy stones. "You can use a food processor like we did for making a big batch, but the old way just tastes better."

After Andrea finished pulverizing the corn, she scooped some onto a light green corn husk, folding the tamale into a small parcel. She picked up a second husk, tearing off a strip, which she used to tie up the tamale.

Standing at the back of the dining room, I signaled for my staff to start passing out the fresh Tamele'chos we'd been steaming in the kitchen.

Andrea fished a bundle of wild tea out of the jar.

"I told Chef Nephi to make some wild tea for everybody." She scanned the room looking for me, pretend-scowling. "Is it ready?"

"Yes, Chef," I exclaimed loudly from the back of the room where we'd set up a large stainless urn.

"Our wild tea is soooooooo special," Andrea continued, "like a favorite friend. Apaches drink this tea all year long—my mom and dad would always have two pots by the fire, one with Cowboy Coffee in it and the other with wild tea."

Andrea's expression shifted again.

"Never ruin it with sugar! Chef Nephi, tell people to not use sugar," she said, emphasizing each word. "Just let it be how it is! Tell people to close their eyes and smell it first before drinking it."

"Yes, Chef," I repeated.

While some Native foods have wild, bloody stories, there are others whose stories whisper softly—connected less to the march of time and the bombastic narrative we call history than the timelessness of a landscape. Like Apache acorns and tsínk'ózhé berries, the plant Andrea called wild tea belongs to this second camp. As I watched the conference participants, who would soon be leaving, take their first bites of a simple, comforting Apache dish and sip this humble, beloved beverage, I felt deep gratitude. Wild tea is a reminder that there can be so much goodness in the ordinary and abundant. It reminds us to appreciate what we have.

I thought about that moment early the next morning, standing in the quiet, empty hotel lobby and carefully untacking my historical timeline from the wall. I was so proud of everything the team and I had just pulled off.

This is what recovery from addiction can look like, I thought to myself. *This is participating in our evolution.*

After three full days of cooking demos, Q&As, and wonderful conversations with so many different kinds of people, I felt more focused than ever, more confident that I was doing what I was supposed to be doing.

As a young chef, I fed off the manic energy of a restaurant kitchen: the chaos, the heat, and the hustle. I'd been enthralled by star ratings and accolades, but I no longer found those things so important.

What mattered was gathering to cook, eat, and share food wisdom together, making the old ways new.

+ + + +

During my first few years at Sunrise Park Resort, I had treated it as a pitstop on my way to bigger and better things. Gradually, I'd come to see that being in this banged-up Rez kitchen had in fact made me into a better chef, someone capable of turning out incredible food with constraints and limitations you'd never find in any high-end kitchen. I was using my professional skills to celebrate and uplift my community.

Inspired by the NACA conference, I sought out opportunities to expand the work we were doing beyond our kitchen. In the spring of 2013, we piloted a mentorship program called the Western Apache Gastronomy Project, where we taught at-risk Apache teens cooking fundamentals like using a chef's knife, practicing good sanitation, breaking down whole ducks and cooking venison, and how to blanch, shock, and sauté. We took them on field trips to forage and gather stones and wood we'd incorporate into our plating.

Around the same time, I decided to finally reclaim a row of empty clay planters at the back of the hotel. My guess was they had once held decorative plants during the summer, but now they were empty and choked with weeds. I asked Emily and Jacob, a white couple who lived just outside our borders and had taught a workshop on farming basics at the People's Farm, if they'd help us create our own kitchen garden. The two of them arrived in a dusty green pickup, and Jacob stepped out wearing a massive straw hat covering his long gray hair, looking just like Gandalf. The two of them taught us how to make "lasagna beds," layering the dark brown soil we'd dug up from the forest behind the hotel with mountain grass, cardboard, and vegetable scraps from our kitchen. We mixed in compost from Ndée Bikíyaa, and our hippie teachers demonstrated how to introduce earthworms to keep the growing environment healthy. When the garden beds were ready, we planted thyme, rosemary, cilantro, and oregano starts; we'd add vegetables the following year once the soil was set and the worms did their job. I loved to watch my staff tend to those planters, continuing a tradition of Apache farming.

The restaurant was busier than ever. We were doing a couple hundred covers a night, and our Chef's Tables were booking up months in advance. One night, my grill guy, Aaron, was getting completely slammed. Arizona is meat-and-potatoes territory, and the orders just kept piling up. Dishes were being sent back and I started focusing on his station, giving him direct commands.

Suddenly, Aaron tore off his apron, throwing it down to the ground.

"Fuck this, I'm not doing this." His face was red and shiny as he marched out of the swinging doors, just like in a movie.

I had no time to think.

"Yo, Randall, come up here," I shouted. "Let's do this!"

I had met Randall in the run-up to the conference, when the recent high school graduate had applied for a scholarship to attend, sending in a long letter about how he'd always loved being in the kitchen with his mom and grandma.

"I get teased a lot for being a boy who likes to cook, but I don't care, I don't pay attention," he wrote. Randall showed up to the conference with his own knife, something that might be normal for an aspiring cook from the city but was definitely out of the ordinary on the Rez. I was so happy when, after the conference was over, I was given the green light to offer him a prep cook position.

Randall emerged from the back where he'd been cutting up three cases of red potatoes. I told him I was putting him in charge of the station.

"Every time a steak comes in, you season it like this and throw it on the grill." I pointed. "Here's the hot spot. Just keep going through these tickets. I'll jump back and forth and help you."

Within half an hour, we had dug ourselves out of the pile of tickets. From that night on, Randall was the grill guy. He joined Juwon, another nineteen-year-old who I'd recently hired as a line cook after he handed me a two-page résumé with glued-on photos of dishes he'd prepared in his high school culinary class. Both Juwon and Randall came from really rough backgrounds, and from the way they threw themselves into the work, it was clear that cooking was their anchor, just like it was for me.

The team and I started to receive lots of invitations to travel and present our work. In March, I received an email from Chef Olson, asking me to cook a special dinner showcasing Native American cuisine at his new spot. Returning to cook with your mentor is one of the best feelings for a chef—someone you admire professionally sees you as a partner and peer. Chef Olson was still running a tight ship—his kitchen was a humming, organized operation—and he was still faster than I was, but I could tell he was impressed with my professional development and, more importantly, with my food. We worked side by side producing a multicourse dinner for two hundred and seventy people, capping it off with the special dessert we'd spent years developing at Sunrise, Masáána bik'os ndeezi bigową or *the long neck apple's house.* As I demonstrated to him and his pastry chef how to assemble the intricate concoction of poached pears, poached pear pearls, raspberry coulis, whipped cream, and piñon shortbread and top it with one of the hundreds of spun sugar domes we'd prepared that morning, I shared the story of how the dish was inspired by my Grandpa Ivins's garden in Whiteriver, and the many happy hours I spent up in an old pear tree. The dish wasn't just beautiful; it had heart.

+ + + +

Love, recovery, and decolonization. Besides food, these were the things that occupied my thoughts during my first two years of sobriety, and I kept noticing the ways in which they were all connected.

Back at the Baltimore Station, Woody had talked about the circadian rhythm of detox, how the process follows a predictable, scientific pattern. A clock starts ticking from the last time you get high, Woody explained to us, and the period of early recovery lasts between eighteen and twenty-four months.

"It takes time to push out the chemicals, to realign your system," Woody had told us. "It's a biological process of healing, a cycle of ups and downs. It follows a rhythm, just like every other damn thing in the whole universe: the plants, the moon, the waves in the ocean."

Chasing sobriety means surrendering to the process, becoming open to change. It's holding steadfast to constructive principles while also learning to just go with the flow. For many years, I believed that I had to leave the Rez to get clean, leaving behind the chaos and dysfunction, but that ended up not being true. Sobriety isn't about geography. It's something that lives inside you.

By the time I was on my eighth or ninth go-around with rehab, I recognized the patterns. I could anticipate when the irritability and the drug dreams would come, when I'd spend whole days feeling antsy, ready to move on to something more interesting. I knew that between days twenty-five and thirty things tended to get intense—I'd feel like crying for no reason or lash out at someone in my orbit—and I also understood that if I could just white-knuckle it, the wheel would keep turning again and I'd feel something different.

Recovery unfolds in the in-between moments, I learned. It's not an elaborate, festive banquet—it's the steps one takes to produce it. My job was to keep recommitting to sobriety with every tool and skill I'd developed, over and over and over, like a prep cook getting a restaurant kitchen ready each morning for the busy shifts ahead. Each time I start future-tripping, each time I hear the addiction talking and whining about how the world isn't doing me right, isn't meeting my needs, I return to cooking as a way to support my recovery. Chopping and browning onions, brewing a pot of tea, watching the ingredients transform into something beautiful and delicious. Every day, I remind myself that I'm making a conscious decision to ride out any difficult emotions that bubble up without using.

It's overwhelming to feel things again. It sometimes feels like the shame, regret, anger, and sadness that come with sobriety might crush me. I often have to remind myself that there's nothing wrong with me, that this is the unseen process of my trauma and hurt unraveling.

I had learned from Woody that the last organ to detox is the brain. Because alcohol is fat-soluble, he told us, it lingers in the body. Your liver cleans out, along with your intestines, your kidneys, your spleen, and your heart, but the organ you most rely on to understand your reality takes the longest to recover.

For too long, I'd regarded the idea of recovery from a comfortable distance, learning the lingo and the science, but not surrendering to the process, to the mental and spiritual reorganization it demanded. It had been the same way with love. I talked a big game about wanting it in my life, but I let go as soon as I needed to roll up my sleeves.

The same was true, I saw now, with my relationship to the concept of decolonization. I first encountered the term in my twenties and my impression of it coincided with everything I was about at the time—aggression, resisting authority, breaking the rules, lashing out against the system. Back then, the word conjured images of masked protesters out in the streets clashing with the outside forces hell-bent on poisoning our land, stealing our water, harming our people. It was romantic and violent.

In sobriety, a new dimension of decolonization was being revealed to me, one that involved unlearning the stupid, young-man shit that had gotten me into mortal trouble—and learning to soften my heart.

Viewing decolonization primarily as fist-in-the-air rebellion ignores the deep spiritual component of the work. The initial rupture of genocide and land theft has led to decades of ensuing injustices, and all this historical trauma is a major factor in our people's sky-high rates of addiction and suicidality. Pushing society to reckon with and rectify this brutal legacy will always be slow-going, heartbreaking work. I had seen myself how activists and warriors burned hot and eventually flamed out.

A big part of decolonization is figuring out how to move through our everyday lives in a way that replaces division, consumption, turmoil, and confusion with connection, creativity, stability, and purpose. The home front is just as important as the battlefield—it's where we can alter our realities by caring for each other and building healthier, more resilient communities.

Two decades of addiction and dependency had shown me that I was tough enough to survive shattering violence and loss, but was I tough enough to be gentle? Was I tough enough to be humble? Was I tough enough to be loving and patient? This would be the ultimate challenge, my version of the Wu-Tang's 36th Chamber.

+ + + +

In the summer of 2014, Nalin and I exchanged vows we'd written ourselves in front of about three hundred friends, colleagues, and family members. We decided we didn't want to hold our wedding in a Christian church. We wanted it to be a celebration of our life on the Rez—in spite of all the hardships, this was the place where we'd both been able to find peace and to actually feel hopeful.

In the Apache tradition, it was my role to build the camp where the wedding party would gather. In the weeks leading up to our big day, I spent every free moment up at Paradise Creek, working alongside Ari, my cousin Lyle, my nephews Thomas and Sean, and other family members. We built two large Apache shades and a traditional wickiup where my family could live during the preparations. We dug a giant pit in the ground, large enough to slow-cook a whole cow, and hauled and stacked enough wood to keep a fire going for days. Nalin and I planned a menu that included as many Native foods as possible. We reached out to a group of Crown Dancers and asked them to join us.

On a warm June evening, Nalin and I stood in the middle of a large circle. She wore a white camp dress and I wore a black canvas vest over a brand-new white shirt and a traditional loincloth over my beige cargo pants. We both wore moccasins and an eagle feather that carried a medicine man's blessing.

It was a spectacular event. People danced for hours. We ate Apache Pit Barbecue, hunks of beef wrapped in burlap and foil and slow-cooked overnight underground. A bunch of my relatives, along with Chef Mark Mason, who came as my guest, jumped into the pit to take out the earth-braised meat and carve it up. We served it with roasted potatoes, squash, and corn, plus Racket Bread and Acorn Stew. For refreshments, we had fresh spring water from the mountains and hot wild tea.

When Nalin and her daughter had first moved in with me—the hotel manager at the time had offered us two adjoining rooms—we had been nervous about blending our families, but we'd quickly discovered that our kids really enjoyed spending time together. It was fun to eavesdrop on their bubbly, nerdy conversations. During the slower months, our new family of four frequently had the whole hotel to ourselves, jokingly calling it our "mansion." It was like *The Shining*, but happy. We explored every hidden hallway, stairwell, storage room, and exit door in the three-story building, playing epic games of hide-and-seek. We spent a lot of time outside, at the lake and in the surrounding forest.

Looking back, I can see how fortuitous the timing of all this happiness was. The stability and security I had found with Nalin was essential in navigating the increasingly challenging conditions at work. Standing alongside someone who shared my values made it easier to stay true to myself as things came apart.

I had always been asked to make do with a minimal support staff during the low season—one or two cooks, a dishwasher, and a couple of servers—but that summer, after Ronnie Peaches stepped down as general manager, I was allowed to hire only a dishwasher. It became my job to not only prep the menu and set up for service, but greet and seat customers, key in their orders, bring them their drinks, and run back to the kitchen to cook their meals. It was a ridiculous and humiliating process, not because of my ego, but because there was no way to provide good service to the guests who came in, around a dozen tables each night, most of whom were Apaches from our community. The diners were usually nice about it, marveling at the fact I was doing it all myself and assuming my staff had called in sick, but I kept firing off emails to upper management arguing that we were doing damage to the hotel's reputation, threatening future business. It took several weeks of increasingly dire messages to get them to act. Finally, I was allowed to bring in a server to help me, but we still got slammed during every dinner service.

Even once the ski season started that year, I was forced to fight to maintain a staff big enough to handle the demands on our kitchen. As the team and I continued to take on high-profile projects—like teaching a workshop on Indigenous foodways at Washington University in St. Louis and consulting on the menu at Mitsitam—we got some media attention. We were featured in *Food & Wine* magazine's 2014 summer issue, where I'd insisted the writer print the names of all the dishes she mentioned in Apache as well as English. In February 2015, the *Arizona Republic* published a full-page spread on the Summit Restaurant at Sunrise in the newspaper's food section. I was profiled in *Newsweek* and the *Huffington Post*.

I tried to quantify the value of all the publicity and press our restaurant was generating—by my calculations, it added up to something like seven million dollars' worth of advertising. I wrote the management team a report explaining why my staff deserved raises, justifying equipment upgrades. I was ignored.

Each time one of my staff members quit that winter, I was asked to move forward without the position. I felt an immense sense of responsibility to protect what we'd built, but I could see that working at Sunrise wasn't sustainable. The stress and lack of support were taking their toll—I worried they might derail my recovery.

I was eager to explore other professional opportunities. I convinced my bosses to give me a week off so I could travel to Chicago and train as a *stagiaire* at Grace, an up-and-coming restaurant that would go on to be awarded three Michelin stars. I had met Grace's chef, Curtis Duffy, at the Roots conference in Ohio, and I hoped that spending time in his kitchen would provide some much-needed inspiration.

The atmosphere at Grace was modern and serene—one entire wall of the kitchen was covered in ash-wood shelves that held clear bins of every kind of dry good. It was the coolest-looking spice rack of all time. I loved the idea of putting the ingredients front and center like that, and I remember coming back and buying big jars to store the Native ingredients we showcased in our Sunrise menus.

In the summer of 2015, I got another exciting opportunity when I was selected to give the keynote speech at the Rainbow Treatment Center's annual substance abuse prevention conference. I had met Rainbow's clinical director, Mr. Walsh, when we hosted a couple's retreat dinner for the clinic's staff and clients up at the restaurant. It was an honor, four years sober, to be asked to stand up in a roomful of more than eighty clinicians and a couple hundred other community members to talk about the behavioral changes I'd witnessed in myself and the dozens of Apaches who had come through the Sunrise kitchen. I called my presentation "Ancestral Landscape: Sustaining Sobriety Through Neuroplasticity, Power, and Purpose."

"Decolonization is not just a political or legal term," I'd told the audience that day. "Did you know that there are Indigenous researchers like my friend Claudia Serrato looking at how the process can impact individuals on a molecular level in the womb?"

The room was silent.

"Our elders and ancestors always tell us that everything is connected—and it really is. The intergenerational trauma of colonization damaged our DNA and our brain health. So did the drugs we used as a way to try to cope with all the unresolved grief. We lost brain cells in the process of getting high and surviving the violence of addiction."

I clicked to a slide with a definition of *neuroplasticity*: The ability of the brain to change in structure and function in response to experience—when we think, feel, and act in novel ways, we change our brains.

"The phrase several of my addiction counselors used with me, 'Nothing changes if nothing changes,' makes complete sense now! I know that learning a new skill in the kitchen or tasting a new flavor or trying a new recipe creates new neural pathways, healing my mind."

The final slide of my presentation was a glossy shot of our Three Sisters salad.

"Embracing Indigenous foodways is one of the behavioral changes we can make to support our recovery. Did you know that eating beans, squash, and corn together gives you a perfect protein, supporting the growth of brain cells?"

I looked around, reading the room.

"Decolonize your food choices, decolonize your mind!" I finished my talk with a sly grin.

Mr. Walsh had come up to me afterward and asked to meet with me at the Rainbow Treatment Center administrative offices, which were housed in a cluster of squat beige buildings in Whiteriver. He was thinking of launching a vocational program of some kind for people in rehab, and in the meantime, he wondered if I was interested in leading some workshops with his staff. They had loved my presentation and wanted to learn more.

The clinical director of the Rainbow Treatment Center leaned forward, smiling.

"You've got a gift for teaching," he said. "Not everyone can break down complicated topics and make them seem relevant."

I agreed to do presentations with the Rainbow clinicians, teaching them basic kitchen skills and exploring how they related to healing and recovery. It was an opportunity to branch out beyond the grueling restaurant work and circle back to my curiosity about the connection between foods and mental health.

+ + + +

Things finally came to a head at Sunrise in early 2016. The day after New Year's, I received an upsetting call from Rene, our morning-shift server, who informed me that a few of my staff members, including Vina, had been involved in an accident. The van that had picked them up from Sunrise after that morning's shift had lost its rear tire, skidding across the road into the oncoming lane of traffic. Luckily, no one had been hurt, but when I heard that, earlier on that same day, a couple of resort workers had complained to the maintenance department about the vehicle shaking and making strange noises, I was furious they had been ignored.

I marched into my office and typed up a formal, three-page report on Sunrise Park Resort letterhead, telling my supervisors everything that had happened and listing all the vehicular safety issues that had been raised throughout the years.

I am disheartened that it has remained this way for our Apache people, who are the majority of the workforce at Sunrise Park Resort, I wrote. *I am disheartened, because many of our tribal members live in poverty, under circumstances that non-Native management can never fully comprehend.*

I noted that, on several different occasions, managers had voiced their opinion that the employee shuttles were a major hassle. I said I'd even heard one of them say the subpar vans were "a problem that the employees will just have to deal with" and "if they don't like it, they can get their own ride to work."

The attitude that White Mountain Apache Tribal people/employees should be in a position to transport themselves to work on a daily basis if the van is not running is a very disconnected and uninformed perception of the realities of White Mountain Apache life on an "Indian Reservation" in this state and this country at large, I wrote.

I ended my letter with a simple statement: *The condition of our Sunrise Park Resort transport vans have always presented problems for this hotel and its respective employees. I am grateful that none of my em-*

ployees were injured. I do not want to see the well-being of our Apache people minimized through failing to maintain safe operating vehicles and vehicular negligence in terms of inspection protocol.

The next day, Roy, the assistant manager, called me into his office. He was sitting at his desk next to our Human Resources director, a Native woman who told me she was there as a witness. I sat down across from them, feeling my stomach turn.

"Nephi, your letter really hurt my feelings. It makes us worry about you. Don't you like your job? Don't you appreciate everything we do?" Roy flashed me his fake smile. "I spoke to a few of your staff and nobody was hurt. They all told me they were okay."

I took a deep breath, determined to keep my voice steady despite my disgust.

"Thank you for bringing me here to discuss my letter, which is actually about the safety of your employees, and not about you." My tone was stern. "Of course people are going to tell you they're all right—everyone knows that management fires people easily. As their supervisor, it's my job to report gross negligence."

The two of them stared in stunned silence. It dawned on me that this could be it for my job, but I was done caring.

"Why do you have to pull the race card, Nephi?" Roy was no longer fake smiling. "I feel like your letter was reverse racism toward me."

I put up my hand before Roy could continue. I felt like I was going to vomit.

"In order for 'reverse racism' to be a real thing, we'd need to get in a time machine and erase the whole history of colonialism and white supremacy," I said.

I looked over at the HR manager, hoping she'd intervene. I noticed the white, pink, and yellow slips of a carbon copy disciplinary form peeking out from the stack of papers in front of her.

Roy started rattling off petty excuses: "budget constraints," "special dispensations," a bunch of corporate, managerial speak. It was unbelievable how they'd twisted the situation, erasing our legitimate concerns.

I walked out of the meeting and went outside to sit in my truck. My heart was racing, anger pumping through my veins.

I remembered how, back in my addict days, I'd driven away in the middle of a busy dinner service without saying a word to anyone. I had no urge to get fucked up like I did that time, but I did wish I could start the car and go. Things were different now, though. I was doing my best to be a good husband, a responsible father and stepfather. I took pride in being able to cover my bills. The only other real restaurant on the Rez was the one in the Hon-Dah Casino and, as far as working conditions went, it would probably be just as aggravating—a big, typical gaming-operation kitchen with management that saw you as a number before you were a human being.

For the first time in a long time, I had the feeling of wanting to crawl out of my skin and leave my life behind.

TEN

GAS STATION SANCTUARY

A few months after my meeting with Roy, I sat in the passenger seat of a shiny black car, being chauffeured like a VIP. As we passed the Washington Monument, I craned my neck to take in the top of the giant obelisk, where it poked the sky.

In a couple of hours, I was scheduled to start meeting with the managers and chefs at various Smithsonian cafeterias, but for now, Albert—the recruiter who'd made my travel arrangements—was shuttling me around leafy residential neighborhoods with names like Woodley Park and Mount Pleasant. When we had talked on the phone about the possibility of my taking a job in DC, I'd told him I had a family to consider. Albert made sure to point out every local school we passed—their pretty brick buildings and jacked-up playgrounds were a world apart from our barebones Rez schools.

Before my first appointment of the day, a meet-and-greet with the staff at Mitsitam Café, Albert and I stopped by the National Portrait Gallery to grab a coffee. The June sunlight poured down through the Courtyard Café's domed glass ceiling, lighting up the green ferns and pink orchids scattered around the well-dressed professionals chatting and clacking away on their laptops. Thankfully, my Americano was strong. I had been going nonstop since arriving at Reagan National Airport on Sunday, which happened to be Father's Day.

Albert and I first connected about the open head chef position at the National Museum of the American Indian back in April. I'd previously submitted a contract bid to be a consulting chef, sending in dozens of sample menus, but nothing had come of it. But now the current executive chef was moving on and the company managing the Smithsonian's food and beverage program was eager to hire a Native chef to oversee Mitsitam full time. He wondered whether I wanted to throw my hat in the ring.

Executive chef at Mitsitam Café. It was the kind of job a chef dreams of—one that came with a six-figure salary, publicity, prestige, and potential cookbook deals. I submitted my résumé, and, after several rounds of calls, Albert had phoned to tell me I was being flown in for interviews.

Even getting to this point in the process was a huge deal. The last time I'd visited the museum, I'd undercut my message of the grounding, restorative powers of Native foods by partying like a maniac. Now, I was being recognized as both a chef working at the highest level and a Native foods expert, and would return solid in my recovery. This was a chance to redeem myself, to take the amazing work we'd been doing at Sunrise and blast it out to the world.

Mitsitam's first two executive chefs had been non-Natives. Richard Hetzler had opened the restaurant back in 2004, when professional Native cooks still seemed like a rarity. Jerome Grant, who'd taken over for Chef Hetzler in 2014, started his career at a resort in the Caribbean—his parents were Filipino and Jamaican. Now, Chef Grant was being tapped to oversee Sweet Home Café, the restaurant inside the brand-new National Museum of African American History and Culture, which was scheduled to open that September.

Chef Grant had greeted me warmly when we'd met in his office. He'd explained how the restaurant was open three hundred and sixty-four days of the year, and served thousands of customers a day, and that his team regularly catered private events and banquets, pulling resources and chefs from other Smithsonian kitchens.

"It's surreal," Chef Grant said, handing me a binder of printed menus from dinners for various embassies and government departments. "You start out as a young kid, and you never think that one day you'll be cooking for state officials in the nation's capital. It's wild to me that some of the most powerful people in the world are eating our food."

Like cooking on the Death Star, *serving the Sith Lords, Vader, and the Emperor,* I thought to myself. I wondered what he'd think of that analogy.

There were two sous chefs at Mitsitam, Chef informed me, and they both assisted with desk work and ordering.

"We're fortunate to have a solid production team—you demo your dish once and the chefs figure out how to execute. Your role is providing structure and oversight, but mainly you just need to bring your spirit to the kitchen. Native American cuisine is a really new concept, so everyone's interested."

I bit my tongue. As I often reminded the journalists who reached out to interview me about the Native American food "trend," ours was the oldest cuisine in the United States, despite the fact that few people acknowledged it. Our Indigenous landscapes were the "terroir" for regional "American" cuisine.

When I came in during the lunch service on Tuesday, Chef Grant introduced me to about fifteen different cooks who were cranking at their stations. I was relieved to see that none of the staff looked familiar—I was worried someone might recognize me as the dumbass who hadn't shown up for his own workshop.

The Mitsitam crew was extremely fast and hardworking. What would it be like, stepping into a well-oiled operation like this? It would be a relief not to have to run up and down stairs every day lugging heavy boxes or cobble together my own marketing. I'd never have to beg for permission to do meaningful programming.

Over the next few hours, Albert and I toured one museum after the next, accompanied by a rotating cast of corporate types wearing black and navy. The trippiest part of the whole experience was walking by the Arts + Industries Building on our way to the Smithsonian Castle; as soon as I saw the ornate red building with its infinite windows, I was flooded with memories of our family vacation in DC during the summer of 1993, when I was thirteen. It was my first time on the East Coast and I remember we spent the day sightseeing, posing for photographs in front of monuments I recognized from movies and books.

I hadn't thought about that trip in years. At the time, I was too much of a teenager to appreciate how impressive it was that my father had been invited to exhibit his *Muttonman* art at the Smithsonian. Now, I saw flashes of Dad getting ready for his show, which was called "Muttonman Discovers Columbus," flipping through folders of his printed comic strips and consulting us on which ones we thought he should include. I remembered hanging out in our backyard while he painted a person-size rendition of his Navajo superhero, which would be installed in the museum lobby. Once he was finished, he custom-built a wooden shipping container because he didn't want to send his artwork across the country in a crappy cardboard box.

I felt myself choke up, but thankfully another one of our companions started quizzing me on the sales volume at Sunrise, puffing his chest as he informed me that Mitsitam brought in approximately $6.5 million a year, an impressive figure, I had to admit.

One thing was for certain—this was, by far, the biggest job I'd ever been considered for, an opportunity to make my mark in a cosmopolitan food city. I imagined Chef Thompson reading about my hiring in the *New York Times*, shaking his head and smiling, relieved to see that I had made it. I thought of Chef Whelan. *Was he still teaching?* I pictured him sharing my bio with his students, telling them he'd been my instructor in culinary school and now I was leading a multimillion-dollar operation. I hadn't spoken with Harry Todachine since leaving the Durango Jail, but I could hear his voice in my head just as clearly as he was standing next to me. *Hell, yeah, Nephi! You did it.*

There was a part of me that still craved this sort of validation. I wanted, once and for all, to erase people's doubts, to show them that I knew what I was doing. Another part of me, though, felt deeply uneasy about leaving the mountains and living in the capital. It felt like moving into the belly of the beast.

+ + + +

I didn't have time to dwell on my visit. The morning after my flight, I was back in my office at Sunrise tackling a long to-do list. Late in the afternoon, I called Mr. Walsh to check in about my most recent presentation for the clinical staff at the Rainbow Treatment Center, which I'd called Apache Cognitive Evolution. The training had revolved around Apache values, traditions, cultural norms, and cultural expectations, and we'd had a lively discussion about "rearranging" existing ancestral knowledge to help individuals recover from trauma. Mr. Walsh said a number of therapists had requested a follow-up session and asked if we could schedule a date. I replied that I needed to wait a couple of weeks—I was waiting to hear about a big job out on the East Coast.

"I'm not surprised," Mr. Walsh said, congratulating me. "What you're doing is very powerful."

He continued. "I'd like to show you something, Nephi. The center recently acquired an empty space for a vocational facility of some sort. We're not exactly sure what to do with it or how it will connect with our other relapse prevention programs, but I'm hoping you'd be willing to come by and give me your thoughts."

The following week, I pulled up to an abandoned gas station on the north side of Whiteriver that I remembered from my years bumming around the Rez—we called it the North Fork Store. The place had closed down a few years back and there were no prices listed on the tall sign advertising UNLEADED, SUPREME, and DIESEL, but there were a number of official tribal vehicles parked in the lot. I parked next to them, stepping over scattered trash as I got out of my truck.

A few people stood huddled by the side door of the shop, which had clearly been crowbarred open. The deadbolt hung bent and useless.

"Tribal Police are on their way," said a guy in an agency security guard uniform. "Looks like we had a break-in last night."

Another white van pulled up, and Mr. Walsh jumped out of the driver's seat, quickly assessing the situation.

"What a first impression, huh?" He shook my hand, letting out a nervous chuckle. "Life on life's terms, I guess."

Mr. Walsh's colleagues assured him it was okay to go inside. They'd wait for the cops, but they didn't think there was any point in launching a formal investigation.

"A bunch of bored teenagers," the security guard mumbled.

The layout was exactly as I remembered it—three aisles of shelves that had once been crammed with convenience store junk food—but everything had been trashed. The soda fountain in the corner was busted, as was the old FUNacho cheese sauce dispenser next to it. Underneath the coffee station, multiple pots lay shattered, and the refrigerated cabinet doors that used to hold soft drinks, prepackaged sandwiches, and basics like bologna, sliced cheese, and eggs had been smashed. There was glass all over the floor and the vandals had stomped on old packets of ketchup and mustard, spattering red and yellow across the linoleum. Every wall had been tagged.

"We're not going to re-open as another place that sells fast food, soda, or Ho Hos," said Mr. Walsh, eager to stay on topic. "There's enough of that already."

"True," I said. I suddenly felt like laughing. My life was crazy—from the grand polish of the Smithsonian to this in the span of a week.

Mr. Walsh dragged his foot across the dirty floor. "I think we could do something interesting here, give people hands-on job skills training."

I looked around, thinking of all the tiny izakaya and ramen shops I'd visited in Osaka. I remember marveling at how organized those tiny eateries were, how they turned out exquisite food in kitchens the size of a broom closet. There wasn't really an inviting gathering space like that anywhere on the reservation—and definitely not one that served beautiful food. Growing up, families ate out at the Whiteriver Restaurant, which served delicious, greasy BBQ beef ribs as big as Fred Flintstone's, but as our community's struggles intensified, the place had gone downhill, eventually shuttering its doors. Sometime after I graduated from high school, a drive-thru Burger King opened in Whiteriver, but the nearest nice coffee shop or restaurant was a good thirty-minute drive into the US of A.

I glanced over at the padlocked front doors just as some clouds shifted, allowing the sun to light up the shards of glass like crystals. I turned back around and, in a flash, my brain conjured up an image of a small, neat kitchen with stainless steel counters and a forest green backsplash. I quickly calculated how many four-tops could fit in the front.

"What if Rainbow ran a café that functioned as an extension of your clinical program?" I wondered out loud. "Hands-on culinary training and nutritional education with a recovery focus?"

Mr. Walsh lifted his head, glancing around the room again.

"It's just twenty-three hundred square feet. Isn't that too small for a proper kitchen?"

I did some quick calculations in my head. Mitsitam's production kitchen was probably three times the size of the entire store. On the other hand, the kitchen at Sunrise was just around fourteen hundred square feet.

"It would be a challenge," I said, "but I think you could make it work. The dining room could double as a space for group meetings."

Mr. Walsh asked me to think about whether I'd be interested in consulting on the project and I hurried back to work. The next day, I received a call from Albert—the Smithsonian team was excited for me to come on board as Mitsitam's next executive chef.

+ + + +

There's a spot along the road from Sunrise Park Resort where, on a clear day, you can see all the way down to Phoenix-Scottsdale, the sprawling metropolitan area Arizonans refer to as "the Valley." The same day I was offered the job in DC, I headed over there to try to clear my head. I parked my truck on the side of the road, angling it so I could sit on the flatbed and take in the view. I grabbed my thermos, took a sip of coffee, and began my prayer.

"Hey, Dad. Hey, ancestors," I spoke out loud. "I don't know what to do. I've come to a fork in the road."

It was time to leave Sunrise, I told the mountains. Two exciting professional opportunities had materialized, and I knew both of them would be challenging and rewarding. It was time for me to commit one way or another.

"One comes with major perks and recognition, but it'd mean leaving this place," I continued. "The other is an opportunity to build something meaningful for us Apaches."

It was a cloudless July night. Light pollution from the city that spilled over the hills and valleys that separated our White Mountains from the sprawling desert below, dimming the stars.

I sighed. Like so many aspects of my life, Phoenix stirred up lots of mixed feelings. It was the "big city" for me growing up, the place where I first got interested in restaurants, where I'd first tried pho, birria, and other favorite dishes. It was the place I became a chef. But Phoenix was also where my addictions had taken over, where I'd been fired and arrested and thrown in jail multiple times. It was where I'd become a father, but also where my first marriage had collapsed.

Recently, I'd reconnected with an older relative of mine, my mom's cousin, who had spent more than a decade as the cultural resource director for Nohwike' Bágowa, our tribe's amazing, underfunded museum, and he'd told me about his role in pushing the White Mountain Apache Tribe Water Rights Quantification Act, a bill that had been passed into law back in 2010. Our ancestral territory encompasses five hundred springs, twenty-six lakes, and some four hundred miles of creeks, streams, and rivers, my uncle told me. This legislation, he said, was intended to protect our access to this sacred resource.

In actuality, though, very little of the seventeen billion gallons earmarked for the Tribe's use remained in our ancestral lands—the infrastructure to store and circulate it on the reservation simply didn't exist. Instead, the White and Black Rivers ran into the Salt River, which, in turn, fed into the Gila. Almost all of this water, he observed, eventually made its way down to the Phoenix-Scottsdale area, where there were seven huge municipal reservoirs.

"Water from our mountains makes all those lawns and swimming pools and golf courses possible," he said, his gravelly voice tinged with sadness.

As I stared down at the populous valley, a thought popped into my head: *I don't want to be like that. I don't want to export our ancestral knowledge.*

I'd spent almost nine years now at Sunrise, learning so much from different community members and elders. I'd witnessed what a group of Apaches was capable of—our team had accomplished so much with next to nothing. I pictured Nancy, Vina, Vinny, Juwon, and Randall posing for a photograph in their matching chef's jackets, their faces beaming with pride. Learning about Indigenous foodways gave our demanding, low-paid jobs deeper significance. We were on a mission, which made us incredibly powerful.

Accepting the Mitsitam job would cement my professional reputation and propel me into a new pay scale, but it would also mean taking all the valuable information I'd scouted—all the lessons learned, the battles fought and won—and channeling it into the specials we served random tourists. I'd have a huge platform to showcase the breadth and diversity of Indigenous cuisine, but, at the end of the day, I'd be working in a cafeteria setting.

The whole time I'd been in DC, I'd been on edge, although I had struggled to articulate why. Here, looking out at the dark, quiet expanse that once filled my ancestors with a sense of wonder, I thought of the uneasiness I'd felt walking through the Museum of the American Indian, among carefully assembled displays of sacred artifacts removed from their rightful landscapes. I'd been surrounded by ghosts.

"I'm gonna circulate all this food wisdom here." I blurted out my decision, letting the cosmos know I'd gotten the message. "I want to give our people hope."

I was positive my dad would hear me, and I knew he would understand.

+ + + +

Albert sounded stunned when I called to turn down the offer. Mr. Walsh, on the other hand, took the news in stride.

"Ready to get to work?" he asked once I told him I'd decided to stay in Whiteriver. "I'll put together a contract for us to review."

I hung up the phone, swiveling my government-issue, squeaky green chair so I could look out the window at the mountains I trusted and loved. I had just turned down the type of opportunity young Nephi had dreamed of—and, mostly, I felt relieved. For a long time, I suspected I wouldn't live to see my thirty-fifth birthday, but now, here I was: thirty-six and more than four years sober. Nothing about my life looked like what I had imagined or planned, but that's how surrender worked.

I was done chasing anyone else's definition of success.

Like an Apache scout, I would use all the tools at my disposal to blaze my own path, as difficult as that might be. I wanted whatever I did next to contribute to the cause of Indigenous food sovereignty, establishing food-based practices that could help Native communities become more self-reliant and self-sustaining.

In my heart, I'd always felt that we were just scratching the surface at Sunrise. I knew that I wanted to do something different, something scary. I thought of my favorite old book *Great Chefs of France*, with all of these greats toiling away in kitchens deep in the French countryside. I knew the right people would find their way to us and, in the meantime, I'd be doing something to help Native people save their own lives.

As often happens, the universe had the last laugh that day, showing me that there had only ever been this one direction.

When Nalin came home from work and I told her about my conversations with Albert and Mr. Walsh, she announced that she also had something important to tell me.

"I'm pregnant," she blurted out as soon as she sat down in our one armchair.

I don't remember exactly the words that came out of my mouth, but I'm sure it was something deep like "Oh, shit. That's awesome!"

I do recall that we hugged each other tight, and Nalin explained that she'd been waiting to tell me the news, because she wanted to make sure I made the decision that was right for me. She confessed she had been worried about the DC job and was relieved that we would continue growing our little family on the Rez.

Finding out that I was going to become a father again, this time in recovery, made it even more clear that I had made the right decision. Our baby would grow up just like we did—Dził Łigai Si'án N'de*e*, *children of the White Mountains.* Even before I gave official notice at Sunrise, Nalin and I found a small three-bedroom near Whiteriver. There were still many unknowns in our lives, but we wanted to make a home, a place that was ours.

+ + + +

My last day at the Sunrise Park Resort was October 11, 2016, and by that point, I was almost done with a business plan for the gas station project, which I'd agreed to take on as a consultant. Mr. Walsh had finally gotten the green light to bring me on full time to launch Rainbow's clinical nutrition program and open a café that would serve the community and provide culinary skills training. We agreed on a dual title: Nutritional Recovery Program Coordinator and Executive Chef.

Moving from the hospitality industry to the mental health sector took some getting used to. As a chef, you're expected to keep crazy hours and operate at max intensity, but my new boss frequently reminded me that he expected me to work at a measured pace.

"We're developing something entirely new, and it's going to take time," Mr. Walsh said during one of our meetings that fall. "Remember that you are more important than the work, Nephi. If you don't learn to prioritize yourself, you're going to run into problems. Longevity is the best way to make an impact."

Nobody in my professional life had ever told me to slow down. Chefs are rewarded for being fast and hyper-focused and, historically, restaurants are the worst when it comes to work-life balance. "Work hard, party hard" is definitely the prevailing mantra—behaving like a maniac is a badge of honor in our industry.

One of the aspects of working in a mental health agency is that you are expected to take care of yourself. After years of neglecting my health, I scheduled routine doctors' appointments, found a dentist, got a prescription for glasses. Mr. Walsh had helped me understand that I still operated like a person living in constant upheaval. I needed to see for myself that I could ease up without everything falling apart.

While we went through endless rounds of reviews for the project, I began putting together the curriculum for Rainbow's new

Nutritional Recovery program, lesson plans where clients would pick up basic cooking skills while discussing topics related to behavioral health. I had a deep knowledge base, but the best thing I could do for them was teach them to stick to the basics.

The first class I developed involved making an omelet. I'd introduce my demo by explaining that cooking eggs was one of the first things you learned in culinary school and that even though it was simple, you needed to follow the steps carefully to get a perfectly fluffy omelet. I'd demonstrate how to crack eggs on the side of a bowl with a firm flick of the wrist, whisk until the mixture was a frothy yellow, evenly coat the pan with butter and oil, and use a spatula to draw the more cooked bits into the center, giving the more liquid parts more surface area. Last but not least, I'd show them how to execute a clean flip without using a spatula.

The theme of the class would be anticipating the challenges of early recovery and taking steps to stay the course, I explained in my lesson plan. *In recovery, the healing is in the doing*, I wrote. Preparing an omelet can remind us to focus on the things we could control. During those precarious early days of sobriety, there usually wasn't much in the fridge, but if you could get your hands on a carton of eggs, you could whip up a meal. It was a simple way for someone to make their life feel a little less chaotic.

We launched our Nutritional Recovery groups in the main building of the Rainbow Treatment Center, which housed up to sixteen male residents at a time.

"How many of you are scared right now?" I asked my very first group after I finished my omelet and told them it was their turn. Almost everyone raised a hand, grumbling and making crude jokes about eggs and sausages.

I fixed the group with a stare, willing them to quiet down. "How many of you trust me?" I asked, relieved when a majority of the men raised a hand again.

"This is how you're going to stay sober," I said. "Watch other people in recovery, trust them enough to let them guide you, and practice humility, admitting when you don't know what you're doing. Recovery is a life skill, just like cooking an omelet."

Cooking had become a lifeline for me in sobriety, keeping me anchored in a daily routine, I explained, as each participant grabbed a bowl and started following the instructions I'd scribbled out on a whiteboard. At the beginning of our session, we'd gone around the circle, sharing how many times we'd each been through rehab; the group average was four.

"Maybe some of the skills you pick up in our sessions together will be helpful to your own recovery," I said, "but you'll have to figure out for yourself what helps you stay clean and grounded."

I watched a guy named Pat fish shells out of his bowl, flashing him an encouraging smile.

"Scientists learn the most from their failures. Breakthroughs only happen occasionally, and only because someone kept testing and testing and testing."

Once the men were done with their prep, I invited them to come up one at a time to cook their omelet. The group volunteered Kaylen—this burly guy with dozens of gang and prison tattoos on his neck and arms, who I recognized as a regular at one of my dealer's houses—to go first, and everyone huddled around to watch.

"All right, gentlemen, he's going to flip the omelet like a pro," I said, once the eggs in his pan had set.

I turned to speak directly to Kaylen, lowering my voice.

"Swirl the pan and visualize yourself flipping and catching the omelet. Don't wait too long because the omelet will burn, but do it on your own terms, brother."

Kaylen sneered at me, exposing the space where he'd lost a tooth in a brawl, but then he turned back to the stove, wrinkled his face in concentration, and swirled the pan in one smooth motion. Before I could say anything more, he lifted his pan, exposing the bright blue flame of the range, and flicked his omelet into the air, which went much higher than I had demonstrated.

It was like watching a field goal kick at the end of the Super Bowl. The whole room held their breath as Kaylen's omelet flipped midair and he caught it calmly in his sauté pan.

The men all shouted in unison, giving each other high-fives and knuckles. "FUCK YEAH!!!" "WOOO!" "Awww, sheeeit!"

Kaylen stood still. When he broke into a huge grin, he no longer seemed like a hardened convict. He looked like a kid on the winning team.

Later, when we all sat down to eat and there was a lull in the noisy banter, I returned to the theme of the class.

"Recovery is about facing our fears and sitting with our vulnerabilities," I observed. "We think it's gonna be this big, scary thing, but it can actually be cool and fun. I mean, look at yourselves, it's like a party up in here!"

I looked around the table.

"Each of you is an expert in your addictions and every time you come back to treatment, you're continuing your education as a behavioral scientist. You're getting closer to figuring your recovery out."

+ + + +

When the student is ready, the teacher will appear, Woody used to tell us, and, over the years, I've definitely found this to be true.

Amaranth is an Indigenous cultivar I encountered late in my cooking path, when I staged at Grace in Chicago, during my final season at Sunrise. Diners at Grace chose one of two prix fixe menus—Flora or Fauna—and that week, I was assigned to help plate one of the Flora courses: pureed amaranth greens topped with a medley of baby winter vegetables and set in a ring of frozen hibiscus. With its vibrant contrast of red and green, the dish looked like a modern painting—and it was finished with a pile of delicate, white-gold puffs that we spooned out of a clear container.

I asked the sous chef I'd been assigned to help what they were. "They look like miniature popcorn!"

He handed me a clean spoon. "It's puffed amaranth—try some."

The texture was, in fact, popcorn-like: airy with a little crunch. I really liked the subtle nutty flavor.

When I returned to the Rez, I read up on amaranth, an ingredient that was becoming increasingly popular thanks to its reputation as a "complete protein," but one that I rarely used in my own kitchen. It surprised me to discover that wild amaranth was a cousin of lambsquarters, a type of greens that grows wild in our mountains and that I used sometimes to make a bright green sauce.

Amaranth had been domesticated in Mesoamerica approximately eight thousand years ago from wild seeds, becoming a staple crop for the Incas, Mayans, and Aztecs, who cooked and ate both the plant's protein-packed seeds and its nutrient-dense leaves. As popular as beans and corn at one time, amaranth was one of the most important food sources in the Americas for centuries—until the Spanish banned its cultivation and use.

For the Aztecs, amaranth was a divine plant. They mixed its seeds with honey to create sculptures of their gods, which might explain why the colonizers viewed it with suspicion and insisted on replacing this revered staple food with more familiar, "Christian" crops like wheat and spinach. By that point, however, amaranth had migrated up from Mesoamerica into the American Southwest, thanks to Indigenous peoples' intricate trade routes. Farmers in the region had adopted it, finding it to be a perfect crop for our arid climate. One of the amazing things about amaranth is how little water it requires to grow, making it extremely drought tolerant. Starting in the 1970s, with the advent of healthy-eating diets, demand for amaranth had started increasing, allowing it to make a comeback as an agricultural mainstay in countries like Mexico, Guatemala, and Peru. It was just another example of Western science catching up with Indigenous science, touting amaranth as a powerhouse food and an invaluable crop for our warming planet's future.

Finding out that amaranth, lambsquarters, and quinoa were all related made me think about our Apache and Navajo clan systems—I liked knowing that these sacred plants were also related through a vast family network and that they shared a rich nutritional language.

I ordered amaranth seeds from a supplier of heirloom ingredients, determined to teach myself how to "puff" them. After a couple of failed experiments resulting in scorched black pebbles, I got the temperature and timing just right. The trick, I figured out, was getting the pan hot, to about 470 degrees, and adding just the right amount of amaranth so the pan wasn't too crowded. Once the seeds start to pop, you cover the pan with a lid and keep moving it on and off the heat so the seeds don't burn.

Popping amaranth quickly became one of my favorite things to do in the kitchen. I found it miraculous, how each tiny sphere exploded, turning itself inside-out into a shape that, to my mind, resembled a fertilized egg, the infinity sign, or the Eta Carinae—a star cluster viewed through the Hubble telescope that gives off four million times more energy than our sun. Shaking the pan, I thought about how I was a conduit, helping to set off a handful of little Big Bangs. I thought about lives beginning and ending, saying, "Ahéhye'é Bik'ehgo'ihi'dań." *Thank you, Creator.*

Now, any time I felt overwhelmed about work—I'd never done anything like this, starting a food operation from scratch—I reminded myself to think about amaranth. *Remember how each little seed contains a universe*, I'd tell myself. *Remember that, all along, you carried the tools for your recovery inside you.*

I was creating something new, but I would be drawing on every experience, discovery, and idea that had gotten me to this point. Like an Apache scout, I'd gone out into the world to gather valuable intel—and now it was time to put it to use.

✦ ✦ ✦ ✦

Each step of the planning process for the gas station project took longer than expected. There was so much paperwork involved in securing permits and approvals and funding—months passed, then a year, then two. There was nothing unique about our situation. It has always been a challenge, getting things done on the Rez. There have always been layers of bureaucracy to navigate at the tribal, state, and federal levels.

On the bright side, I was busy gaining valuable experience as a clinician with Rainbow's Nutritional Recovery groups. A few months in, Mr. Walsh encouraged me to attend his behavioral health technician training so that I could get credentialed and collaborate on treatment plans for the center's clients.

"You'll be observing individuals in a very different setting," he explained. "Only a licensed therapist can make an official diagnosis and clinical recommendations, but a BHT provides additional perspectives, which leads to better outcomes."

"Like prep cooks," I thought out loud.

Mr. Walsh looked confused.

"They've got technical skills and real-life experience in busy kitchens. They make the head chef's job easier."

It wasn't the first time I had considered becoming a counselor. My whole life, I'd loved collecting new words and learning their meanings—and years of dipping in and out of different therapeutic and drug treatment programs had introduced me to an entire new language I came to embrace. The question of what made me the way I was had always fascinated me. Even in the throes of addiction, I had remained curious, determined to understand my bad decisions. *Why did I use? Why can't I stop? How have I arrived at this place?* Mr. Walsh informed me that a portion of the hours I had spent in treatment centers myself would count toward my BHT certification, and so I decided it was time to cut the bullshit and finally walk the walk.

I quickly discovered that I was just as passionate about this work as I was about cooking. There were so many connections to the culinary and cultural knowledge I already had. I signed up with the Gorski-CENAPS organization to become an Advanced Certified Relapse Prevention Specialist (ACRPS).

In order to fulfill the case study requirement, I needed to find a client to work with, someone who wasn't in formal treatment. A friend of a friend connected me with a twenty-nine-year-old named Sam whose drugs of choice were alcohol and meth. He'd grown up down the road from me, in the town of McNary, very poor, with both his parents drinking and drugging. Sam and I worked together for nine months, going through his whole story, discussing his struggles and difficult family dynamics. A big part of the work was interviewing him about how he pictured recovery. I explained that his perspective was critical to creating a treatment plan that could really stick.

Sam's entire life was out of order. He was juggling legal issues related to a few different car wrecks, he'd just experienced the destabilizing loss of a close family member, and in the last few months we worked together, he'd started vomiting and defecating blood. My recommendation was that he enter an intensive inpatient program, and I submitted a complete report as the last step in receiving my accreditation. It made me a little sad when I found out that the young man had opted for one-on-one therapy through Behavioral Health Services instead, but it was a good reminder that I couldn't control what the people I worked with decided to do. I wasn't their savior.

A big part of early recovery and long-term sobriety is learning to look out for yourself—and not in the street-life, gangster way. It means going back to the lessons that, if you're lucky, they teach you in kindergarten: drink more water, get enough sleep, eat healthy, exercise, find things that make you happy, and ask for help when you're down. For a grown person who's emerged from the war zone of addiction, it can be very difficult to admit you don't know the ABCs of self-care. That stress and shame can actually contribute to relapse, further enforcing an individual's perception that they're a lost cause. Getting a handle on the basics is the key to crossing over into the maintenance phase of sobriety.

I brought something to the table that no other Rainbow staff member did—I wore a chef's hat. Not only could I help people in different stages of recovery make better food choices, I could train them to work in restaurant settings, helping them find employment once they were stabilized. I could teach anyone how to whip up easy, tasty meals, equipping them to take good care of themselves and the people they loved. It was so gratifying to use my passion for cooking to help others get their lives back on track.

+ + + +

Clara Craig joined us on a freezing night in February 2017 at the hospital in Show Low, on ancestral Apache Land. When Nalin and I first found out that we were having a baby girl, I was nervous and excited. I'd grown up around a bunch of boys and the main way I interacted with my cousin-sisters was acting all tough around them and "protecting" them whenever we were playing in a big group. Watching Nalin raise her daughter made me wonder what the experience would be like, and whether I'd be good at it. My concept of "a man's role" had changed dramatically over the years, particularly in recovery. I'd gotten a crash course in toxic masculinity working in professional kitchens and hanging out in rough circles, and by the time I got sober, I'd figured out I didn't want any part of it.

I didn't want to be one of those shitheads who somehow got a pass because they were raising a daughter. I wanted to earn my reputation as a responsible parent. Clara had huge brown eyes and the same dimple I got from my mother's family. Right from the beginning, it was clear to me she was sweet, strong, and creative. She started walking right around her first birthday, trailing me through the house in these little pink moccasins. Once her thick hair was long enough, we tied it in a tiny ponytail on the top of her head. I loved being the first one awake at five thirty every workday, waking up my daughter, getting her changed and ready for daycare. I loved mise en place–ing her diaper bag and driving her to Whiteriver, listening to acoustic guitar music by John Frusciante. I couldn't wait to hold her hand in public, learn to braid her hair, and buy her a mini chef's toque for her to wear when she helped me in the kitchen. Being Clara's father was a gift to my recovery. She was my reminder to stay diligent, to remain caring and soft.

Soon after Clara turned one, Nalin and I found out we were expecting another addition to our family, and that this time, it was a boy. Donny Craig was born in October 2018, and just like I'd done with both Ari and Clara, I was the first one to wash baby Donny's hair after he was born.

Donny Craig had the biggest baby cheeks I'd ever seen, with a slanted dimple on his right cheek that he inherited from Nalin's father. Sitting quietly in his bouncer, he'd observe our household with dark brown eyes that seemed to see everything.

In recovery, I had fully grasped the enormity of my own father's influence; he helped save me. Since getting clean, I was more present in Ari's life, and in 2019, he moved in with us full time. I was glad I could show him that I really meant what I'd said, that we'd always stick together.

Fatherhood in sobriety, I've discovered, is an experience that blows open your heart, your mind, and your spirit. During the first few years of our little ones' lives, I lovingly stocked the freezer with quarts and quarts of homemade baby food. I stacked the plastic containers neatly, labeling and dating each one just as I would in my restaurant kitchen: Acorn squash. Butternut squash mixed with toasted white quinoa. Purple potatoes. I introduced my kids to as many Indigenous foods as possible. I hadn't learned much about my ancestors' culinary traditions until later in life, but I wanted my children to grow up with these familiar flavors, to see them as old friends.

This is the most important dinner service in the world right now, I'd think, spooning pureed Apache squash into little Clara's mouth or feeding little Donny his quinoa porridge, his big, brown eyes lighting up with anticipation. I thought about how decolonization can happen on a molecular level—I was activating my babies' taste buds and their appreciation for Native flavors. After going through hell, these moments reminded me it was possible to create our own versions of heaven.

+ + + +

While it might have been easier to hire an architect, I knew I was capable of putting together a simple design for our gas station conversion. I had years of experience working in restaurants, but, most importantly, I understood what we were trying to accomplish—and it wasn't like any other food establishment I'd ever heard of. Our casual eatery needed to double as a therapeutic environment for Indigenous people in the process of transforming their lives.

Our space needed to be beautiful, but it wasn't really a matter of aesthetics. Our spot was, in mental health lingo, a site for trauma-informed care—every individual who walked through our doors was someone who was directly impacted by the historical violence rained down on Native Americans and its aftereffects. Our staff, clients, and customers would all be dealing with issues related to poverty. They might be recovering from addiction themselves, or have loved ones who were struggling. Many would be experiencing health problems, or dealing with anxiety, grief, or depression.

My hope was that our café could be a turning point, a place that provided comfort or even a fresh start. But I also knew the reality of Native people's lives, and, as bleak as it sounded, I knew that, for some people, our services might constitute end-of-life care, a brief respite from hardship and struggle. I wanted to make each and every person feel welcomed and respected. I wanted them to understand that they were worthy, that they belonged in the kind of intimate, thoughtful restaurant that I loved.

I traced the existing convenience store layout onto a pad of graph paper, filling page after page with different placements of ranges, exhaust hoods, counters, and sinks, and drawing arrows to indicate the traffic flow of customers and deliveries.

One of my drawings featured a small central cooking island with different workstation counters organized around it, but a contractor I consulted pointed out that it would necessitate cutting into the ceiling in a way that would compromise the structure of the roof. I sketched a short, straight, American-style kitchen line, but realized it would be too cramped, plus, having cooks standing side-by-side wasn't a great way to foster learning or collaboration.

I flipped to a fresh page, placing an L-shaped island in the center. I imagined people clustered around it, looking each other in the eyes and chatting comfortably. I sketched a hotline along the back wall: a dual French flat-top next to a double-burner range with a griddle. Under those, I drew boxes for the top-of-the-line Jade convection ovens I would place beneath them. Finally, in the corner, near the crowbarred side door, I drew a hearth where we could cook, Apache-style, on an open fire. I figured that placement would be easy to vent.

Each iteration got better. I loved how the L-shaped prep counter not only maximized our workspace but made it easy for a cook anywhere in the kitchen to turn around and pass a dish they were working on so that the next person could add to it, topping a salad with warm ingredients or putting a composed sandwich on the grill. This setup, I believed, would promote interdependence, getting cooks out of that selfish me-and-my-station mode and teaching them that everything ran more smoothly when they collaborated and looked out for each other.

We purchased the All-Clad cookware they used at Mary Elaine's, which were a revelation after working with aluminum pots and pans. I also installed the Eco-Grip floors I'd first seen when I was given time off from Rainbow to stage at SingleThread and the Restaurant at Meadowood, two celebrated restaurants in California that operated their own farms. After decades of hauling out dirty floor mats to be scrubbed and pressure-washed, this flooring seemed miraculous—in addition to being easy to clean, it was nonslip and giving, all-around better for workers. I also planned to re-create SingleThread's cooled prep area, which was kept at 55 degrees. We'd be working with an abundance of wild Apache foods and produce from the People's Farm, and I wanted to treat these Indigenous ingredients with special care and respect, making sure nothing wilted in our hot kitchen. This refrigerated prep area would also be the perfect environment for cutting meat, poultry, and fish.

Above all, I knew I wanted an open kitchen, separated from our dining area by a half wall that even the shortest Apache grandma could see over. The appeal of an open-kitchen plan is that guests can see for themselves that a team is prioritizing cleanliness and food safety. In the context of the café we were building, however, it would mean so much more. Every person who came into our restaurant would be witnessing Natives becoming skilled cooks. Guests would be able to hear every conversation happening in our kitchen, which would keep the team accountable, communicating mindfully and respectfully.

Transparency became the guiding principle for my design. What would it look like to extend that idea to every corner of the space we were conceiving? Grace's spice wall was part of the inspiration for my sketch of a large window so people could look into our walk-in and cooled prep room and see our beautiful ingredients, carefully organized, and our staff working cleanly.

Addictive behaviors go hand-in-hand with secrecy, dishonesty, and shame—and so, for people in recovery, transparency is a conscious choice, a behavioral skill they must practice and strengthen. I wanted to give people in my kitchen the ability to live their recovery in public. Beyond serving delicious, healthy food on the Rez, it was the reason for this place to exist.

+ + + +

Settling on a name proved more of a challenge.

Initially, I'd considered a catchy, one-word name for the café, a hot trend at the time with restaurants like Grace, Alinea, and Noma getting named to various best-of lists. *Amaranth? Sumac? Or, maybe, Mogollon?* While I already knew that the restaurant we built was going to be beautiful inside, I didn't want it to come across as fine dining. I wanted to avoid names that could come across as fancy and pretentious.

Almost every person I consulted advocated for a straightforward name that leaned into our gas station location, something like North Fork Kitchen or Rainbow Café. I liked the term *café*, because it made clear that this was a place where you could stop by for a bite without a whole lot of fuss and because our plans included a full-service espresso bar.

Although I knew that the kind of clean, seasonal dishes I wanted to serve weren't what most of my neighbors thought of as "Native" food, I wanted our name to reflect that our entire operation was rooted in Indigenous culture.

Gozhóó. This familiar Ndee word presented itself, reminding me of its meaning: balance, harmony, and beauty. Even for a person with a very limited grasp of the Apache language, *gozhóó* was part of my vocabulary. People used it in daily interactions, like "gozhóó łbii" (*good morning*) or "Shił'gozhóó" (*I'm happy*).

A name like Café Gozhóó would not only marry the Western term for a welcoming, daytime eatery and this soulful Indigenous term, but also—for those in the know—communicate that our mission was much broader than just slinging sandwiches and lattes.

Deeply interwoven into the word *gozhóó* is the concept of cosmic balance. When you're out foraging wild foods, you're in tune with the landscape, that's gozhóó. So is prayer and participating in sweat lodge. Every ceremony where we sing and dance in unison, every enlivening conversation with a friend—all of that is gozhóó. We're in harmony with ourselves and each other.

In my own life, gozhóó represented the lived experience of recovery, which I understood as a process of figuring out how to regain balance. As a word, *gozhóó* is both deep and light, conversational and heavy. It's like that with sobriety, too—a weighty, charged term that really just means putting one foot in front of the other.

Whether anyone else understood it that way, calling our restaurant Café Gozhóó was an act of resistance and resurgence. It was a reminder that we are the experts on taking care of ourselves, that traditional Indigenous knowledge doesn't need a clinical or government stamp of approval. It doesn't need validation from Western science.

By staying in the White Mountains to build this program, I had faced my fear of failure. I'd taken a giant leap of faith in *us* and not the system. I hoped I could inspire people who came through our groups and the café to do the same.

+ + + +

We finally broke ground in late 2018, working from my hand-drawn sketches. Next, I needed to put together a team, which, like everything else about the creation of Café Gozhóó, was anything but straightforward.

We advertised for a range of positions, including a *chef de cuisine* to help oversee kitchen operations and collaborate with me on menu development, several *commis* (apprentice cooks) and *chefs de partie* (chefs of a station), a barista, and a manager and assistant manager to take care of logistics and everything front-of-house.

Mr. Walsh had once remarked that the people I hired for the gas station project would need to be "really special," and that definitely turned out to be true. Many applicants sent in résumés thinking they were applying for typical food and beverage positions. They had strong work experience, but they were taken aback when, during the interview process, I explained that one of the requirements of the job was no drinking or doing drugs, on- or off-site, since we were under the auspices of the Rainbow Treatment Center. None of the positions at Café Gozhóó were straight-up hospitality roles, I told candidates. Every member of the staff, from cashier to sous chef, would be expected to take an active interest in the mental health piece of our mission, hopefully taking advantage of opportunities to get some basic clinical training so they could participate in our Nutritional Recovery programming.

A few of the individuals we brought on initially didn't work out. As part of their onboarding, employees were required to attend mandatory Rainbow staff training and it was quickly clear they didn't get it. "Why do I need to know what trauma-informed care is?" "I don't see any connection between cooking or Native foods and staying sober." "Who cares if people see me and my friends getting rowdy at the casino Saturday night?" These were some of the comments I got. It quickly became clear Gozhóó wasn't the right place for those people.

I adjusted the interview process. Applicants for the more skilled kitchen positions—*chef de partie*, sous chef, and *chef de cuisine*—already had to complete a timed knife skills test, but I incorporated a mystery-basket task, where candidates were required to create a dish or two from a collection of ingredients, including yellow squash, tomatoes, Apache acorns, wild lambsquarters, cooked beans, chili flakes, asparagus, eggs, and an assortment of fresh herbs, and serve them to a panel of agency staff.

Observing how someone tackled this challenge told me about their life skills, whether they were adaptable, resilient, and self-directed. At the end of the day, technique and organization are things that can be taught; curiosity, humility, and respect are attributes individuals have to bring to the table. While sobriety wasn't a requirement of the job, it came as no surprise to me that several of the employees who ended up staying and working out were in recovery.

By late 2019, we had a core crew in place, but we were still waiting, ironically, for our gas lines to be connected. Finally, right after the New Year, the kitchen was fully functional. I began to organize some soft-opening events to give the team opportunities to test our equipment, and have the team prep and cook the kind of dishes we'd serve once we opened our doors to the public.

The priority at Café Gozhóó would be serving clean, delicious, and affordable food to our community. Whenever I got overly ambitious with my menu planning, I reminded myself I wasn't cooking for my ego; I was cooking for therapeutic purposes. I wanted every auntie or uncle who walked through our doors to feel welcome, even if the kitchen design and high-end coffee machine were new to them. That meant simple dishes executed beautifully.

We'd be open, initially at least, for breakfast and lunch service, and in addition to standard fare like omelets and sandwiches, we'd always offer one or two grandma-style soups, which was a way of training the team to "recycle" whatever ingredients we had in supply. We'd also serve rotating seasonal specials that would introduce diners to Indigenous ingredients and flavors that might be completely new to them.

One of the dishes I knew would be a staple on Gozhóó's menu was the Apache Dip, a grilled steak-and-roasted-green-chili sandwich on Racket Bread (Bundi'tunneh) served alongside a cup of Acorn Stew—a fun, delicious mash-up of two dishes that pretty much every single person in Whiteriver knows and loves.

Whenever I brought in ingredients that my staff hadn't encountered before, I reminded them that part of our mission was broadening people's food vocabularies and educating them about Indigenous cultivars they might have considered "white" or "American."

"Expanding your palate and incorporating more colorful ingredients into your repertoire is going to pay off in terms of physical health and longevity, and it's the same with mental health," I said as we prepped fresh kale, lambsquarters, and beetroot greens from the farm, which we'd wilt and mix with roasted potatoes. "If you only have four emotions that you can identify, you're going to stay stuck in a pattern; but when you develop your emotional intelligence, you have a better chance of staying clean and balanced."

\+ + + +

In late January 2020, right around the time the first confirmed COVID case was reported in Arizona, my staff and I hosted a celebratory tasting dinner for thirty-five guests, mostly family members and friends as well as the staff of the People's Farm, who had been bringing us weekly deliveries of fresh produce.

That morning, I came into work before dawn to talk to my father.

"Hey, Dad, check this place out," I said as I set a couple of tote bags on the counter. "We're here now, the café is finally real—and it's beautiful. I buried corn and salt in the cement with the water lines for protection, just like you taught me."

In the weeks leading up to the event, we had settled on a lineup of dishes that reflected the vision for Café Gozhóó. In addition to the Apache Dip, we would serve tasting-size portions of Dijíízhi stew, Three Sisters fritters, and a toasted white quinoa salad with fresh greens from Ndée Bikíyaa, tomatoes, cucumbers, pine nuts, cilantro, and mustard blossoms.

The dessert course was where I wanted to do something really inventive, celebrating Indigenous ingredients and flavors that might be less familiar to diners.

I watched the servers present each guest with a tart, refreshing glass of tsínk'ózhé slushy, which they brought to the tables in a glass bowl filled with fresh snow we'd gathered up near the Sunrise Park Resort. I took a deep breath and closed my eyes. I owed this precious moment to all of my mentors: Chef Whelan, Chef Olson, Chef Thompson, Chef Rusty, Woody, Harry, and David; to my brothers, Dustinn and Shiloh; and my parents, Mariddie and Vincent. Above all, I owed it to younger Nephi, who refused to give up, even in the darkest, most terrifying moments of life, even when fear, self-doubt, and addiction threatened to paralyze me. I thanked the universe for sparing my life, opening my eyes, and inviting the entire team to come out into the dining room with me.

Before we brought out one final dish, I gave our guests a short overview of Café Gozhóó's mission and the Nutritional Recovery program, proceeding to introduce every person who had helped create this special dinner one by one.

"Mostly we're excited to serve the community," I said. "We plan to open soon, and hope you'll tell everyone you know to come visit us and have some fresh, amazing food."

Our guests applauded.

"We have one more surprise for you," I said, nodding at the team to go finish plating.

"My late father, Vincent Craig, taught me about the Navajo Problem Solver, a decision-making and planning philosophy that was a gift from Creator to help people to live good lives. It's taken me a long time to understand, and maybe I still don't."

The elders in the room chuckled. I smiled at sixteen-year-old Ari, who stood across the room, listening intently.

"What Vincent was trying to teach me, I think, was that the answers to a lot of the problems we face as Native people are already here, within and among us. The answers live in traditional ecological knowledge, in the way our ancestors related to the world, the way they moved through this landscape, the way they ate."

I turned back to the kitchen, giving my chefs the signal to bring out our second dessert. The evening's grand finale was an original creation of mine—a Western Apache Seed Mix Fritter that I placed on a rectangular white plate along with chunks of honey-braised butternut squash, poached butternut squash pearls, chocolate sauce, roasted butternut squash chutney, and piñon whipped cream, topped with marigold flowers and puffed amaranth. Each chef carried a rectangular white dish in each hand and they set them down in the center of each table.

People's eyes got very big. A couple of them even gasped.

"Do we eat it?" asked my friend Twila, the person who'd first taught me about our Western Apache Seed Mix. "It's too beautiful!"

I laughed, adjusting my glasses.

"I think of this dish as a sacred sand painting. It tells an epic story of self-determination, resilience, and healing. The fritters are made from ground and crushed acorn, pine nuts, parched Apache white corn, squash seeds, and sunflower seeds, which, as you taught me," I said, smiling at Twila, "is the traditional seed mix that our people would have kept around to tide them through lean times or when they were out scouting."

Each of the Native foods that composed the dish, I explained, represented a powerful element of Indigenous history and societies. The chocolate represented the sophisticated trade routes developed by Indigenous peoples, which reached from Mesoamerica into Western Apacheria and beyond. The squash was female, carrying inside her the seeds of her survival, a nod to our matrilineal Apache and Navajo cultures. The Piñon Cloud, as I'd called the flavored cream on the menu, was an "Indigenized ingredient," I said.

"Dairy from cows is not Indigenous to the Americas, but piñon, or pine nuts, are. It's an ancestral and widely favored taste."

I watched one of my aunties bring a spoon to her mouth and close her eyes in contentment.

"The Aztecs saw the marigold as a symbol of the invasion of the Spanish and the near-eradication of an ancestral way of life," I continued. "In the language of flowers, *marigold* means 'pain and grief' and also signifies a wish to comfort a person who is grieving. I see this ingredient as a symbol of working toward ancestral justice."

"That's beautiful," said Candice, a girlfriend of one of the cooks. "And what are these cool, itty-bitty puffs?"

I smiled. I appreciated someone else being wowed by their first encounter with amaranth.

"Those are popped amaranth seeds," I said. "Amaranth is an Indigenous plant that originated in Mesoamerica, but it's a relative of a plant that we use in our prayer bundles here in the Southwest. Indigenous peoples revered amaranth as a nutrient-rich food—you can prepare it like a grain, instead of rice or quinoa."

I listened to the happy sounds of people scraping their plates clean, and cleared my throat. I wanted to add one last remark.

"Every time I use amaranth, I'm giving a big middle finger to Hernán Cortés and other Spanish conquistadors who ordered to chop off the hands of anyone found possessing or cultivating this sacred ingredient."

Ari chuckled.

"The amaranth is my act of resistance."

AFTERWORD

RECIPES FOR SURVIVANCE

\+ + + +

It's five p.m. on a Thursday and I've just downed an espresso. My kitchen crew has left for the day, and the heavy metal they cranked after lunch service ended is still blasting. All the food's been wrapped up, labeled, and put away, the stainless steel counters polished, the floors scrubbed. We've sanitized every handle, pull, knob, and dispenser. Four-plus years since we officially opened the doors of Café Gozhóó, the joint looks brand-new.

I commandeer the music, pressing play on my favorite album ever, *Enter the Wu-Tang*, and take a moment to admire our work. The café smells like every high-end kitchen where I trained up as a young chef—clean and metallic with a soap-and-vinegar tang.

Just like everything about Gozhóó, our meticulous cleanup regimen is intentional. It's as important as the nourishing meals we serve to our community and our focus on local, Native ingredients. Working clean is particularly important for anyone recovering from addiction, which is a majority of the people who come through this kitchen. *Clean kitchen, clear mind.*

There's still an hour to go before my Recovery Cooking group rolls in. These sessions usually run twice a week, drawing men and women ranging in age from eighteen to sixty, all of them in treatment at Rainbow. Wednesdays are for outpatient clients and Thursdays are for in-patients. Almost all of the participants are members of the White Mountain Apache Tribe. I know some by their family names. I know others because they once sold me bootlegged alcohol.

"This is our family of choice," I'll often tell my groups. "Our family of origin is where we did the most damage—they saw us burn it all down and now they don't trust us. It's our responsibility now to build a network of support if we're gonna process all this intergenerational trauma."

Some classes are livelier than others and when I'm dealing with a group that seems checked out, I remind them to not look at their rehabilitation as a punishment.

"The cooking isn't gonna get you sober," I explain. "But the skills you build are an opportunity to practice healthy behaviors. They're a way to show you can take care of yourself."

I still get excited before each class. I love witnessing the transformation that happens when someone who's never even cracked an egg discovers the satisfaction of preparing a meal from scratch and sitting down to share it with their community. When we cook and eat together, I see who my clients are beyond their habits of addiction, observing their willingness to throw themselves into new experiences, their courage to try a food they've always told themselves they didn't like.

I want so badly to help all of my clients commit to their recovery and write their own recipe for living it. As part of Rainbow's clinical staff, I'm familiar with each individual's diagnosis, drug of choice, and treatment plan. More importantly, I know how it feels to experience the kind of violence and suffering they've endured—and that healing is possible. I also know, of course, that not everyone will make it. Many of the people who participate in my groups will relapse. Some of them might die.

Every week, the group votes on the dish they want to prepare the following session; tonight, we're making gumbo. As I get up to gather ingredients—vegetables and sausage from the chilled walk-in, jars of spices, the giant container of all-purpose Blue Bird flour that lives in the cabinets beneath the worktable in the prep room—I reflect on the fact that each one of my Recovery Cooking groups is a microcosm of life on the Rez.

It's beautiful, dynamic, and full of swagger, but it will continuously break your heart.

\+ + + +

In retrospect, the soft opening of Café Gozhóó was a rare bright spot in what would become another difficult chapter of my rollercoaster life. In the early days of the pandemic, as life on the Rez and beyond contracted, my relationship with Nalin collapsed under the weight of the stress and the unresolved issues that we had both carried into the marriage with us.

While Nalin and I slogged through custody arrangements and other aspects of dissolving our marriage, I moved into a three-bedroom with Ari. We were both knocked sideways when his mother, Kim, passed away after a lengthy battle with a serious illness. Our home was flooded with grief.

The fact that I was able to hold fast to my sobriety in the midst of all this devastation is one of my proudest accomplishments. All through the quarantine months and afterward, Ari and I found solace in the abandoned skatepark in Show Low, where we practiced our tricks, got out of our heads, and hung out together doing something we loved. I'm happy my son inherited my passion for the sport—watching him ride, I knew he was practicing confronting his fears. He became stronger, more capable. We'd sit on the curb, talking about the philosophical side of skateboarding and how it related to our lives, helping us pick ourselves back up even when things seemed impossible. I am grateful that my older son got to witness his father survive the tragedy of divorce in a healthy way, that he's gotten to see me laugh and cry, be afraid and angry, that he was aware I was talking with my therapist and practicing self-care.

Once again, cooking came to the rescue. In 2020, I launched Wu-Tang Wednesdays, a series of Instagram Live cooking demos that came out over the course of thirty-six consecutive weeks, a nod to the Wu-Tang Clan's *36 Chambers* album. In each video, I taught viewers how to make a home-cooked meal, everything from Apache dumplings and chili-glazed butternut squash to a simplified pho or paella, sharing a recipe and an ingredient list. I tried to make sure each featured dish could be completed within an hour.

While I cooked, I explored themes of decolonization, Indigenous resurgence, recovery principles, and knife skills as life skills. I gained hundreds of followers, some Native, some not. It was pretty uplifting to get notes from individuals all over the country—and as far away as Italy, Brazil, and Sweden—telling me that my videos were helping them get through the pandemic and that they were excited about everything they were learning. Against the backdrop of the racial justice protests that broke out in response to George Floyd's murder—along with all of the public health challenges our communities were facing—the topics I was discussing felt relevant and urgent. On top of that, my followers were appreciative for all the ideas and tips on how to feed themselves and their families well.

Wu-Tang Wednesdays were good for my mental health, too. It felt like a gift, to be able to do something creative and useful from within the confines of my home. Just like I'd once done for my own father, Ari played the role of production assistant, helping me set up lights, prep ingredients, and make fun playlists that played in the background during each episode. It was a trip to see Wu-Tang Wednesdays get written up in the *Arizona Republic*—a reminder that pain is temporary but Wu-Tang is forever.

As soon as we were able to fully open Café Gozhóó in late 2021, I became laser-focused on showcasing Native ingredients and flavors in a way that was inviting to my community. There can be so much legal, political, and academic jargon around the concepts of decoloniality and Indigenous food sovereignty that it scares off everyday people. The food we served in the café—our Indigenous Feast Platter, for example, a simple, rotating entrée that's always served with a cup of Three Sisters soup, roasted red and purple potatoes, seasonal greens from Ndée Bikíyaa, and a dessert of macerated berries—needed to be accessible to the widest variety of people. We regularly ran specials like Acorn Stew, wild tea, and Apache Kool-Aid. The dishes and drinks we served were meant to activate people's food memories and spark conversations about their childhoods and family traditions.

We always have a multitude of wild, Apache, and Indigenous cultivars on display in our kitchen. We hang bundles of wild tea and chilies from the ceiling, along with dehydrated wild onions and wild potatoes. We keep dried corn kernels from the People's Farm in Apache baskets on the counter that separates our kitchen from the dining area, and jars of Apache acorns and edible sumac, or tsínk'ózhé. The ancestral foods are everywhere. Parents point out the onions and tell their children about digging them up when they were young, customers inquire if they can buy bundles of tea. Every Apache, every Native, who walks through the doors of our café should feel proud and connected to their culture, and I hope non-Natives feel curious and inspired as well. The Native foods are central to what we do at Café Gozhóó—change happens gradually, but the foods are skillful ambassadors, reminding our customers and Rainbow clients of our connection to the land and the importance of surrounding ourselves with things that feed our spirits.

Of course, running a restaurant of any size is never easy, and, over the past four years, we've confronted many obstacles, big and small, including a water main break that shut us down for a year. Still, we didn't give up—the restaurant might have been closed, but the kitchen stayed open. During that time, we continued to run our therapeutic groups and food education events for the community.

+ + + +

Right before six o'clock there's a knock at the front door. I'm pleased to see that it's Kenny, this huge homie I used to run with toward the end of my active addiction. He claps me on the back and heads straight for the staff room to hang up his coat and grab an apron. I greet the rest of my clients, thirteen of them in total this time around.

Once everyone is suited up, we gather around the L-shaped island, and I enlist a few people to chop bell peppers, celery, and yellow and green onions, and two others to pick and chop parsley. I put Josie, a young mother who hasn't seen her babies in months, in charge of browning the andouille sausage that I bought at the supermarket up the hill in the predominantly white town of Show Low, because I knew it wasn't something we could get here on the Rez. Two people will work together to make cornbread from scratch, while another duo will prepare a simple side salad.

Before we go to our stations, I give a little speech about roux, the foundation for tonight's dish. It's composed of just two ingredients—flour and butter—and it takes concentration and patience to get the right, doughy consistency and rich brown color. You add more flour or butter as you go, I tell the group, and you babysit it, even on a low flame.

"It's like that with recovery, too," I say. "You have to be mindful. You can't be on autopilot, because that's when you fall back into your habits. That's when you get burned."

I assign Kenny and a few of the other rowdy-looking guys to work on the roux together and while everyone's doing their thing, I walk around offering pointers. The conversation flows freely—this group's been together for about six weeks, and they've gotten comfortable. People talk about different movies set in New Orleans they've watched: *Chef*, *The Princess and the Frog*, and *Interview with a Vampire*.

Everyone grabs a bowl and serves themselves from a sixteen-quart All-Clad pot. We've pushed four café tables together to make a big square dining table, and, once we're all seated, I ask for a volunteer to bless the food. Delshay, a tall, skinny teenager in a too-big, old-school Bugs Bunny jersey, raises his hand.

I always tell my groups they can pray however they want to. Some of them go the Lutheran, Christian, or evangelical route while others, usually the elders, will offer up a prayer in Apache. Delshay keeps it simple.

"Bless this beautiful food and let this food strengthen our bodies and our spirits. Bless Chef and his team."

+ + + +

Even with all of the personal and professional setbacks I've experienced in recent years, I remain optimistic about the work we're doing at Café Gozhóó. In addition to pioneering the practice of using Indigenous foods and professional cooking as an integrated care modality for addiction recovery, we're showing what it looks like to prioritize mental health in a restaurant kitchen. I'm proud to be part of a groundswell of food professionals committed to addressing racism, sexism, arrogance, and violence in the industry.

With the compounding demands of clinical work, kitchen supervision, and single parenting, it's been a challenge to invest much time in growing NACA, but I continue to connect with others doing impactful work around food sovereignty and Indigenous resurgence. I dream of other cafés and restaurants like ours popping up on reservations and in cities across the country. I hope to one day realize my dream of establishing a Center for Indigenous Cuisine and Agriculture, where we'd train the next generations of Native chefs and Native farmers to go out into their communities and make an impact.

+ + + +

The Thursday-night Recovery Group is back in the kitchen, sweeping and mopping and wiping down surfaces, getting things back to their spotless state. Every time I look around at my groups, I'm struck by their faces. They look so much like the Apaches who stare back at me from the old black-and white photos I collect—the same high cheekbones, squinty eyes, thick, bushy hair, and tough expressions.

"Okay, let's talk about what we're going to cook next week," I say, picking up a marker to write on the whiteboard.

Josie turns around from the sink where she's washing the last of the dirty dishes.

"My sister's always telling me that salmon is one of the healthiest things I can feed my kids." She pushes back a thick strand of hair that's escaped from her bandanna. "She's a nutritionist."

I nod. "It's a very sacred food for Natives on the West Coast. We often have a nice, simple preparation of roast salmon with a side of Three Sisters on the café menu. That'd be a good thing to make."

Kenny leans on his deck brush. "I don't fuck with no fish," he announces.

The group laughs—we've all encountered people who hold on to the old Apache superstition about scaly things.

"Don't knock it until you try it," I remind him. The importance of expanding our food vocabulary is something they've heard me talk about a lot. "Expand your flavor palate to expand your emotional palate" is a metaphor I often use.

Kenny shrugs. "Whatever you say, boss."

I love having Kenny in group. The first time he showed up at the café, he was in complete shock.

"Kaaay-yeah . . . NEPHI! You're still alive? What the fuck?!" His voice was deeper than I remembered. "You were in bad shape the last time I saw you, running around with your backpack, selling your tools and knives. You wouldn't stop talking shit about missing your dad and not wanting to live."

Now, here we are, two battle-weary Apaches trying to make something good of our lives, trying to stop numbing out. It wasn't that long ago that I was in Kenny's shoes, navigating the treacherous waters of early recovery. It wasn't that long ago I walked all the way up to death's door.

When I first entered recovery, I was scared that I'd become a duller, dimmer version of myself. I still didn't feel safe or comfortable in my skin. I still wasn't sure who I was, but embracing Native foodways helped me recognize that, beyond the trauma and heartbreak, there was so much power resting in Indigenous communities all across the Americas—and it helped me realize my own power, too. After years of questioning my identity and seeking connection, Native foods helped me feel safe being exactly the kind of chef—and person—I wanted to be.

For far too long, Native Americans, and other Indigenous peoples all around the world, have been struggling to keep our heads above water and tend to the deep wounds of historical trauma while also facing ongoing discrimination and injustice.

Like so many other Natives living in the postapocalypse, I've spent much of my life in survival mode, turning to alcohol and drugs as a way to cope with the tragedy of what has happened, and continues to happen. It took fully grasping how addiction was actually supporting the status quo—the rampant alienation, the erosion of families and community, the intergenerational cycles of poverty and despair—for me to see recovery as a form of rebellion. There's nothing more badass than staying sober in a world that's hell-bent on watching you fail.

No matter what it is that you are trying to recover from—a toxic kitchen, apathy, burnout, low self-esteem, grief, depression, incarceration, capitalism, or white supremacy—the trick is figuring out how to move beyond just staying afloat.

The term *survivance* was coined by scholar and writer Gerald Vizenor, an Anishinabe Native from Minnesota, who was interested in capturing the vibrant, creative, and defiant nature of the Indigenous experience. Without denying the immense tragedy and loss suffered by Indigenous peoples, survivance points to the ways in which they have channeled their culture and spirituality—not to mention the adversity itself—to shield themselves and resist oppression. If survival is the slog of just getting by, survivance is an art form, an intuitive, inventive, evolving practice of empowering ourselves and embracing the glorious messiness of life.

As I tell the people in my groups, there is nothing shameful about being in survival mode. It takes a lot to make it through the trauma and heartbreak many of us are born into and addiction is one way of managing that pain. The problem is getting stuck there.

Survivance is realizing that you're doing your best, often with little to no resources, in dire circumstances. You're still here, street-smart, creative, resourceful, intelligent, and tough as nails. Moving through adversity and chaos has given us powerful insights and skills—the trick is taking all the heartbreak and channeling it into living more fully, expanding our capacity to hold both the dark and the light.

Survivance is moving from addiction to recovery. It's getting stronger as you get softer, and finding humor amid the pain.

Survivance is caring for the people around you and letting them care for you. It's nourishing yourself in all the right ways.

Like all living beings, we humans need to eat for survival, but the foods we consume are so much more than a list of nutrients and calories—they're fragments of history and memory, manifestations of our ancestors' wisdom and intelligence, a tangible connection between our bodies and the cosmos.

In this era of violence, polarization, dehumanization, and unchecked extraction we find ourselves in, we all feel stressed and frazzled and frightened, caught in a *Groundhog Day*–loop of fight-or-flight. Cultivating a more mindful approach to food—learning the stories behind the ingredients we use every day; supporting Indigenous, ecologically sound farming practices; practicing kitchen skills that help us be more grounded, present, and kind in other parts of our lives—can help us move out of this cycle of suffering.

What are the things that can help you move from survival to survivance? And how can you speak up and take accountability for what is happening to Indigenous landscapes and communities across the United States, supporting Indigenous organizers and talent and diverting resources, with no strings attached? How will you turn your rage and grief about the world into your superpower? Grab a knife, grab a cutting board, grab your friends, grab a chair. There's work for each one of us to do.

ACKNOWLEDGMENTS

First, I want to thank my cowriter, Hagar Scher, who spent countless hours listening to my stories, revising my written memories and reflections, and shaping the ups and downs of my life into the scenes that color this book. Thank you for traveling to Apache Land to meet my family, visiting the house I grew up in, and experiencing a traditional Apache Sunrise Dance and Crown Dance on our beautiful White Mountain Apache Rez. Thank you for accompanying me into some of the darkest moments in my life to find hope and strength, and for helping me capture my message—of grief, vitality, creativity, Apache humor, recovery, and revitalization. Over the course of writing this book together, your perspective helped me to find clarity and better understand my past as I look to the future.

This book is an expression of love. Over the course of my twenty-eight-plus-year career as a chef, I have had numerous opportunities to create a cookbook, but I never felt "ready" for such a project. In recovery circles we say that our most powerful tool is our voice—and I believe the same to be true in the Indigenous experience. I wanted to write a book that reminded other Indigenous people that their stories were not just valid and important, but profoundly valuable and necessary in shaping our resurgence after centuries of colonial violence. Remember to take care of yourself.

To my son Ari, thank you for being one of my greatest teachers and examples of strength. Thank you for allowing me to write about our lives together with Mom. From the moment you came into my life, I have been so proud to be your dad. As you have grown into the man you are today, I look back on our life together, and I am deeply grateful for all that we share: our love of music, art, cooking, and skateboarding, and our strong work ethic.

I think of every single Sunrise Dance Camp we have built together, me proudly watching you work so hard that I had no doubt that you would grow into a strong, intelligent young man. I love you to no end. Mom and I are immensely proud of you, Son. You are my hero!

To my little daughter: At the time of publishing this book, you are nine years old. When I look into your eyes, I see depth, humor, wit, kindness, love, and courage. I share your love of books, funny cartoons, art, painting, music, cooking, and, of course, Dad's huge bowls of pho! Thank you for teaching me about the pretty little things in my life and coloring my world with love. I love you to no end.

To my little son, who is now eight: When I look into your eyes, I see intelligence, kindness, love, curiosity, humor, and a sense of toughness that I recognize as our ancestral strength. I love our shared passions for Legos, art, skateboarding, Transformers, *Calvin and Hobbes*, music, cooking, and you guessed it . . . Dad's pho! I love you, Son. Thank you for teaching me about patience and humility, and reminding me to be a good dad. I love you to no end.

I wanted this book to be a tool for any individual in recovery and for the professionals and family members who are interested in supporting them. I am telling my recovery story not to brag, but because I am no longer ashamed. My story unfolded in parallel to my journey to understand the power of Indigenous foodways. I hope it will inspire Indigenous people everywhere and all the home cooks and chefs out there.

I want to thank the countless mentors in my life, be they professional, personal, romantic, spiritual, or cultural. Thanks to my mother, Mariddie Johnson Craig, for your lifelong example of dignity, eloquence, tenacity, courage, love—and for teaching me to make sure people knew we are specifically White Mountain Apache. To my late father, Vincent Craig, aka Muttonman, thank you for being our family sentinel, an advocate for sobriety in Native America. Your wisdom, humor, creativity, ingenuity, and love for our people live on in everyone you connected with on this earth. Thank you to my older brother, Dustinn, for bringing skateboarding into my life; ride through genocide, bro, I know you can land it. To my younger brother, Shiloh, thank you for being my lil partner in crime when we were growing up and for being an amazing example of what a good Indigenous father looks like.

I want to thank the millions of Indigenous people around the world who have been fighting back for generations and passionately resisting the forces of colonialism. Your bravery, strength, grit, determination, and deep love for our people fuel the pursuit of ancestral justice and healing. And to my countless White Mountain Apache and Navajo ancestors, I stand on the shoulders of giants.

Thank you to all the people and organizations that believed in and supported my work over the years. Thanks to my literary agent, Rachel Neumann of Wave Literary, who has been with me every step of the way. Thanks also to the team at Penguin Press for all that they have done to help bring this book to life. Rest in peace Ann Godoff.

Thank you to all the chefs that I worked with in my early career: Chris Olson, Russell "Rusty" Risher, Micheal Rusconi, Bradford Thompson, Fernando Davina. Thank you also to all the chefs who have welcomed me into your kitchens to visit, dine, or be a stagiaire: Daniel Boulud, Curtis Duffy, Kyle and Katina Connaughton, Christopher Kostow, Jason Shields, Michael Tusk, Patrick Henriroux, and Alan Passard.

A huge thank you to the "first generation" of Native Chefs: Sandy Garcia, Lois Ellen Frank, Walter Whitewater, Loretta Oden, Arlie Doxtator, and Jack Strong. Twenty-seven years in, I'm proud to be standing among you and helping to train the first generation of Native-trained Native Chefs in North American professional kitchens.

Thank you to the entire Rainbow Treatment Center staff for all your important work helping our Apache people achieve sobriety, liberation, and wellness. A huge thank you to the courageous Apache community members from Whiteriver, Arizona, who make up our RTC Nutritional Recovery team at Café Gozhóó: Café Manager Jasmine Hilton; Assistant Manager Denneilynn Childs, aka DJ; Chef de Cuisine David Williams; Barista Caitlan Fall; Cashier Kyle Quintero; Chef de Partie Adriano Colelay; Chef de Partie Jonathan Ethelbah; and the numerous staff and clients who have contributed over the years. Gozhóó!

Thank you to my brothers and family in Dinetah: Nancy Mariano Craig, Bob E. Craig, Harrison Craig, Vivian Craig, Elvira Craig, Emerson Craig, Rena Mae Craig, Tiny Craig, and the extended Craig/Etcitty family in the Eastern Agency on the Navajo Nation. And also to my brothers and sisters in Navajo Land: Lyle Ironwater, Gregg Perry, Michael Perry, Aaron Craig, Ryan Pete, Tonya Craig, Jenneth Begay, Brandon Craig, Tyrell Benally, Eric Tso, Lavelle Benally, Nikki Benally, Torri Benally DuQuesnay, and all my other cousins and extended family.

Shout-out to the hundreds of Indigenous cooks, chefs, and food warriors I have met in my journey: Crystal Wahpepah, Kickapoo Nation; Valerie Segrest, Muckleshoot; Claudia Serrato, Purépecha; Alexa Numkena-Anderson, Hopi/Yakima; Chris Rodriguez, Chicano; Joseph Haber, Mohawk; Flora Deacon, Deg Hit'an Athabascan; Joseph Shawana, Odawa; Nico Albert, Cherokee; Amara Lopez Enciso, Purepecha/Latina; Bleu Adams, Diné/Mandan/Hidatsa; Mark Mason, Diné/Mandan/Hidatsa; Christopher Fujimoto, Native Hawaiian; Sean Sherman, Oglala Sioux; Lee Garam, Chinook; Bertina Cadman, Diné; Harrison Watchman, Diné; Ed Mata, Yurok; Freddie Bitsoie, Diné; Denella Belin, Diné; Jero Tso, Diné; Derek Nicholas, Red Cliff Band Ojibwe; Destiny Moser, Ojibwe Rainy River First Nations; Diosa Hall, Mohawk; Rowen White, Mohawk; Andrea Stanley, Diné/Acoma/Honduras; Vincent "Vinny" Way, White Mountain Apache Tribe; Vina Reidhead, WMAT; Nancy James, WMAT; Justin Pioche, Diné; Tia Quintanilla Pioche, Diné; Laurencita Billiman, Diné; Twila Cassadore, San Carlos Apache; Karlos Baca, Diné/Tewa; Elsie DuBray, Oóhennunpa Lakxóta/Nueta/Hidatsa; Rob Kineen, Tlingit; Ben Jacobs, Osage Nation; Kealoha Domingo, Native Hawaiian; Kimberly Tilsen-Brave Heart, Oglala Lakota; Elena Terry, Ho-Chunk; Ramon Shiloh, Black/Filipino/Creek/Cherokee; Stephanie Pyetwetmokwe DeSpain, Native American/Mexican; Teri Ami, Hopi/Tewa; Ciara Minjarez, WMAT; Shy Alchesay, WMAT; Denee Bex, Diné; Andrea Beatty, WMAT; Divonne Mason, WMAT; Tina Archuleta, Jemez Pueblo; Walter Cloud, Diné; Neftali Duran, Oaxaca; Tawnya Brant, Mohawk; Sammy Gensaw, Yurok; Felicia Cocotzin Ruiz, Chicana/Tewa; Cynthia Wilson, Diné; Reagan

Wytsalucy, Diné; Mike Henry; Clayton Harvey; Cheryl Pailzote; and Danya Carroll, PhD, from Ndée Bikíyaa. Keep pushin'! And to all the talented emerging Indigenous food people who I have yet to meet: I can't wait for all of us to continue to learn and grow together.

Lastly, I wanted to name and thank some of people who have inspired my work and this book (this list is in no way exhaustive): Maria Yellow Horse Braveheart; Devon A. Mihesua; Michael Yellow Bird, PhD; Joseph P. Gone, PsyD; Sanjay Rawal; Thomas Francis; Sean Francis; Danita Macy; Ed Lauritsen, PsyD; Taiaiake Alfred, PhD; Eduardo Duran, PsyD; Keith Basso, PhD; Gabor Mate, PsyD; Anthony Bourdain; Valerie Vande Panne; The RZA; The GZA; Raekwon the Chef; U-God; Ol'Dirty Bastard; Ghostface Killah; Inspectah Deck; Method Man; Nasir "NAS" Jones; A Tribe Called Quest; Immortal Technique; Antithesis Crew; Gene "GENO" Declay; Ramon Riley; Ann and Herman Skidmore; Beverly Malone; Harris Burnette; The Red Hot Chili Peppers; Gangstarr; James Junes and Ernie Tsosie III; Tatanka Means; Adae Briones; George Smith, PhD; Simonetta Moro, PhD; John Zacher; Solco Schuit; Pat McElroy; Kenrick Davis; Farmer Lee Jones; Chef Silvana Salcido Esparza; Chef Brian Tatsukawa; Evan Sung; *Calvin and Hobbes*; Bill Watterson; Paulo Coelho; Paulo Freire; Frantz Omar Fanon; Bob Marley; Marc Brackett, PhD; Jennifer Mullan, PsyD; Jennifer Nez Denetdale PhD; Nicholas Gill; Jedi Mind Tricks; Sam King; Social Distortion; Mike Ness; Eli Sussman; Megatron; Alton Brown; John Frusciante; Chef Alex Lee; Geoff Rowley; Andrew Reynolds; Donny Barley; Ed Tempelton; Rodney Mullen; Natas Kupas; Steve Caballero; Adrian Lopez; Rune Glifberg; Ricky Oyola; Clyde Singleton; Kareem Cambell; and many more.

I want to thank you, the reader, for having an open heart and mind as we traveled through my American experience as an Indigenous man, father, brother, son, and community member who happens to be a chef. Thank you very much if you laughed, cried, felt optimistic, and reflected on our shared humanity in these pages. Take care of yourself one day at a time forever. Onward!

+ + + +